DOES
ANYBODY
ELSE LOOK
LIKE ME?

DOES ANYBODY ELSE LOOK LIKE ME?

*A Parent's Guide to
Raising Multiracial Children*

DONNA JACKSON NAKAZAWA

PERSEUS
PUBLISHING

A Member of the Perseus Books Group

Library of Congress Control Number: 2003103474
ISBN 0–7382–0605–9

Perseus Publishing is a member of the Perseus Books Group.
Find us on the World Wide Web at http://www.perseuspublishing.com.
Perseus Publishing books are available at special discounts for bulk purchases in the U.S. by
corporations, institutions, and other organizations. For more information, please contact the
Special Markets Department at the Perseus Books Group, 11 Cambridge Center,
Cambridge, MA 02142, or call (800) 255–1514 or (617) 252–5298, or e-mail
j.mccrary@perseusbooks.com.

Text design by Jeff Williams
Set in 11-point Bembo by the Perseus Books Group

First printing, May 2003

1 2 3 4 5 6 7 8 9 10—06 05 04 03

For Christian, for Claire.

CONTENTS

Introduction   ix

CHAPTER ONE
"Does Anybody Else Look Like Me?"
The Preschool Years   1

CHAPTER TWO
"Who Do I Match—Mom or Dad or Anyone?"
Moving from Preschool into Grade School   43

CHAPTER THREE
"What Do I Do When Friends Say Hurtful Things?"
Navigating Friendships in the Middle Childhood Years   77

CHAPTER FOUR
Facing the "What Are You?" Question
Moving Through the Turmoil of Adolescence   121

CHAPTER FIVE
The Big Picture
My Community, My School, My Culture   157

CHAPTER SIX
A New Multiracial Generation in America   189

Notes   201
Recommended Reading for Children   211
Recommended Reading for Teenagers   215
Acknowledgments   217
Index   219

INTRODUCTION

THIS BOOK WAS BORN in the aisle of a bookstore out of both frustration and wishful thinking.

Having grown up as a white woman in white America, nothing had quite prepared me for the daily encounters that would be part of my life with my husband, Zenji, as we began our multiracial family a decade ago. Gratified that we lived in an era when acceptance of all colors (and combinations thereof) was becoming more the norm than the exception, I hoped multiracial families and children like ours—Japanese and Caucasian—would hardly warrant special attention. After all, weren't magazine covers proclaiming that by the middle of the twenty-first century there would no longer be a white majority in America?[1] Wasn't our family just one small speck in a seismic shift of racial amalgamation?

Nonetheless, that spotlight caught me off guard at almost every turn when I ventured out with my children, in the form of lingering stares in the supermarket and intrusive questions from strangers ("What *are* they?" "Where did you get them?" "Wow, do you ever get used to the fact they don't look anything *like* you?" "Ohmigod!—your little girl has blond hair and *Asian* eyes!"). Not surprisingly, as my children grew past toddler-hood, they faced their own confusing encounters, yet each time they turned to me for comfort, I couldn't help but feel that my maternal instincts alone were insufficient to meet their needs. What could I know of ameliorating the hurt my son felt for being singled out by another boy on the swing set because of his unique mix of Caucasian and Asian features? Or because his mom and dad didn't "match?" These emotional knee scrapes were as subtle as they were sporadic, and more often born out of curiosity than cruelty ("Hey, Christian, your eyes go up like this: *Vroop!*" "What *are* you anyway?" "Do you speak *Chinese?*" "Why do you only have black holes for eyes?" "*That's* your mom? No way!"). Still, each time these scenes occurred, they confounded my children, breaking through the cocoon of our family life and puncturing their self-assured image of who they were (as my son once verbalized it, "I'm just a kid like any *other* kid").

Each of these scenarios was a reminder that even though mixed-race families like ours were becoming more and more common, and we increasingly had other mixed families around us, much of the world still reacted to us (and to our kids) with some discomfort or at least visible surprise. A fact that made the Richter scale of my maternal instincts run wild: My kids were quickly gleaning the message that they were somehow "other"—so different, so outside the range of normal that friends and strangers alike would never stop pointing it out to them.

As any mother might, I worried about how my children might be unwittingly shaped over the years as so many in our society unfailingly struggled to categorize them—even as toddlers still strapped in the grocery cart—into one of five standard racial pigeon holes: Caucasian *or* African American *or* Native American *or* Asian *or* Latino, and, upon failing, made them feel they were the odd birds out.

I needed a game plan—a way to help our children successfully deflect and reframe this negative message—to give them tools to emerge undaunted from their interactions with those around them, from the preschool sandbox to the high school cafeteria. I needed to better understand how this singling out might affect their psyches and their core identity as it developed and what we as parents might do to raise our kids to be fully confident *bicultural* individuals, inherently aware of and proud of their dual heritage—*and* to have fully integrated these heritages into one rock-solid identity. I needed to know how to talk to my kids about who they are and about the world we live in, both appropriately and knowledgeably.

In search of these answers, I headed to the bookstore. Surely, I thought, I was not the first parent in a multiracial family to pose these questions; after all, as a nation, aren't we in the midst of an unprecedented multiracial baby boom? Aren't we witness to a century that will see the face of our nation rapidly change its complexion? But combing the shelves only led to disbelief: Where were the books geared to parents of multiracial children? And so my mission began: to write the book I longed to hold in my own hands.

This book is an answer to the many questions that have arisen for me since my husband and I began our family. In it you will find the story of not only my own journey toward answers, but also the powerful and generously shared insights of more than sixty multiracial children, young adults, and parents (in all types of racially mixed families, from all parts of the country), whom I interviewed for this book. They walked this walk before me or are embarking on it now, as am I. Their stories are coupled with extraordinary insights and cutting-edge research from numerous experts who have devoted themselves to studying America's growing generation of multiracial children and whose work has helped me to provide parents with an understanding of the crucial developmental tasks our multiracial children face at each stage of their identity development.

Each chapter in this book offers numerous dialogues and sample scripts that I hope will be of great use to you in your own living room by helping you respond appropriately and knowledgeably to your children at each age in their development, as they work to achieve a healthy identity despite the confusing situations they will no doubt face. These insights from parents and experts alike—who offer innovative and effective approaches to parenting our multiracial children—provide the foundation on which this book is based and a roadmap for all of us taking this extraordinarily rewarding journey.

Before we begin, however, there are several notes of import to the reader.

The Emerging Numbers

With the 2000 census, Americans for the first time ever had the option of identifying themselves as "one or more races" to indicate their racial background, and nearly 7 million Americans did just that. Remarkably, 42 percent, or 2.9 million, of these multiracial individuals were *under* 18 (comparatively, in the "one race" population, only 25 percent are under 18),[2] a fact of great interest to demographers who look to the under 18 population to predict ways in which the profile of our country is growing *and* changing. And changing it is: multiracial youth now compose one of the fastest-growing segments of the U.S. population, signaling the most significant cultural and ethnic sea change in our country's brief history. Moreover, according to a 2002 report by the Population Division of the U.S. Census, the 2000 census may actually reflect a vast underreporting of the potential pool of multiracial children, which may be closer to 4.5 million. In 2000, the parents of 2.9 million children reported that their child was of two or more races; an additional 1.6 million *more* children who were reported as being of a single race did not racially match their interracial parentage, as noted by the reporting adult in their home (the caveat being that there is no way to know whether the second adult in the home—who was of a different race from that child—was actually that child's *other* biological parent).[3]

This caveat notwithstanding, as these numbers emerge, they point to the fact that, in the United States, more than 1 in 16 children under the age of 18 are now multiracial[4] (a number drawn from data already three years out of date). When looking at current *birth* rates, that number is significantly higher, especially in some areas of the country. Today, as many as 2 in 10 babies born in some U.S. cities are multiracial.[5] As the rate of mixed marriages increases dramatically with each decade—from 1.5 million in 1990 to more than 4 million in Census 2000—the number of multiracial births is likewise skyrocketing.

Meeting the Needs of Our Multiracial Children

The old "rap" on multiracial children has long held that the sheer fact of *being* of two or more racial heritages means that a child *must* be inwardly confused about who he or she is and thus more prone to lifelong adjustment problems.[6] But the *reality* is that any confusion our children may feel is a result of the disturbing reactions people in our society so often have when they can't racially compartmentalize our kids, all too often sending them the message that they are different and "other," which can't help but impact their developing sense of self. Because of this reality, parents in multiracial families face pressing issues that do not arise for children in monoracial families—issues that have not been sufficiently addressed to date.

Because the growth in multiracial families is such a rapidly occurring change in the long static fabric of our society, there still exists an enormous lag time between the information parents have needed to help us address issues our children face and what has been readily available. In the pages that follow, we hear from many adolescents and young adults in multiracial families whose parents are successfully meeting the challenge of mindfully addressing their children's emotional, psychological and educational needs and thus are helping them form healthy, integrated and confident self-identities. The wealth of their insights amounts to powerful inspiration.

The Terms Used in This Book

As I began my extensive interviews for this book, I discovered that there exists a war of terminology or, at the very least, a heady debate in this arena. On the one hand, some of my interviewees were uncomfortable with the term "mixed race." They felt it echoed too closely the erroneous idea that multiracial people are somehow inherently "mixed up" because of their dual cultural identity or that it implied they were a self made up of the sum of separate fractions rather than a whole person, and thus they preferred the term "multiracial." On the other hand, some of my interviewees reacted negatively to both the terms "mixed race" and "multiracial." They noted that cutting-edge genetic research has, in the last several years, shown unequivocally that we *all* genetically originate (whatever our "race" may be) from a small handful of people in sub-Saharan Africa, and that the "races" have been mixing throughout millennia of human migration across the globe. Recent research into the human genome highlights how the standard five racial categories into which human beings are typically lumped—Caucasian, African American, Asian, Native American and Latino—do *not* match up to corresponding genetic differences. In other words, neat categories of race simply do not exist. Race is, rather, an artificial distinction[7] that reflects very little genetic difference, perhaps one one-hundredth of 1 percent of our DNA.[8] Indeed, skin color variations—which are so often used to create social boundaries—have only emerged in the last 100,000 years, a mere blink of an eye in evolutionary terms.[9] As more than one interviewee put it, "We are *all* mixed." For this reason, many preferred the term "multiethnic" because it leaves out artificial racial distinctions and highlights only the more valid differences of culture and ethnicity.

While this makes sense, it is nevertheless true that as long as we live in a world in which race is one of the most salient factors of day-to-day life in determining how we are treated by others, it remains a real fact of life. For that reason, in this book, I have chosen primarily to use the term "multiracial," though the terms "mixed-race" and "biracial" also appear in this text in order to avoid the overuse of any single term.

In addition, it is important to note that when I use the term "multiracial child" in this book, I use it to not only refer to biracial (of two races) and multiracial (of two or more races) children, but, in many contexts, I stretch

American heritage. There is no clear consensus, but I have done my best to honor each interviewee's wishes.

This effort extends, in some cases, to adding the term "Jewish" to the parenthetical identification for some interviewees, if and when they cited it as integral to their mixed identity. Indeed, although it may seem overly politically correct to cite each person's self-identifying ethnic/cultural/racial heritages in the pages of this book, it is relevant to see what perspectives each interviewee brings to his or her insights.

Whenever interviewees requested that I change their names (which very few did), I have done so.

Yet another discussion emerged during the writing process regarding the use of the words "minority" and "majority," given that these terms are growing increasingly blurred. For instance, in some small segments of our country, the majority has become the minority, at least according to traditional terminology, and vice versa. When I use the term "minority" in this book, it is simply to refer to all people who have had experiences as "minority" groups in an America which, though changing, has traditionally had a distinctly white majority and, in most parts of our country, still does.

I would also like to note that the age ranges here, as with all parenting books, are approximate. As any parent knows, certain children go through some developmental stages much earlier than others, and yet all pass through them in their own time frame. As they pass through the key stages of multiracial identity development (phases carefully outlined in this book), during which their self-image can be so positively or negatively forged, they need our support and guidance all the more.

Finally, I use the word "parents" throughout this book to refer to a child's primary caretakers, well aware (or at least hopeful) that this book will also prove useful for grandparents, extended family members, caregivers, school administrators and teachers, and all who care about the emotional well-being of our growing generation of multiracial children who are, in the very fact of their being, changing the way we view and live race in America.

CHAPTER ONE

"Does Anybody Else Look Like Me?"

The Preschool Years

AT THREE AND A HALF MY SON—Japanese American and Caucasian—experienced his first emotional paper cut as a multiracial child.

That summer, Christian attended a multiage camp two mornings a week, where kindergartners and toddlers played together outside during recess. One day, when I picked him up, he said—his voice gulping as he gestured with both hands to his eyes—"One of the big boys asked me why I only have little black *holes* for eyes. Do I only have little black *holes* for eyes, Mommy?" His eyes were filled with a desperate questioning I had never seen in them before. My heart did a free fall in my chest. As a multiracial family, we had experienced our share of awkward comments and intrusive stares, but this was the first time anyone had made my son feel—face to face, child to child—that something about him was odd, different. My mind raced through a thousand responses: What could I—what *should* I—say to him? And what should I *not* say?

When we got home, I guided Christian to the mirror, where I pointed out his beautiful soft brown eyes, his acorn brown hair. "Besides," I said, "the color and shape of your eyes don't matter. Even if they were black, it wouldn't mean a thing. Daddy's eyes are dark brown and mine are blue and yours are the color of honey. Our eyes are all different colors in our family. Does it make any difference in how we love each other?" Dutifully, he shook his head no. Still, I was grasping at straws: Was this anything close to what he needed to hear? I felt painfully ill equipped.

I thought (well, I hoped) I had helped him process the incident. A few days later, though, Christian was busily sketching loopy "happy faces" when, just as he finished, he scratched out the eyes he'd just drawn in one furious scribble. For weeks, no matter how quickly I tried to salvage his drawings, he worked his marker back and forth until the eyes were all but obliterated, the paper torn through. Drawing after drawing looked like stick figure fugitives with their eyes blackened out to mask their true identities. Although he didn't understand what had happened on that playground—and although that kindergartner's words were almost definitely not *intended* to be hurtful—it had wounded him all the same. He was venting his hurt and confusion and anger in the only way he knew how.

Again, a feeling of complete ineptness as a mother washed over me. I didn't feel I had helped him process the incident at all. And I shuddered at the idea of having to stand by and watch as small seeds of insecurity were planted and encouraged to take root by the overtly race-conscious world in which we live. Minor incidents we had encountered as a family ran through my mind: a "friend" who had questioned whether my "conscience" was clear about bringing a multiracial child into the world in the first place; an acquaintance who advised me, when Christian was two, to do something different with his hair so he didn't look "so Asian"; the constant search of my son's features so a family member or acquaintance could somewhat triumphantly declare, "He doesn't even look that Japanese!"; people sizing up the three of us a few uncomfortable moments too long in restaurants or in line at the grocery store; and, when Christian and I were out alone together, seemingly endless queries about whether he was adopted.

And I well remembered, too, how once, when I had been out strolling with Christian—still not yet a year old—a seven-year-old neighborhood boy had come up and asked me, "Why does he look so . . . different?"

"Christian's daddy is Japanese," I said. "You know my husband."

"What's *Japanese*?" the boy asked.

"People who come from Japan. Do you know where Japan is?" So far, so good, I thought. We'll turn this into a geography lesson.

Then he raised his hands in front of him, as if he were aiming an imaginary machine gun in an imaginary World War II movie, and shouted, "Pekuw, pekuw, pekuw . . . *I'm gonna kill him.*"

Before I could stop myself, I reached down and put my hand tightly on his shoulder and said, in an outraged whisper, "If you ever hurt him every *inch* of you will *regret* it."

I was as shocked by my own mother-bear response as I was by this boy's clear rejection of my son because he appeared "different." The words had flown out of my mouth unbidden and apologize as I might, both his reaction to us and mine to him had left me shaken.

Still, Christian's playground incident was the first time he, as a young child, had to face an unsettling situation on his own—and I feared that, as he got older, this might prove only the tip of the iceberg. Over the years ahead, I wondered (worried, really) whether my child would have to navigate his way through myriad uncomfortable "multiracial moments" without my being there as solace or guide.

Zenji, my husband, and I had talked many times about our desire to help our son forge a strong self-core; to be able to look out into the world around him and bring his eyes back to his own mirror with self-love, with a clear-cut knowledge of who he was. Our goal was to imbue in him a deeply rooted self-identity—so that no matter what others might say, no matter what might occur, *he* would be crystal clear about his identity, about his absolute worth, within the greater world. We wanted to fill his emotional bank so full to the brim it would well-withstand any withdrawals the world might make by way of stinging questions or comments by fostering in him an unshakable faith in his own beauty and value and worth.

We wanted to grow *that*. But how? Where to begin? Where were our role models? Our sages?

Christian's playground incident, coupled with earlier uncomfortable moments we'd encountered, had culminated in a clarion wake-up call.

Indeed, most parents (among the more than 60 multiracial children, young adults, and parents whom I interviewed for this book in search of answers to these questions) talked with me about experiencing just such wake-up-call moments, often when their children were quite young, when they realized that although race was a complete nonissue within the four walls of their own home, it most certainly was an issue *outside* those four walls; people's insistent curiosity and stereotypical assumptions made being multiracial a very real factor in the lives of their children as they sought to attain a healthy and positive sense of self.

Take Jason Sackett (Caucasian), a clinical social worker in practice in West Los Angeles, and his wife, Karen (Carribean American), a high school counselor—parents of two young biracial boys. While taking their one-year-old son Austin out for a stroll one day, "about half a block from our house, a woman in a passing car stuck her head out of her window, stared us all square in the eyes and yelled, 'Ugheww! *Disgusting!*'" Jason describes feeling "a burning anger" that his family would be the target of so much hate. That evening he and Karen—concerned about Austin's self-esteem as he grew older should he witness more of the same—went back and forth about how they might respond should there be a similar scenario down the road. Karen says, "I admit it would have been tempting to yell back, 'Hey, biracial families are growing in number, so either get used to it or go somewhere else!' But while it would make my point, it wouldn't teach Austin much except how to be sarcastic." Although Austin was too young—thankfully—to know what was going on, "What if he hadn't been?" asks Jason. "The incident made us both realize we have a lot of work ahead. We need to pay more attention to communicating with Austin; to help make sense of others' attitudes for him."

Laura Rittenhouse (Caucasian), adoptive mother of Lianne (Chinese), tells about her "wake-up call" moment. One night, while reading a bedtime story to her young daughter, Lianne, "I was shocked when Lianne suddenly began hitting herself in the face. I cried out, 'What are you doing?' Lianne said, 'I don't like my face.' I protested, 'But I love your face, you have a beautiful face. I want your face.' Lianne looked straight through me and replied, 'I want *your* face . . . I want your *eyes*.'"

Immediately, says Laura, "I moved ethnic diversity closer to the top of my list of nursery school book selection criteria. I got a book that has lots of photographs of different kinds of noses, mouths, and eyes and cleverly shows how dull the world would be if everyone looked alike. I'm now a great deal more conscious of telling Lianne how beautiful she is." Still, months later, Laura says, Lianne's words "still echo in my head."

Such moments—whether prompted because our children witness glimmers of other people's discomfort with their multiracialness, or because our children express confusion about their own appearance and identity—nudge along a disquieting realization: While the world inside of our cozy home may be a "race-free domain," it is too simplistic to assume that the love we foster within the four walls of our home will be enough, in and of itself, to give our kids all the skills and wherewithal they need as they build their own identity and interact in a vastly monoracial world.

The fact is, the society in which we live is a society in which race just keeps coming up.

the term to refer to any child who lives with family members who represent more than one race due to parents' interracial marriage, remarriage, a transracial adoption, or foster parenting. This is for the sake of simplicity—to avoid repetitiously writing "multiracial children and those in transracially adopted families." Thus wherever their issues are similar, I use a unifying term, "the multiracial child," in reference to children who are multiracial as well as children who are transracially adopted and living in multiracial families. I hope the reader will forgive this stretch in terminology, as I well appreciate that the issues for transracially adopted children differ from those of multiracial children in significant ways that fall outside the scope of this book.

Another note must be made regarding the use of terms to refer to various "races"—such as we currently view them. These terms are increasingly the subject of some debate. At one point, in a room full of multiracial individuals and parents of multiracial children, at a national conference on multiracial families, each person in the room articulated what terms they liked to use to refer to their racial background and which they resisted. Comments included, "I don't like Caucasian because it leaves out my ethnicity—I prefer Euro-American." Others felt this was a bogus distinction; if, like so many "whites," you had little awareness of your ethnic heritage, and if your ethnicity was not a salient factor in your day-to-day life, and if you benefited from white privilege, shouldn't you identify as "white?"

Even more complicated are the terms for those of African American/ black heritage. As one woman said, "I'm not *African* American in America. That ethnicity was lost to me a couple of generations ago. I'm *black* in America and my experience is as a *black* woman in America." Others felt the term "black" connotated dark or negative imagery and, moreover, lost touch with their ethnic heritage, thus blurring them into a group of people from many varied cultures who just happened to share their same skin shade. Again, decisions had to be made. In this case, I generally favor the term "African American" as a means of ethnically identifying an interviewee's heritage, when appropriate. If an interviewee was of, say, Caribbean American descent, I used this term instead. Because I struggled to give a sense of each person's specific ethnic heritage, I gravitated toward these terms rather than the term "black." In other contexts, when discussing individuals of these heritages as a group, I often used the term "black" because it is a more inclusive term, referring not only to blacks in North America but also to those of Caribbean, Central and South

For many parents who are raising children in multiracial families, one question looms paramount: What do we need to know in order to do all we *can* do during these formative years—as our children first shape their attitudes and beliefs about themselves and those in the world around them—to help ensure they develop a secure and healthy sense of self?

A child is a work in progress. As the renowned preschool Italian educator Loris Malaguzzi emphasizes, when talking about the fragile—but critical—process of helping any child to develop a secure identity from the earliest stages of development,

> A child is born. Then through the long and difficult process of "constructing" his/her identity the child is reborn: he gives himself a face, a body, gestures, movement, speech, thought, feelings . . . in short the awareness of being and means of expressing his/her "me-ness." . . . [our] child's most sought after goal is to recognize himself or herself in others and to see parts of himself in the world around him. This is a most complex and delicate process. . . . This sense of self, of one's own self, is a vital component of self-esteem, learning and development . . . it is a quality that the child must set in motion with adult help and cooperation as soon as he/she can.[1]

A most complex and delicate process. Although constructing a healthy and confident self-identity is a complex process for all children, for multiracial and transracially adopted children this process is even more complicated. As our children's identities develop, and as they struggle, in Malaguzzi's terms, to recognize themselves in others and see parts of themselves in the world around them, their inner experience (who they see and believe themselves to be, "just *me*") and outer experiences (who others perceive them to be based on their comments and observations, "*what* are you?") are not always in harmony with each other. It's often within this window of cognitive dissonance that our multiracial kids encounter confusion and distress that interfere with the process of securing a confident self.

So, as we set out to do the most important job we'll ever do—imbue the children we love with a richly rooted self-identity—what insights and tools of discourse do we need to ensure that our children feel comfortable within *themselves*? How do we help our young multiracial or transracially adopted children discover who and what they are? How do we help them respond to the ever-present comments from strangers and peers about the shade of their skin, the hue and texture of their hair, the shape of their eyes, or the "mismatched" colors of mom and dad? Or, to speak back with confidence to the inevitable question that may well haunt them throughout their lifetime, "What are you?" How do we help them to feel *good* about being multiracial? About growing up in a "different" type of American family?

I began this project with a quest to understand how and when children who are multiracial (of two or more racial heritages), or transracially adopted (adopted into a family of a different race than their own) develop their first inklings of racial differences. I wanted to know: When do children begin to notice differences in skin color, hair, eye shape, and other characteristics? And if and when they do begin to feel "different," how can we keep those tentacles of "feeling different" from gaining a lock hold?

For instance, when that kindergartner badgered Christian on the playground about the shape of his eyes, did Christian, at three, already have some dim perception of racial differences? Of himself as "different?" Or was he as clueless about racial differences and skin color as I was about how to deal with incidents stemming from those racial nuances? And even if he were clueless about race, how did such incidents nevertheless affect his developing self-perception?

Like most parents in multiracial families, before I began examining these issues, I had little concept of exactly when changes in racial awareness occur, how they impact our children, or, moreover, the profound influence we wield on our children's burgeoning multiracial identity from the very earliest stages. Yet only by gaining this understanding could I competently—and confidently—begin a natural dialogue with my own children regarding their racial identity and racial differences in general. Only by getting inside their world and understanding their racial understanding developmentally would I know how much I should say and when I should say it, and how to do so in an age-appropriate way without overemphasizing these issues.

Is "Color-blindness" the Answer?

One nagging question remained. As I wrote this book, my mind vacillated in an inner argument of ideas. On the one hand, in this day and age, I asked myself, Why shouldn't we strive to raise our kids as "color-blind?" Why shouldn't we ignore society's artificially imposed categories of race altogether and emphasize to our children, instead, that we are all members of one race, the *human* race. Why not "let go" of the race issue? After all, the differences between races—based for the most part only on a little more or less melanin in the skin—are scientifically meaningless. *Race* is not what makes people different, or, for that matter, the same. We are all members of the human race. Haven't scientists proved, through genome research, that almost every speck of our DNA—race to race to race, regardless of what our ethnic heritage may be—is more similar than it is different?[2] Besides, in this melting pot of America, aren't most of us some mixture of ethnicity and/or races? So why should we imply to our kids that race *does* define some part of who they are—or, worse, how they or others ought to be labeled? Why can't we usher our children forth into the world as ambassadors of a race-free society in hopes that their color-blind hearts will help change our world for the better?

Goodness knows, we don't want to overstate or overplay the role that being multiracial might play in our child's life. Promoting our children's self-growth involves mindful attention and open communication regarding *all* issues in our kids' lives—attention to their emotions, their needs, their development in *all* arenas—and race-related issues are only one part of that tapestry.

As Susan Fu (Caucasian), who has three biracial (Chinese/Irish Caucasian) kids, Alex, Kayla and Chloe, puts it, "My husband's and my goal is to give our children the best possible education we can . . . and to do everything in our means to help them to become successful, nice, independent and happy people." This goal, she emphasizes, "is very different from saying, We are a multiracial family trying to raise three multiracial kids in a 99 percent Caucasian area, to feel like they fit in with the majority around them, arming them with strategies to cope with the fact that they are different, so that they might become successful, nice, independent and happy people."

To be sure, *avoiding* raising our kids primarily through the lens of race is crucial; our children's multiracialness is only one aspect of what we need to be mindful of in parenting. There is, as any parent knows, so much more. Nor is being multiracial a *problem* that needs fixing. Being multiracial is *not* the problem. But society—a society which often reacts in unexpected ways to multiracial families and individuals—*is* problematic. Because so many multiracial kids do report experiencing core identity issues as they come of age in our race-obsessed society (according to not only my interviewees but also the findings of numerous experts in the field, as we will see detailed in further chapters), it is critical for us to pay close attention to that aspect of their development.

Very early into this project, the answer to the question of whether parents need to openly address being multiracial with their children became startlingly clear. After interviewing over sixty individuals in multiracial families—including numerous young adults who have related their own experiences to me—and after reviewing recent research in the field, it became markedly apparent that raising kids to believe color *doesn't* matter in our society leaves them vastly underprepared and unnecessarily vulnerable as they come of age. As Maria Root, Ph.D. (Filipino/Chinese/Spanish-Portuguese/German/Irish/Caucasian), editor of *The Multiracial Experience: Racial Borders as the New Frontier,* explains, "When kids grow up in a family where they're repeatedly told that race doesn't matter, that we are all the same and you're no different from anyone else—so don't let it bug you if people say you are," that may appeal to our ideal sense of how the world should be for our children, and how we long for it to be, "but that doesn't help the child to be able to handle the fact that race does make a difference in how people are treated."

Wouldn't it, then, be naïve to lead our children down the garden path of believing that they are growing up in a society where the idea that "we are all one race" rules?

What a child needs to know, rather, is how to be prepared for non–color-blind peers and people who *will* query them repeatedly regarding their racial identity—from the texture of their hair to the shade of their skin to the family in which they live. What a *child* needs to know is how to speak up for himself with utter confidence and an unflappable sense of self, whether he encounters one incident of race-questioning in his lifetime, or one thousand.

And although it may seem to intuitively make sense that because preschool children don't yet notice racial differences, *we'd* be foolish to bring these differences to their attention, in fact, children's peers and the society in which our kids live—both of which wield a tremendous influence on their sense of self—*will* bring it to their attention, especially as they move from preschool into grade school. Isn't it far preferable that we do so first, in an educated, measured and developmentally appropriate way that shores up their self-esteem and sense of who they are—again, filling *up* that emotional bank—rather than leave the job of educating them about racial labels and what their significance might or might not be to their playground counterparts?

In truth, if we don't talk about race with young children, it's very possible our kids may attach too much importance to the racial differences they notice between themselves and others. Only we, as parents, can help our kids internalize their absolute worth as we help them process the racial differences that they will increasingly notice between themselves and those around them. If, by remaining silent, we (in effect) deny that those differences exist, they are likely to only grow in importance in our children's minds and may even seem more significant than they actually are.

Even more persuasive, toward the argument for helping to prepare our children—through mindful, measured dialogue—about their multiracial identity, are the sentiments of multiracial young adults who were raised in supposedly color-blind homes. Upon looking back, these young people candidly talk about their experiences growing up. In one University of Memphis study of multiracial college students, those raised in families that did not discuss the fact that they were members of an interracial family or whose parents did not address the issues their children might one day face, later reported feeling that, although their parents' messages (such as "color doesn't matter") were *meant* to be loving, such a perspective was *unrealistic*. Most of these young, multiracial adults felt their parents had neglected to prepare them adequately for what they eventually faced. As one multiracial young adult describes it, "Sometimes parents want to communicate to their children that you are just a wonderful person and they do the 'color doesn't matter' thing and that is so damaging because color does matter . . . and if you grow up thinking 'color doesn't matter' and you are a person of color, you are going to find out pretty soon and it's going to be hard."[3]

The vast majority of multiracial students in this study emphatically voiced the wish that their parents "*had* helped prepare them to deal" with the incidents and issues they would later encounter.[4] Ditto the findings in a study conducted by clinical psychologist Maria Root. When adult children from multiracial families were asked, "Do you think your parents were prepared to raise mixed children?" the overwhelming majority replied no, their parents had not been.[5]

Clarifying why so many young multiracial adults may feel disappointed in this aspect of their upbringing is the work of psychologist Willie B. Garrett (African American), father of two adopted African-American/Native American children and three African-American/Caucasian birth children. Garrett relates how his experiences with counseling transracially adopted children have informed his approach in working with biracial children. Garrett began his work as a psychologist at a center for emotionally troubled kids in Minnesota in the 1970s. He noticed a distinct trend, he says, that spoke volumes about the need for children who are racially mixed and/or transracially adopted to be raised with a clear sense of their whole racial identity. In working with troubled kids, Garrett found that a surprising "number of children who were having emotional problems were minority children adopted by white families." As Garrett worked with these children in multiracial families, he began to search for why this might be the case. The answer quickly emerged: "At that time, in the seventies, the prevailing theory of raising transracially adoptive kids was to raise them as if there was nothing different about them, and to ignore the issue of race altogether. Parents were reassured that 'all you need is love'—and 'love will be enough'—that racial/cultural issues needn't be addressed." As a result, says Garrett, "These kids had tremendous identity issues; they felt that they weren't accepted or loved by their parents—because, they believed, if their parents *did* love and accept them for who they were, then there would have been some open discussion about their racial identity. But because the subject of their racial identity was never talked about, they felt that not only were they not accepted by their parents, but that there must be something *wrong* with them."

Kelley Kenney, Ed.D. (African American), cofounder of the Rainbow Support Network (for multiracial families) and parent of two African American/Caucasian daughters, underscores what these young adults voice, from the perspective of one who routinely counsels interracial couples in multiracial families: "I always feel wary when couples tell me race doesn't matter, or that they're color-blind, or when they say their kids are color-blind. I feel they're in deep denial about race, and that they've sold their children short by setting up this false perception that their child's race—and how they look—*isn't* going to matter in their lives. That's just not the reality—questions will come up. And when those questions do come up kids who aren't properly prepared for them will feel suddenly alienated from and rejected by those around them."

When parents send their child the message that race is not an okay subject to talk about, they set their child up to feel ashamed of their true racial identity (and, therefore, of who they *are*)—and to feel compelled to hide one entire aspect of themselves.

Twenty-two-year-old Nicole Brown (African American/Caucasian) expresses how important having this ongoing discussion regarding one's multiracial identity is, from her vantage point: "I *wish* we lived in a color-blind society, but that's not happening. So you had better prepare your kids. You had better delve into race with them so they understand who they really are and the complications that can come with being multiracial. It would be totally unfair to pretend that your kids will have no problems; that everything is going to be just fine. It makes for a really naïve person who's going to go out into the world without the necessary skills and knowledge and rhetoric they need to defend themselves from the stupid and hurtful things some people will say and the confusing responses the world will give them."

Indeed. And yet, despite this reality, a surprising number of parents whom I interviewed seemed to believe that raising their multiracial children to be "color-blind"—as if race doesn't, or shouldn't, matter; as if "love is all that matters"—or simply not discussing race at all, was *best* for their kids.

Through the course of our conversations, however, some parents began to ask themselves important questions regarding the way in which they were addressing (or rather *not* addressing) race with their children—and wondered how they might begin to bring an awareness about the reality of race into their children's lives.

But before any of us can bring an age-appropriate awareness of race to our young children during their preschool years—acknowledging racial differences without focusing on them disproportionately, preparing our kids for the realities of what may occur in their lives without overstating these possibilities—we have to understand the stages our children pass through as they initially become conscious of race.

Understanding the Two- to Five-Year-Old Multiracial Child

To what extent do very young children—as young as two and three—truly take note of racial differences?

Race is really a grown-up notion that is meaningless to the vast majority of preschoolers. Most do not have the slightest inkling of their race, says Marguerite Wright (African American), research psychologist for the Center for the Vulnerable Child at Children's Hospital in Oakland, California. For instance, in her research, when Wright asked three-year-olds, "What color are you?" they were just as likely to mention the color of whatever *clothes* they were wearing as they were the color of their skin. Three-year-olds who were aware of their skin color (as some kids this age are) tended to describe themselves in terms they were familiar with, such as pink and peach or brown and chocolate, rather than use terms like black, African American or white.[6] Yet all too often when we hear three-year-olds describe their skin *color* we assume their self-description means they are already aware of their *race*—and such is not the case.[7]

When my son, Christian, was three, one of his first preschool projects was to cut out pictures of eyes, ears and noses to make collages of his family members' faces. One of the teachers mentioned to me that when she has students of Asian or African-American descent—or any other minority—she has magazine pages showing people of that race for that child to cut features from. But preschoolers usually have so little awareness of race that the African-American boy might choose a blond-haired mother; the blond-haired boy of European descent might cut out Asian eyes for the collage of his mom. He's more likely to go for the mouth smiling wide or the sparkle of the eyes, which captures his mom so much more than the color of her cheeks or the slope of her eyelids.

Wright tells the story of a three-year-old preschooler, Jetasha, who was asked to hand her interviewer "the photo of the child that looks the most like you" out of an array of photos of racially different children:

JETASHA: This one.
INTERVIEWER: Why does she look like you?
JETASHA: Because she goes to school with me.[8]

Although it is only a few years down the road—at five and six—that children begin to be attuned to and try to process racial differences, at the age of three, Jetasha's racially unaware response is overwhelmingly common.

At the same time, typical three-year-olds can tell you without any hesitation whether they are a boy or a girl—and are often endlessly intrigued by the topic. But gender identification develops earlier and more naturally to young children than does identification by color or by race.[9] Gender is clear-cut from the get-go. It doesn't take a toddler very long to figure out that there are two physiological camps: boy or girl, penis or vagina. But what is so clear-cut about race? There are hundreds of permutations, combinations and variations of skin hue and eye shape to observe, process, mentally code and label. Children have to be *coached* to code racially varied skin hues and ethnic features into racial groupings according to the stereotypes and prejudices they hear adults articulate.

As a song from the film *South Pacific*, set during World War II, portrays so poignantly (in a scene where a white officer wrestles with his own deep-seated prejudices toward the Polynesian woman he is contemplating marrying):

You've got to be taught to be afraid
Of people whose eyes are oddly made,
And people whose skin is a diff'rent shade,
You've got to be carefully taught.[10]

As we come to understand very early racial awareness, it is helpful to also understand the developmental awareness of the typical three-year-old in general. As the work of Swiss psychologist Jean Piaget—who launched the landmark study of how young children come to understand the world around them more than 50 years ago—shows, preschoolers are overwhelmingly convinced that they are the absolute center of the universe. They fail to grasp that people around them have different points of view or different sources of knowledge. They are, in Piaget's terms, egocentric (e.g., if my soup is hot, everyone's soup must be hot).[11]

Additionally, until the age of three and a half, children simply cannot classify something as belonging to more than *one* category at the same time. For instance, a red ball can't be categorized as a round ball and the color red at the same time. Likewise, three-year-olds given a novelty toy such as, say, a

large sponge shaped and painted to look like a rock, find this kind of sub-
tlety too confusing. In their mind, the object possesses only one characteristic, not both at once. It is a rock, *or* it is a sponge.[12] Children this age don't
yet possess the sophistication to categorize people—or themselves—along
nuanced, *mixed* racial lines.

Kelley Kenney (African American) shares a story about her daughter
Olivia (African American/Caucasian) when she was almost four. Kenney
was sitting with her in front of a store when, she says, "some black people
walked by us and Olivia said, 'Oh, look mommy! There are some *black* people!'" Kelley says she was understandably surprised that, growing up in a
biracial family where her own mom was black and Olivia herself was half
black, Olivia would exclaim with surprise about seeing "black people." But,
she explains, "When we thought about it, it made sense." Developmentally,
she observes, "to Olivia, Mommy wasn't 'a black person'—she was just
Mommy." To Olivia, Mommy couldn't, in that single moment, be categorized as "a black person" and "Mommy" at the same time (double categorization). Moreover, why else would anyone see mommy as black (rather
than just Mommy) if *Olivia* didn't? (Egocentrism at play.) Therefore there
was, in her mind, no relationship whatsoever between "black people"
strolling by and her own mom. And, finally, Olivia didn't yet have the developmental and cognitive ability to see *herself* as being mixed—as being part
black, part white (double categorization again).

This tendency toward forming absolute, singular categories makes the
concept of being multiracial especially difficult for very young children to
grasp. It is confusing for children of three to understand that they themselves
are more than one thing—that if mommy is Asian and daddy is white, then
they themselves are *both things at the same time*. The concept simply doesn't
click. Consider this conversation between a mother and her three-year-old
child struggling to conceptualize that her friend could be a member of two
different groups at the same time:

CHILD: Why is F. half Chicano and half Japanese?
MOTHER: Half and half is whole.
CHILD: Is she a whole?[13]

This internal confusion, however, does not mean that a child's multiracialness *shouldn't* be brought up and discussed. It is only by discussing these

issues that we can unobtrusively and yet effectively set the groundwork for future conversations (exactly *how* to have these early conversations with your preschooler is the focus of the second half of this chapter).

Although three-year-olds are not yet operating under the same set of influences and preconceptions as older children, they are busily and quietly gathering salient information to form conclusions about the world around them every minute of every day, soaking in a broad array of cues from their environment. For this reason, their seeming ignorance of racial issues should not lull any of us into a false sense that our children will remain "blissfully ignorant of race," as many parents understandably hope. Just around a minuscule corner in their development, race will increasingly inform the way our children view and categorize those in the world around them—including themselves. Even though, at this early age, they may not possess the verbal abilities to articulate their perceptions of color and race, these perceptions are already beginning to "color" the way they think.

Consider one study, in which three- to five-year-old children were asked to describe photographs of classmates familiar to them and children unfamiliar to them. In describing photos of children who were familiar to them, they often listed details such as clothing, hairstyle, facial expressions and activities that a particular child did, *rather than* described children by larger categories such as gender or race. However, when children were asked to say who was *different* from them, they often explicitly used skin color as a defining factor. This study suggests children may be more likely to consider the color of another child's skin when determining who is "different"—and less likely to cite it when determining who is "the same." It may be, say researchers, that children's nonverbal racial perceptions (their inklings that skin color may differentiate people in some way) exceed their verbal understanding of racial categories.[14]

This is not to imply that even four- and five-year-olds are overtly conscious of *race* itself. Grouping others by *skin color*—as a precursor to grouping others by racial characteristics—may increasingly inform the way in which children see others as they age. But most four- and five-year-olds are still more or less unaware of *racial* categories per se. According to Marguerite Wright's research, while children may (usually, in her experience, only with prompting) group photos of African-American, Asian and Caucasian children into three skin color groups—dark, brown and light-skinned children—once this grouping is done, preschoolers do not spontaneously use a

color or racial word to describe these children. Even when they group people into families based on skin-color similarity, they are just as likely to put
light-skinned African American and Asian children in the same family with
Caucasian children as they are to select white children for that group.[15]

To wit, Wright points out that although most African-American children describe their skin color as *brown*, some with light complexions may
describe themselves as *white*. "Their use of this word seems to be based
purely on their perception, on what they see as the similarity of their light
skin color to what adults call 'white,' rather than because of racial awareness
or an emotional identification (the infamous 'wish to be white')," she
observes. Although some African-American parents assume that if their
children call themselves "white," they must feel inferior, Wright emphasizes
that such parental "concern is needless. They are confusing their child's
quite accurate *color* identification with an adult's *racial* identification."
Similarly, when children are asked to color their skin in self-portraits, children who choose colors like green or purple are making choices that have
little to do with their self-image.

But, again, the eyes of preschoolers are only unaware of such physical differences for a mere flicker in time. At ages four and five, young children are
increasingly *eager* to compare themselves to others in endless ways. Not only
are they more interested in who they are, they're more interested in the specific characteristics of those around them. Francis Wardle, Ph.D. (African
American), executive director for the Center for the Study of Biracial
Children and parent of two African-American/Caucasian girls, points out
that at this age, kids are starting to "ask all sorts of questions . . . about skin
color, parents, age of parents, clothes, where their friends live" and so on.
They are particularly interested in how their physical characteristics compare to those of other kids around them. Who has the longest hair? The
curliest? Who among them is the tallest? Who can run the fastest? Jump the
farthest?[16] And—whose skin is the darkest?

Four- and five-year-olds are simply comparing themselves to everything.
For instance, a child coloring with crayons might try to see how the color
of her skin compares to the colors in the crayon box. (My own son was five
when he announced one day with a sense of proud discovery that he
matched the "tumbleweed" crayon in his classroom's Crayola set. Even now,
at eight, he still refers to his skin as being "tumbleweed.") Fours and fives
frequently begin to ask about their own racial identity—their curiosity

often triggered by questions other children ask them, such as, "Your daddy's white and your mother's black, so what are you?" or "Are you black or are you white—I can't tell?"[17] Or, their questions may be triggered by confusing statements they've overheard about the way they look. Often these questions occur for the first time when young children enter a new day care or school setting. Not surprisingly, it's during this time of intent self-comparison to others that the foundation for our children's beliefs—about who they perceive themselves to be (tall, short, fast, slow, black, white, mixed and so on), and about who those around them are, and the values *ascribed* to those labels ("It's good to be fast" or "It's the worst to be the shortest one in the class" or "It's weird to be half this and half that")—begins to be built.

Four- and five-year-olds' growing interest in skin color and racial differences is readily observable by the questions they ask at this age:

"If I'm black and white and the new baby is black and white, how come he is so much lighter than me?"

"I didn't know that black babies could come out of white mommies!"

"Why did that little boy call me black if my skin is *brown*?"

"Why does Jimmy say my skin is yellow when it's not yellow at all?"

Moreover, the way we, as parents, *respond* to these first race-conscious questions lays the initial building blocks for our child's *lifelong self-concept*. At four and five, as children learn to determine what is authentic and what is not, what is true and what is not, what is to be believed as fact and what is to be discarded as false, it is paramount that our ongoing dialogue with them about race is both conscious and carefully considered. At this stage our children's antennae are so tuned to issues of differences that stereotypic and inaccurate information can be *particularly* damaging.[18]

Meanwhile, by four and a half and five, children are increasingly able to understand the concept of two different characteristics being "mixed together," which allows us to begin to use terms such as biracial (two races) or multiracial (two or more races) when we introduce conversations about racial identity—although children need our guidance in understanding these labels at this young age. Nevertheless, having a verbal label can be enormously useful in helping children not only understand who they are but also respond to questions other children might ask about "what" they are.

It is also at about four and a half that children begin to realize their skin color will remain the same. Until this age, kids often engage in "magical thinking" about their skin shade—believing that it can or will change over time. For example, when asked to point out photos of babies who "match" them, four-year-olds often choose photos of babies with skin colors that are obviously quite different from their own. And when asked to predict what skin color they'll be when they grow up, their predictions often fall far from the mark.[19] Yet at around the age of five they begin to solidify their concept that their skin color is part of their long-term identity—which means we need to be certain that their self-image regarding skin color is unquestioningly positive.

Encouraging a Multiracial Identity for Our Kids

It is sometimes tempting to approach the issue of our child's multiracial identity by avoiding the topic, perhaps out of fear that discussing it will draw unnecessary attention to our child's racial uniqueness in a world that might prove to be more than willing to do the same, or out of hope that identity issues will never arise for our particular child because they haven't thus far. Or perhaps we remain silent on the topic because we simply feel inept— and saying nothing at all feels less circumspect and dangerous than saying the wrong thing.

Frequently, however, parents have more specific reasons for avoiding discussions of race with their children—yet when this is the case we need to examine carefully our motivations. For some parents—often minority parents (but certainly not always)—their own experiences in the past were so traumatizing that they simply avoid discussing race with their children because it stirs up too many deep-seated emotions. They hope that "things have changed," and meanwhile the less said the better. In order to avoid talking about their own past experiences—which are too painful—they avoid talking about race entirely. This is often true when a parent's culture includes a painful history (e.g., the Native American experience, African-American slavery, or the Japanese internment during World War II). Parents sometimes fear that if race *is* an open topic, their kids might learn about these traumatic events in their culture's history and that the knowledge of what was once perpetrated against their race might damage their sense of self, cause them to feel inferior or create fear that such atrocities might happen again. They would rather keep these floodgates closed. And their instincts, at first glance, are good ones. Young children are not an appropriate audience for lessons about the face of racial hatred in our history. We don't teach children about other horrors of the world—nuclear bombs, rape, murder—when they are this young, so why should we teach them about racial hatred? But ignoring the topic of racial heritage and racial differences for fear it might involve discussing racial hatred and race crimes is analogous to the proverbial throwing of the baby out with the bath water. Instead, we should hold on to the one tightly, while letting the other go.

Other parents in multiracial families may avoid discussing race because they arrived in this country as immigrants and don't yet fully grasp the race issue in America. They don't know *how* to converse with their kids about it, and the identity that they're most concerned their kids internalize is that they're "an American." Race is secondary to the issue of becoming part of mainstream American culture.

But perhaps the most troubling reason why some parents avoid the topic of race is because they want their multiracial children to accept one heritage while rejecting their other racial background. According to psychologist Maria Root, this may happen more frequently in African-American/Caucasian families, "where there is the desire to socialize one's children as black. Parents might tell their kids that if you are *part* black in America, then you *are* black. They hope that this process of socialization will help their children to be politically active and involved in what it means to be black in this country." Parents may also fear that if their children identify as being part white, they won't be fully accepted by the African-American community in which they live. Hence, rather than have conversations with their child regarding their mixed identity, these parents dictate their child's identity *to* them. They may even hope that their child will "pass"[20] as fully black. Conversely, a white parent in a predominately white community may wish—especially if their multiracial child is very light-skinned—to play down, or even hide, the fact that their child is part African American, hoping that the child will be accepted as white and thus never face racial prejudice or stereotypes.

However, telling a child that although they're multiracial they should identify with only one race is all but guaranteed to set them up for a state of inner turmoil and identity problems over the long haul. It says to them that while we know they are really one thing—*both* races—they must pretend to everyone that they are something else—a contradiction that can't help but ignite powerful self-doubt ("I'm white? What about the part of me that's black? Is being both *bad*? It must be bad if I can't talk about it with Mom and Dad . . . "). This confusion, in turn, perpetuates the erroneous stereotype that multiracial kids, as a whole, are destined to have problems, that because they *are* multiracial, they will, as a matter of course, be inwardly conflicted and maladjusted about who they are. In truth, the confusion about our multiracial children's racial identity is *society's* confusion—most people simply don't feel comfortable when they don't know how to racially pigeonhole our children. That confusion and discomfort about multiracialness should be owned by *society*, not by our multiracial children.

Take Bethany Fry (Native American/Italian/Caucasian), age 24, who tells the story of being asked to reject her Native American heritage by her own grandmother. "I look completely Caucasian, although in the summer I get a lot darker than some of my friends. But that's about it," she explains. "When I'm with my dad's Italian family I look like I could be very Italian. I *am* Italian. I'm also Native American and I'm very proud of being Native American. But when we were growing up, when I was with my Italian grandmother and we would go somewhere with her Italian friends, my grandmother would say, 'Now remember if anyone asks you, you're *Italian*, right?' She coached me to make sure I didn't mention being partly Native American. She wanted me to pretend to be someone I wasn't. It was so confusing and awful—it made me feel that there was something wrong with *me*. You would think your grandmother would love you no matter what. But she didn't. I had to hide that side of my family—of *myself*—in order to be with her. It was really hurtful."

Fortunately for Bethany, she was raised by two aware parents whose inclusion of both her cultures helped counter much of the damage done by her grandmother, who was also a strong presence in her small-town life. But even so, negative memories of that early time of confusion and disillusionment remain to this day.

But when the person dictating a one-race identity to a child is a parent, the scars run even deeper. One young multiracial and transracially adopted girl cites just such a formative growing up experience. "I was adopted by a white family who was very racist," she explains. "They thought I was white or so they claim, but I assure you that I didn't look like a white child. I looked biracial (black/white). My parents always spoke negatively about people who were nonwhite; therefore I grew up feeling like I had to conceal who I was by lying to myself, telling myself I was white, but I never looked white. I always tried—and still do to some degree—to measure myself against white standards of beauty—which is something I can never achieve."[21]

Judith Ashton (Caucasian), executive director of the New York State Citizens Coalition for Children, and mother of an adopted African-American/Caucasian son, emphasizes that the importance of promoting a transracially adopted child's racial and cultural heritage during their upbringing is obviously just as critical as it is for children in interracial families. "Transracially adopted children usually don't have a parent of their own ethnic background in their adoptive family to help give them a clearer sense of their own identity. So this issue has to be out there for us all the time. Even if our children *are* biracial, it's not as useful to help them focus on being half this and half that because what our kids need to be most clear about is their heritage of *color*. For instance, when it comes to matters of race, my [adopted] son who is half black is not going to get as much benefit out of identifying with his white biological father as will a kid who is biracial from an interracial marriage. My son needs to identify with his African-American heritage more than his white heritage, especially since there is no one else of African-American heritage in his own home."

Ashton agrees it's also essential to realize from the get-go that "love is *not* enough. Race matters. That junk that comes and confronts our kids is real; we can't raise our kids as if it isn't there. If your child's own experience is denied they will be forced to tell themselves: 'This must not be happening because no one else can see it happening, therefore I must not be experiencing it—so I must be crazy. Something must be wrong with *me*.'"

Coping with Curious Comments and Supermarket Stares

Multiracial children often appear quite exotic to others. Indeed, their physical appearance is frequently a source of special attention that can lead to jarring incidents as we go about our everyday routines. Sometimes these interactions are very subtle. Now and then, when my children and I are standing in line at the grocery store, I'll see—no, I'll *sense*—a couple observing us with more than a little curiosity. They'll glance at us, glance at each other and glance back our way before I intercept their gaze. At which point one of them will usually exclaim to me, "What *beautiful* children!" While I appreciate their sentiment, I can't help but notice their awkwardness or that, before they noted my children's beauty, they had to stare.

Over time, such incidents can be not only startling but disturbing, to say the least. Leceta Chisholm Guibault (Caucasian), board member of the Adoption Council of Canada and adoptive mom of two, explains her feelings: "I used to love when my daughter [Mayan Indian/Guatemalan] was a baby and people would stop me and exclaim, 'What beautiful black eyes she has! Look at that straight black hair! And nice brown skin!' Although I thought these were positive comments, by the age of four, my daughter Kahleah had had enough. One day, after having numerous people make these same observations over and over again, Kahleah buried her face in my stomach, overwhelmed. She said she was tired of people 'always' pointing out the same things: her hair, eyes and skin." At that point, says Leceta, she began to view these comments from her daughter's vantage point, asking herself, "What child deserves to be made to feel different, simply because of race?"

Although frequent comments about a young child's unique physical appearance ("What beautiful curls!" or "She has such beautiful golden skin!") may initially seem flattering and enjoyable (and we might even assume they are positive for our child's self-esteem), eventually—as these comments singling out our child are repeated over time—they become objectifying, causing a child to feel not only awkward but "other."

Why do people so often make comments about multiracial children? Of course they are beautiful—we as their parents know that. But why is it that our children garner so much extra attention from strangers when other, clearly adorable kids don't garner as much?

Perhaps when people encounter a biracial child they often are compelled to look, and look again, in order to figure them (and their family situation) out, yet at the same time they feel awkward staring without saying a word. In order to mask their discomfort, they may overreact, touching our child's hair or commenting repeatedly on how beautiful our child is.

Even though our child is getting the *verbal* message that he or she is beautiful, by being repeatedly singled out, she is also getting the *nonverbal* message that she is *different*. And whenever children receive mixed messages, it tends to cause them inner anxiety. This combination of being treated more like an object than a person and receiving mixed messages, explains psychologist Willie B. Garrett, "is so damaging to the child because over time they're going to internalize these unpleasant feelings, which take the form of the child thinking of themselves as *un*attractive." They "get it" that their appearance falls outside the norm.

Indeed, children whose appearance is frequently scrutinized and overreacted to often report feeling "like a puppy."[22] Even three- and four-year-olds can begin to perceive that if everywhere they go people raise the magnifying glass to them, while other children are not undergoing such public scrutiny, they must be odd, no matter how positive the words being said may sound.

One noteworthy aside here. While it is disconcerting for *all* children—including monoracial kids in monoracial families—to be singled out for an aspect of their appearance (e.g., "What big, beautiful, blue eyes you have!") over and over again (certainly *no* parent wants their child to absorb the warped message that the superficial details of how one looks, rather than who one is inside, are what makes one special) the *context* of such stranger-exchanges is clearly different for multiracial children. For our children, such praise-under-scrutiny is all too often an apology for staring at our children in the first place and is sometimes coupled—as our children come of age—with experiences of *rejection* based on the way they look.

As psychologist Maria Root puts it, "It is the combination of inquisitive looks, longer than passing glances to comprehend unfamiliar racial-ethnic features . . . and comments of surprise . . . *along with* disapproving comments and nonverbal communication that begin to convey to the child that this otherness is undesirable or wrong."

Meanwhile Mom or Dad (unaware of what their child is experiencing) might unwittingly collude with strangers during such intrusions by keeping the conversation going. Garrett talks about counseling parents who often get into "these types of conversations explaining intimate details of their adoption or their interracial family with a complete stranger, and that's another violation of the child's world. If the parent is colluding with strangers by discussing these issues right in front of their kids, then the child becomes accustomed to not having their boundaries respected." Later in life, says Garrett, that lack of respect toward a child's needs may contribute to "setting a child up for a pattern of allowing themselves to be mistreated by others who also don't respect their boundaries." Garrett also believes that not protecting our children from stranger interactions can hurt the parent child relationship itself: "A child *expects* their parent to protect them from any pain or discomfort. Yet when strangers are intruding and parents aren't saying anything, the parent isn't protecting them from that situation. Which is why I advise parents: Always remember, your child is listening and watching. You should not feel you have to explain the circumstance of *having* your child."

I have become doubly reacquainted with such intrusive comments since having had my daughter, Claire, four years ago. It never ceases to surprise me how many people see Claire and exclaim, "She has *blond* hair!" or "Oh! Look at her beautiful hair! With those dark eyes and white skin—stunning!" Even among those who see her frequently, her appearance is so often reevaluated: "Her hair is getting lighter!" or, "Her hair is getting darker!" or, "Wow! Look how shiny and blond her hair is now!" or even, "She doesn't even look that Asian!" Wherever we go, we are guaranteed to get comments about Claire—and especially Claire's "blond hair." But ironically, my daughter doesn't *have* blond hair. She has brown hair—light brown hair—but it is quite clearly brown all the same. Yet because onlookers don't expect an Asian-eyed child to have light hair of any shade, they exclaim over how blond she seems without seeing her as she truly is.

I have come to realize that exclaiming over Claire's hair—benignly intended as people's comments may be—gives strangers (unconsciously) something to say while they do a double take to decode her racially. If they rescrutinize her, me, the two of us together, well, isn't that okay as long as they're remarking on how beautiful she is? What can be the harm in that?

Stopping Obtrusive Comments in Their Tracks

Over time, our daughter has developed a kind of public shell she retreats into when others approach. She refuses eye contact, sucks her thumb and puts her head against my side, her arm grasping mine. How much of this sudden shyness, when we are out and about, is due to innate personality, and how much of it relates to having to squirm under each stranger's magnifying glass, we will never know. But I do know that it is critical for Claire that I quickly take her out of the uncomfortable limelight when people make intrusive comments. For this reason, when people comment on her, or my son's, appearance, I often smile warmly and say, straight from my heart, "Oh, aren't all children so *beautiful?*" in an all-child-everywhere encompassing way to deflect the excessive attention from my children and make all children the topic of our brief exchange—and to stop people in their tracks before they say more.

It's also important to respond to the curious in such a way that we *model* the behavior we want our kids to learn from us; behavior they can draw upon later, when they navigate their way through our race-conscious world on their own.

Louise Lazare (Caucasian), mother of eight adopted children (six of whom are biracial) recalls, "When our children were younger we would take them to a Chinese restaurant and all the people there would stare at us. I didn't notice it that much—for me, being stared at was just a part of our daily life—but the kids did; they couldn't stand it. We also got a lot of stares when we were on the subway in Boston. Once, when we were going downtown to the public gardens, as we got off, a black woman came running up to me and pressed five dollars in my hand and said, 'God *bless* you.' Being stared at was just part of our life."

Nancy Brown (Caucasian), M.N., C.N.S., is president of the Association of MultiEthnic Americans (AMEA) and mom of two African-American/Caucasian girls, Nicole (22) and Rochelle (17). She counsels parents in multiracial families that "getting those out-of-place comments and curious stares is part of the territory of being a parent in a multiracial family. If we are going to be in a multiracial family we have to be prepared to withstand public attention—and we can't be afraid to open our mouths. Our mission isn't to put a stop to all this but to know *how* to deal with the extra attention that can make our children feel objectified." And to do so in such a way that our children can learn from watching us.

So how exactly do we gracefully deflect this special—and all too often objectifying and discomforting—attention our children receive? It can help, for starters, to remember that every glance that comes our way when we're out and about with our kids is hardly loaded with racist subtext. There is simply no socially agreed upon etiquette for closely observing those around us—no agreed upon social construct for "looking." And yet it's part of our human impulse to look at others and observe them out of curiosity. As social beings, we are constantly assessing and coding others (whether unconsciously or consciously), making guesstimates about their age, gender, economic status, marital status—and race.

Curiosity is human. *Looking* is human. And sometimes the person glancing our way is simply being human. As one mom puts it, "Sometimes I feel that a warm look comes from a liberal point of view; that people are trying to let you know in a liberal sort of way, 'Hey, you have a multiracial family and it's okay with me.'" In other words, a passerby who offers a simple nod and smile may even be trying to make a supportive connection.

Still, for our children's sake, we have to be careful to avoid buying into the premise that because we made certain life and love choices that don't fit into traditionally prescribed racial lines, strangers who feel compelled to query us until they assuage their curiosity can assume our life—or our children's—is an open book.

Accordingly, many of my interviewees cite different but equally creative means of closing that book gently when others seek to open it. Take Agnes Horowitz (Caucasian), adoptive mom of five-year-old Maggie (Chinese). Because Maggie comes under a lot of scrutiny in public, which makes her uncomfortable, Agnes has started her own experiment: "I've begun to avoid other people's eyes a little bit when I'm out with Maggie. I just keep looking at her and staying involved with *her*. I don't like to have to do it, but I do it. I create a kind of cocoon around us because I think it's better for her. That cocoon that surrounds us is so strong and so palpable that others wouldn't dare to interfere."

Cassandra McGowen (Chinese), adopted by Caucasian parents forty years ago, and now mom of two Chinese/Caucasian daughters, talks about how her husband has taught her to use humor when their children are scrutinized, in order to deflect attention from their girls. "My husband, Ty (Caucasian), has developed this wonderful response when he's out alone with our two mixed-race daughters," she says. When people say, "'Oh, what beautiful children!'—which couches so many questions like, 'What are they? Are they *yours*?' and is so objectifying—Ty's answer is always, 'Oh, you should see their *mother!*'"

Ginny Miller, Caucasian mother of two African-American/Caucasian adopted children relates, "Every single time my son and daughter and I go to the shopping mall or grocery store someone always says to them, 'Where did you get that curly hair?' or, '*Wow!* Women would kill to have that hair!' Both of my children know that they are biracial and adopted, and we talk about it all the time. When someone asks them, 'Where did you get your beautiful hair?' they have a standard answer we've prepared them with at home: 'From God.'" This response usually ends the conversation in such a way that Ginny's biracial children feel good about who they are—as well as about their ability to speak up for themselves with pride and with a finesse that quickly moves them out of the spotlight.

It can take courage to speak up and make it clear to strangers that we prefer they stop asking questions or making obtrusive comments—or, especially, touching our child. But psychologist Willie B. Garrett emphasizes we need to always bear in mind that our children do not have the ability to stand up for themselves. We, as their parents, need to assertively set limits—even if it means offending a stranger—by saying something like, "Thank you, but I feel uncomfortable when people touch her hair." Or, we may find that the only way to nip insistent questioning ("Where is she from?" or "Where did she get those eyes?") in the bud is to respond directly: "This is a personal matter that I don't care to discuss," and then move on.

Carrie Howard (Caucasian), adoptive mom of six-year-old Tessa (Chinese), articulates her experience in setting just such limits: "There are times when I can't get through the supermarket without being stopped by a stranger or two exclaiming over Tessa's beauty; little old ladies have practically chased me down the aisle to make sure they had a chance to tell me that my little girl is adorable." But Howard is especially disturbed "when strangers call Tessa 'a little China doll,' as though she were a fragile piece of *chinoiserie* [or] an exotic object d'art. How much are the compliments inspired by her personal qualities, and how much by the obvious contrast between our Caucasian faces and her Asian one? Since we can't read minds, it's impossible to know what people are thinking when they compliment our kids. But it's safe to say that what brings our children to most people's attention is the fact that they look different, and children pick up on that distinction."

In response, says Howard, she has learned to deflect strangers' comments by shifting those moments into an opportunity to remind Tessa that she is "a three-dimensional person with many gifts to offer" *other* than physical beauty. "When strangers gush over Tessa, I just smile and say, 'Thank you, we think she's beautiful too,' and keep pushing my cart down the aisle. Then when we're out of earshot, I remind her that she is smart and strong too—not a China doll at all."

Often, incidents that make our children feel "other" may seem completely un-noteworthy to everyone *except* that child and his or her parents.

It may even be hard to determine if your child really notices what is occurring; sometimes all that betrays their confusion is a momentary loss of a smile or a flicker of discomfort shading her eyes, or a quick glance at us, to see how we're responding (and to validate *her* sense that a situation infringes on her growing sense of personal boundaries).

I remember once, as Christian (four and a half at the time) and Claire (nearly two) and I were walking down the street with a group of Christian's friends, a little Korean boy peered out of a nearby window. One of my son's Caucasian friends, six-year-old Adam, was walking beside him and pointed up at this little boy. He exclaimed loudly to my son, "Wow! He looks a lot like you! He does, he *really* looks a lot like *you*! *Look* at that boy, Christian!" My son, having discussed different racial facial characteristics with us often enough, ventured an unsure smile. I could see his split-second confusion. Did he look so different that it warranted amazement from friends if another child looked *anything* like him at all? In truth, the boy in the window looked nothing like my biracial son except for the fact that he had seemingly monoracial Asian features, which only served to confuse Christian further.

Our First Dialogues About Race

How, then, do we begin to talk about race in a way that subtly prepares kids for the realities of what may come up in their lives and include and celebrate all their cultural heritages without overemphasizing the issues?

Meeting the challenge of fostering a healthy multiracial identity in our preschoolers begins with engaging them in a positive dialogue about racial differences. Then, when they do begin to register those differences for themselves, they already possess a solid, healthy racial self-concept that enables them to discard any negative views others might espouse.

This involves, says AMEA president Nancy Brown, "answering kids' questions about race and being multiracial in a developmentally appropriate way—the same way as we might answer questions about fire safety or crossing the street—sharing the matter-of-fact facts, without making it into a scientific discussion that goes over the top of what a child might understand."

It can also be very helpful to let your child know that you understand how uncomfortable it must make them feel to be the focus of so much attention. For instance, when Christian seemed disturbed by his friend Adam's comment, I took that moment to lean down and say, "I don't think

Adam has ever been to Japan the way we have, has he? If he had I bet he'd know that although most people in Asia have dark hair and beautiful brown eyes that doesn't mean they look *alike* anymore than everybody who is blond in America looks alike."

Another tack to take is to ask your child, "Why do you think so-and-so made that comment?" or, "Why do you think people always want to say something when they see families like ours?" Then talk about people you know who are also in mixed families and how normal that really is.

As parents in multiracial families, our job is to create a forum for a positive discussion of racial differences between our child and ourselves to the extent that such stares and comments lose their ability to cause our children discomfort or confusion, or to stir up even the smallest seeds of self-doubt.

Consider the way Nicole Brown (African American/Caucasian), age 22, sums up how her mom, Nancy, helped her develop a healthy racial self-concept: "From as early as I can remember, my parents always talked to me about both sides of who I am and supported both sides of who I am. I feel that I was so well-prepared for the world and so well-exposed to all of who I am that, most of the time I was growing up, even when someone did make a hurtful comment to me, those comments didn't even penetrate. I already knew who I was and felt good about who I was, so those comments had no effect on me."

How do we begin to imbue *our* children with inner confidence?

Using Props and Tools

One of the most natural ways to embark on that early conversation is by filling our home with props and tools—a range of appropriate play items and storybooks, amid our child's toys, that reflect their unique racial heritage as well as diversity in general, and to use these as a point of departure for discussions about differences. It's critical for our children to see reflections of *themselves* in their day-to-day setting (it's easy, sometimes, to forget that if you're, say, Chinese American and your spouse is Caucasian, your child's two greatest role models do not reflect his *own* unique racial identity).

Leo (African American) and Diane Dillon (Caucasian) have illustrated more than 40 books, including two Caldecott Award–winning children's books *(Ashanti to Zulu* and *Why Mosquitoes Buzz in People's Ears).* They talk about how when they raised their biracial son, Lee (now in his 30s), "there were few, if any, quality books that included races other than white. We looked for books with good stories and illustrations, along with some classics like Mother Goose. Then, at night, we would stay up coloring in the characters to reflect children like him." In the morning, they would hand Lee a new book—full of Mother Goose characters and others who bore his skin shade, his biracial characteristics. Ironically, Diane recalls, "Years later, when Lee was a teenager, he was at a conference where we were speaking and we were talking about having to color his books. Afterward he came up with a grin and said, 'I used to wonder why some of my friends had the same books but theirs were different from mine.'" Seeing how few books were available which reflected multiracial and multicultural children, "We decided to dedicate our career to include varied cultures and races whenever we could," says Leo.

Naomi Reed (African American/Russian Jewish/Caucasian), age 20, talks about how, growing up, "A few of my books were about black or white characters and one or two were about Jewish characters, but none were about mixed-race characters. I would get so excited, though, when some of the animal characters in my stories would have families in which different kinds of animals lived together." To this day, Naomi recalls how reassuring those images were.

Agnes Horowitz tells how one book came to mean the world to her adopted daughter, Maggie. "I found this wonderful book, *A Mother for Choco*, about a little bird who wants to have a mommy, but the different animals she asks say no, they can't be her mommy because she doesn't look like them. Then a bear says, 'Why can't I be your mother?' And Choco says, 'But you don't look like me.' The bear takes her home and says, 'Choco, here are my other children!' And none of them are bears. When I first read it to Maggie she was just three, and when I finished the book she said, "I am Choco, Mommy. I am Choco."

Consider, too, the recollection of Rochelle Brown, age 17 (younger sister of Nicole), about some of the books her mom and dad read to her early on. They reflected multiracial families that "made a huge difference for me. I loved these two books: *How My Parents Learned to Eat* and *You Be Me, I'll Be You*. I remember *so well* every time my mom would read them to me. I also loved this book, *People*. On one page everyone has gray suits on and at the bottom it says, 'What would the world be like if everyone looked the same?' And then you turn the page and everyone has different colors and it shows how much we all need that diversity. I still have these books. I don't look at them so often now, but I know they're there." (For a list of books geared toward children in multiracial families, see the recommended reading section.)

As parents, we need to make that extra effort to borrow books that reflect multiracial issues from the library or buy them for our children's bookshelves and have conversations about the images in them. "It's our responsibility to make these books available," emphasizes Nancy Brown. In order to make sure that her daughters were surrounded by appropriate images of other children, she once went so far, she says, as to "make sure to select gift wrap for presents that featured toddlers of every conceivable hue."

In addition to bringing positive images into our children's lives in the form of props and tools, we also have to challenge stereotypes whenever we see our children encounter them. Even at this very young age, children internalize messages from the media and other social institutions that too often imply white or light is best. For this reason, Jason Sackett and his wife even screen TV shows and videos. Jason explains: "My son was recently going through my bookcase and he pulled out *Dumbo*. He was watching it and my wife says, 'Jason, come here—I think we're going to have to lose this film!' The black characters were like Amos and Andy—and we don't want him to see black people portrayed like that."

Psychologist Willie B. Garrett cautions that it's essential for parents to step in and speak up when they see such negative, stereotypical imagery. "If you prefer to let your child watch public television because that's the only place you see families like yours, it's important to let your kids know why you prefer PBS," he says. "If the programming on other channels only features people with blond hair and blue eyes, which is damaging your children's sense of themselves, tell your kids *why* you're turning it off." If we don't challenge these images and talk about why we're challenging them, our child may unconsciously buy into such stereotypes.

Leo and Diane Dillon talk about how they were able to point out negative, stereotypical imagery to their biracial son, Lee, when he was a very young child, to the extent that *he* began to see stereotypes quite quickly on his own. "It's amazing how many times we hear people in the media say, 'Oh, she was so beautiful with her blond hair and blue eyes,'" says Leo. "People don't realize the harm they're doing. What does a child with brown eyes and dark hair feel hearing that? The message is that you are not valued as much.

Lee noticed those things as a child. He would be watching TV and say, 'They've done it to us again!' meaning they had shown black people in a bad light or completely left them out. Children don't always talk about these things but if they do it's terribly important to validate what the child has seen or heard. We wanted Lee to know he wasn't paranoid or crazy."

Because mixed racialness is barely visible on TV and in the movies (except for a handful of emerging stars such as Halle Berry, Cameron Diaz, Alicia Keys and Vin Diesel), and because as parents we have little control (once the TV or movie is on) over stereotypical imagery that may pop up and surprise even us, in our home we focus vigilantly on collecting *books* featuring multiracial children and families. We have greater control over the stories on the bookshelf—and a wider variety of imagery to choose from— than we do with the standard TV and video fare.

With less success, we have also tried to find dolls that resemble our fair-complexioned, Asian-eyed daughter, Claire. Asian dolls are too dark in skin shade, and Caucasian dolls have eyes of an entirely different shape. (We once ordered an "Asian" doll, only to discover when it arrived that the doll's eyes were round in shape, like any other Caucasian doll's eyes—only the skin tone had been changed to an odd tan unlike any Asian skin I have ever seen.) Psychologist Beverly Daniel Tatum, Ph.D. (African American), President of Spelman College and author of *"Why Are All the Black Kids Sitting Together in the Cafeteria?" And Other Conversations About Race*, tells the story of one grandmother, who, unable to find a doll that matched her biracial grandchild's complexion, made a Raggedy Ann doll using fabric in a shade that matched her grandchild's skin. Like many experts in the field, Tatum emphasizes: "The more the preschool child sees herself reflected in her environment, the more positive that is for her identity."

Sometimes it takes a little extra effort to fill our child's environment with multiracial images. Michelle Watson (Caucasian), mother of two African-American/Caucasian children, says she, too, has had tremendous difficulty in finding multiracial dolls for her six-year-old daughter. "When Alex sees Barbie dolls she'll go for the one with the long blond hair. At Christmastime I steered her toward the new multicultural Barbie ["Kayla"] to add to the ones she already had. Now she wants to have an American Girl doll. But they don't look like her. At first she wanted the blond doll but just recently she started talking about getting Addy, the black doll. She's changing over the last few months." But, says Michelle, the African-American girl doll

doesn't look like Alex either. "Today I went through the mail and saw a cat-
alogue for My Twin Dolls" (dolls made to resemble their owners), she says.
"We may even go so far as to get one, so she has a doll that resembles *her.*"

While research shows that biracial black/white children under the age of
four and a half tend to group dolls of different colors together in imaginary
doll families without caring much about what color each doll might be,
between the ages of four and a half and eight, this changes. As children
increasingly realize that their own skin color will remain the *same*, biracial
children tend to show more definitive preferences in dolls—often choosing
blackness while rejecting whiteness, then showing a preference for whiteness while rejecting blackness. Researchers theorize that this ambivalent
shift back and forth is necessary so that a child can reconcile both racial elements of their identity—each of their racial identities *individually*—into a
more unified identity.[23]

It can be particularly helpful, during these early years, to be sure that we
not only have dolls of different racial ethnicities available to our children,
but that we also have at least one doll who resembles our child, as they
become more aware that their skin color is permanent, and search for images
which mirror *them.* When children learn through play that people come in
different combinations of light and dark—and with different shapes of eyes
and other facial features—seeing those differences will very likely cause
them to ask questions that spark important conversations about how natural these racial differences are.

In our own home we have had easier success finding appropriate "props";
our dress-up box has an array of Japanese Samurai warrior clothes, Kendo
(Japanese swordplay) costumes, festival coats, head scarves, parasols and
kimono, all of which are, happily, enormously "cool" to the eight and under
play date crowd. This clearly makes both of our children feel validated; their
faces light up with delight when they see their friends dress up to playact in
Japanese costume.

However, props and tools are just that—their real importance lies in the
way in which we as parents make *use* of them as points of departure for discussions about differences. Toddlers learn a great deal about the world
through literature and pretend play—especially when interacting with a parent who is using these tools to make connections to the own child's life. For
instance, you might be reading a book that depicts a rainbow array of children, some of whom are clearly biracial, and—as you point to the biracial

child who most closely resembles your child—say casually, "Oh look, this girl has light hair and dark eyes just like yours!"[24]

The goal is to set the groundwork for a continual dialogue about differences during the critical years when a child's initial sense of self-esteem is being developed. Creating that open forum not only allows your child to bring questions to you, but also, by giving them words to explain who they are and the constellation of their family, you are giving them the power to communicate who they are to their peers and the world around them—skills they will increasingly need as they come of age.

Scripts for Discussing Racial Differences and a Child's Identity

Trying to find dolls, toys, books and other props that are interesting to your child and that reflect your child's identity, and then having those small conversations about physical likeness and differences, can make all the difference for the biracial child. And, although it's always preferable to wait until children ask questions that jump-start a conversation about their appearance and racial differences (making the discussion that much more natural), sometimes we have to nudge that conversation into being. Here are scripts, drawn from experts and parents alike—different types of conversations that can easily be worked into your day to day family life.

All of these conversations

1. provide answers that are simple, specific and truthful
2. tailor our explanations to the question our child has asked
3. tailor our answers to our *child's* comprehension level

You and your three-and-a-half-year-old are watching *Sesame Street*. Elmo is talking about family and a little Asian/Caucasian girl with a white mother comes on and says, "I love to have my mom *tickle* me!" Her mom tickles her and the girl dissolves into giggles. You point to the little girl on the TV and say to your daughter, "Oh, look, she looks mixed like you. Look at her curly brown hair—just like yours! She has a mom who is white and a dad who is Asian, just like you!"—and then you give her a big tickle too.

At church you see another family like your own. You lean down and say to your four-year-old son, "That little boy over there has a black mom and a Caucasian dad. His family is like our family!"

Kelley Kenney (African American) tells how once she and her then three-year-old, Elena (African American/Caucasian), were in the ladies room when Elena looked curiously at her mom's partially bare legs and then at Kelley's black stockings and asked, "Mommy, you black?"

"Yes, Mommy's black," Kelley said.

"Mommy is black, daddy is white, and I'm . . . ?" asked Elena.

"What are you?" Kelley asked her, smiling, turning the question over to her daughter to help her think about her own identity.

"I'm brown!" said Elena.

Your biracial Chinese/Caucasian four-year-old daughter is rolling out play dough on the kitchen table while you cook several dishes for the Chinese New Year celebration you'll be attending at your Chinese in-laws' home that night. Your daughter comes over to "help" you and starts asking, as she stands on tiptoe to see the dishes you're preparing, "Is this Chinese? And is this Chinese?"

"Ummhmm," you say, telling her the names of the dishes and what the ingredients are. You pause and ask her, "Are *you* Chinese?"

"Yes!" she says.

"What *is* Chinese?" you ask, ruffling her hair. She looks at you, confused. You can see her grappling to offer you the right answer. You wash your hands and pick up some of the homemade play dough on the table. You take a little bit of a whitish shade and a little bit of a tanner shade and ask her to knead them together. You tell her "If you take two different colors and mix them, they make a new color!" She holds up the new beige she's made. "You have some of Daddy's darker Chinese coloring, kind of like that tan play dough, and some of Mommy's coloring, kind of like this white. And when you mix them together from Daddy and Mommy, you get beige! Like you! Yes, you are Chinese. And you're also Caucasian, like me. You're both mixed together."

One mom tells how one day she and her two young biracial adopted children "were talking about how people from Africa have intermarried and their skin color has changed and how my kids' skin color is like that, too. That day we sat down in the sandbox and mixed two different shades of sand and they could see how two colors together make a new shade. It was very accurate."

You and your family are having Neapolitan ice cream for dessert. "Look," you say to your two preschoolers, "Here is some vanilla, and here is some chocolate. Look what happens when I mix the two together! It becomes a little bit white and a little bit brown—just like you are because Mommy is white and Daddy is brown!" (Or, if your child is, say, white, black and Native American, you might mix chocolate, vanilla and strawberry.)

You have just had your parents, who are Filipino, over for dinner. They shared photographs of their recent trip to the Philippines with you, your Caucasian husband, and your biracial children. After they've gone you ask your Filipino/Caucasian daughter, "Are you Filipino?"

"No," she says, shaking her head.

You smile and say, "Actually, you are Filipino and so is Grammy and so am I. And you're also white and so is Grandpa and so is Daddy." And then you ask, "Is your baby brother Filipino?"

"No," she says again.

And again you smile and repeat what you've said, "Yes, he is. And I am too. And he's also white. And Daddy is white too. You are both Filipino *and* white."

Maria Root shares one story of how her goddaughter—who is half Chinese, half Caucasian Jewish—drew a picture of her face and then put a line down the middle, telling her mom, "*This* half of me looks like Mom and *this* half of me looks like Dad."

Her mom quickly countered, "You look a lot like your friend who is half Chinese and half white, don't you? Does she look different on one half of her face than she does on the other?"

Her daughter said, "No."

"No? Well neither do you," said her mom.

Often, dialoguing with our children at this age means asking simple questions to find out *what* they are thinking—so we know what information they are lacking. For example:

CHILD: How do people get their colors?

MOTHER: How do you think they do?

CHILD: You tell me.

MOTHER: Well, people have a special thing inside their body called melanin. If a person has a lot of melanin, then they have brown skin. If they have a medium amount, then they are tan, and if they have a little they are white.

CHILD: (Laughs):You mean they eat melon?

MOTHER: No, the word is melanin. It sounds something like melon, but it's different. It's something we are all born with.

CHILD: Well, I was wondering about pens.

MOTHER:What do you mean?

CHILD: You know, the pens you can put red or blue on your skin if you want to.

MOTHER: You mean Magic Markers?

CHILD: Yes.[25]

Your three-year-old is drawing a picture of a family and is spending a lot of time choosing crayons from the crayon box. She looks up at you and asks a barrage of questions, "Why are you light and Daddy is dark? Why am I the color I am? What color *am* I?"

You reply, "You're a mixture of Mommy and Daddy, kind of like the way it looks when I add milk to my coffee in the morning and I let you help me stir it in." You look through the crayon box with her until you find one that matches her skin. "Look at this crayon!" you say. "Amber gold! That matches *you!*"

Another quick and effective way parents can begin important, small conversations with preschoolers is by encouraging children to openly discuss any physical differences they notice between themselves and others. Invite your children (in appropriate moments) to hold up dark arm to light arm, to gaze in the mirror, Amerasian eye next to West Indian eye. For instance:

You and your spouse (who are in an interracial marriage) are having a cookout. Your biracial (Chinese/Caucasian) son and your adopted (Chinese) daughter are playing in the backyard on a sunny day with several friends' children—one is Sri-Lankan/Caucasian, the others black. As the five kids come rushing up to the house to line up for hamburgers and hot dogs, they start giggling and forming a sort of train line, each hugging the one in front of them from behind. You say to them, "Wow, you guys are like a whole lot of colors standing together in the crayon box!" They hold their arms out and compare the different shades of their skin with each other, seeing who is what shade.

It's this type of ongoing, open discussion policy that brings racial differences into an accepting forum for questioning, observation and conversation, and as a result physical differences become increasingly *un*important. Again, it's when we don't talk about them that we send children the silent message that such differences, since they are never discussed, must be a source of shame or embarrassment.

Keeping up that conversation means never sidestepping an issue regarding your child's racial identity by saying, "We'll discuss that later," or "We don't ask questions like that! You can't want blond hair!" (a knee-jerk reaction similar to the one adults often have when children ask questions about sex). Although kids are just becoming conscious of color, that budding consciousness runs deep; they are merely trying to find out what these differences might mean, and whether they mean *anything at all*. Hence, you might simply respond, "Parents pass down their skin color to their children and what skin color you have depends on what part of the world you come from. If your mommy and daddy come from different parts of the world, then you get a little bit of each of their skin color; it's mixed, and that's the color you are."

Praise Your Child's Physical Features

In addition to having these general conversations about skin, racial and color differences, it's critical to make it a habit (within moderation, of course) to *praise whatever features of your child you fear will be the most disparaged in the future*. While praise of a child's physical features—when coming from a staring stranger—can't help but make a child feel oddly singled out, there is no such mixed message inherent when the praise emanates quite genuinely from one's mom or dad, and is fueled by their unconditional love.

If your African-American/Caucasian child has dark skin, make it a point to talk positively about her skin—"I *love* the golden hue of your skin." Beverly Daniel Tatum, Ph.D. (African American), explains, "The very feature that you feel is most likely to be targeted by others in a negative light is the feature about which you want to work to build the *most* self-esteem."

Similarly, if your child is Asian/Caucasian, the more you talk positively about his eyes—"I love the shape of your eyes; they're beautiful just like Granddaddy's"—the more he will internalize that positive message.

My children's eyes have been an ongoing source of unsolicited attention and comments since the day each was born. I recall walking into a family party when Christian was only a month old—our first excursion out of the cocoon of our home with our newborn—when an older second cousin (five at the time) bounded up and exclaimed, "Oh, the baby!" As Christian peered around the room, his cousin looked up at us and asked, perplexed, "Why can't your baby open his eyes *all* the way?"

At that moment I felt much of my elation at introducing my child to his extended family dissipate; her words were a daunting reminder that the world we live in saw my son's mixed features as so very different as to give pause.

In hope of building their self-esteem about their eyes, I have from time to time had some rendition of the following conversation with both of my children:

"You have the world's most beautiful eyes, guys," I tell them, looking in their faces, usually when we are all snuggling in bed after reading a story. Sometimes I even trace my fingers around their eyes, slowly, gently. "I look into your eyes and they are so deep and brown and full of light, I feel like I want to fall right in them," I say. Inevitably, they touch their own eyes as I am talking, soaking in each word.

"They're kind of a little bit like yours and a little bit like daddy's," ventures Christian.

"That's right," I say. "Do you know that every time I look in your eyes I think of how I fell in love with your daddy when I met him, with the way his beautiful eyes smiled at me?"

"You were on the street, walking Percy!" (our dog), announces Claire. "And Percy wrapped you up in the leash, like this!" And she stands and whirls around on the bed and falls down and we all laugh.

We are in and out of the conversation in less than a minute, over and out (for now), before moving on to talk about something entirely different. But the point has been made: Their eyes *are* lovely. And one day, I hope, they will internalize my words into their own feelings—about *themselves*.

None of this is to say that I advocate talking about race all the time. Hardly. Overdoing the conversation can be as troubling for children as ignoring it altogether. Maria Root, who wholeheartedly advocates early conversations about race with young children, also cautions parents that overemphasizing race to a child (e.g., "you're mixed, you're African American and white, you're half this and half that") and commenting repeatedly on their difference "can make the child feel alienated from everyone around them—even if it's done out of good intentions." She cautions parents from dwelling on race, especially with very young children who can't yet process the information. Some parents, she feels, may be tempted to read race into situations because of their own experiences, assuming all interactions are fraught with racist overtones, "which distorts things for the kids so that they see the worst in everyone, everywhere. After a long enough time of hearing this kind of thinking from their parent they can't turn off those feelings—they see racism everywhere, too."

It's a matter of being comfortable with the subject of race—as a parent—and willing to talk about the diversity of our world freely so that the conversation comes about *naturally*. It is a conversation that is neither forced nor force-fed, neither ignored nor overdone. As with all things, it is a matter of measured moderation.

Although it is never appropriate to *not* expose children to their full heritage, no matter what their appearance, the frequency with which you keep coming back to this conversation may depend, to some degree, on both the appearance of your child and where you live. For instance, if a child is very clearly biracial and lives in a nondiverse, white neighborhood, these small conversations might be more necessary and thus more frequent than for a multiracial child who appears to be white and lives in a very diverse area. (For more on issues relating to children and the community in which they live, see Chapter 5.)

Again, these sorts of conversations are occasional and brief—five minutes or less. Over the years, one conversation links up to the next in a kind of stitched-together tapestry that creates an indelible image celebrating all the racial differences in the world, including our child's. When that kind of dialogue is part of one's day-to-day family life, it provides a tremendous source of reassurance and a wellspring of self-understanding for a child forming his *own* identity.

Helping our children to be confident about who they are racially is a *process*. Children are constantly making sense of differences; it's our job to provide the information they need to do so in a healthy way. And in truth, it's not only about exactly *what* we say, it's also about simply being there;

being available when questions are asked and taking the time to carefully answer them from a place of honesty. Naturally, it's impossible to always know what to say and when to say it, how much to react, or whether to react at all. As much as we love our children, we can't always know the right thing to say or do for them. Remembering that this is a process, not a matter of saying the exact right words at an exact point in time, can help give us the confidence to plunge forward.

One morning, two years ago, I gave a speech at a local high school about racial identity and multiracial teens. Christian, then six, attended the first few minutes. The next day, when I took him to school, as we were getting out of the car, he asked me, "Mom, what do people mean when they say the word 'race?'" I paused for a moment, as we walked toward his classroom, afraid of blundering. Although I knew he was not yet ready for a full-fledged discussion of the way the concepts of "race" and "culture" have become blurred in our society—or how artificial the construct of race truly is, genetically speaking—I wanted my explanation to be not just simple but truthful.

"Race is a term we use to refer to a group of people who look something alike because they've inherited similar physical characteristics," I said. "And race is usually related to the part of the world a group of people originally come from. People whose ancestors come from Asia—like Daddy's family—are said to be of the Asian race."

"What about people from America?" he asked. "Is there an *American* race?"

"Well," I said. "That's the amazing thing about America. Everyone's family—except the Native Americans, who were here before any of us, all come from different places and different races. We're a country of many races blending together."

"What race are you?" he asked.

"The Caucasian race. Caucasians are mostly from European countries."

"Like Denmark? And Great Britain? And Sweden?" he asked. He was aware that my father's family had emigrated from England hundreds of years earlier, and that my mother's family had emigrated from Sweden and Denmark a century and a half before.

We looked at each other for an instant, my eyes quietly reading his face as his mind worked quickly over the facts. Then he looked up at me again. "What race am *I*?" he asked.

We were now at his classroom. We paused outside the doorway. "Like a lot of Americans, you're a little of two races—Asian, from Daddy's family from Japan, and Caucasian, from my family from Europe."

We walked into his almost exclusively white—save for one black boy and one part Native American boy—classroom. He looked visibly perplexed as he did a cursory survey of his friend's faces around him, already knowing what he would find.

We exchanged a glance—his still questioning—as I kissed him good-bye. But then the melee of the morning drop-off routine began in full swing, with friends bounding up to tell him their latest news, and I turned and left the room, unsure what he had processed—or *half*-processed.

Still, as I communicate with my young children about race, I hope they are absorbing some of my own feelings about race—thoughts slightly too complex to convey to them just yet (though as they grow, that will change). I hope they are beginning to absorb the sense, from my husband and me, that although different races may celebrate their own cultures and history (and that it is so important to do so) race *itself* is an artificial construct. In terms of our DNA (and, for many of us, in terms of our hearts and minds) one race differs not at all from the next. Nevertheless, differing racial features, and the degree of melanin in each human being's skin, cause some people to see race as very significant and to seize on it as a dividing tool between people.

Therefore, although race is a nonissue in many, many people's hearts (including our own), some people who are less enlightened may imply that because a person is multiracial, or because a family doesn't fit into a traditional one-race family mold, our children are *themselves* odd, strange. Those of us in multiracial families, including our children, need to be aware of and prepared for these questions and incidents before they arise.

In the meantime, we, as parents, can work from the very start of our children's lives, conversation by small conversation, to engage in that fragile but critical process of helping them to assimilate these truths: that if and when others try to impose the idea on them that they are "other," the problem lies within *that* person and that person's misconceptions; misconceptions no doubt gleaned from living in an overtly race-conscious world. The problem does not lie within our child. They are unique, yes, *and* perfectly made, just as they are.

CHAPTER TWO

"Who Do I Match—
Mom or Dad or Anyone?"

Moving from Preschool into Grade School

FOR MOST NEW PARENTS, pregnancy is a time of unprecedented joy intermingled with unspoken fears of the unknown, and parents expecting a mixed-race child are certainly no exception. Expecting a multiracial child can spark a wide range of complex feelings—from curiosity about what he or she might look like and who he or she will (or won't) resemble, to concern over how to help their child achieve a strong sense of identity, to fears over how he or she might be treated by peers and the larger community in which they live, to a wellspring of anticipation about welcoming this wondrous new being into the world.

All of these thoughts danced through my mind in often strange duets while I was expecting our first child, Christian. Increasingly, as I neared term, coupled with my burgeoning excitement over this new life entering ours, was my curiosity about how my husband's Japanese features and coloring and my Scandinavian/English traits might blend. But my musing was also laced with concern: Would our son look "different," and if so, would he *feel* different because he *looked* different? I imagined our child on some future playground and worried whether he would be left out or teased or treated differently by friends, teachers or girls he would one day have adolescent crushes on. I distinctly remember wondering, during one stream of consciousness worry-fest, whether he would have as many dates in high school as his buddies. Would my son one day work up the nerve to phone a girl he thought divine, only to be rejected because his features were vaguely Asian? Or, if she were Asian, would she reject him because his features weren't Asian *enough*?

And then Christian was born and he was beautiful, oh he was beautiful. Suddenly it wasn't about the world and our son anymore, it was about us and our son, and we existed within a cocoon of our own making. When he was placed wet and slick on my belly, I stared into his eyes and we recognized each other in that instant, mutual claiming that all new moms, I suspect, experience. A jolt of love—unprecedented, unexpected, wholly unfamiliar—raced through me, filling me to the brim as if it had been there all my life, awaiting his arrival. And then my eyes combed over my son from head to toe and I remember thinking: *he doesn't look a bit like me. I* was surprised at how different from me he looked.

Still, as I nursed and cared for my newborn son night and day and fell deeper into his spell—as my days were suddenly filled more with doing than with ruminating—that thought faded further and further away, until it simply didn't exist at all. When I held him in my arms and peered at our reflection side by side in the mirror, the physical difference between us, Asian, Caucasian, would blur to nothing. I do not know how to explain this, but it was simply not in my mirror.

Around that time, I read in a science journal that when a woman is pregnant, descendants of the fetus's cells escape into her bloodstream and continue to exist there *for decades* after she gives birth to a child. Researchers have found male DNA in the blood samples of mothers 27 years *after* the birth of their baby boys.[1] Suddenly it made perfect sense to me why all delineation of race had been erased by motherhood. It seemed, in a way, I had become part Asian too. I am walking around with Asian DNA in my blood. If someone feels inclined to be prejudiced against people who are Asian or part Asian, they might as well just go ahead and hate me too.

The difference not only doesn't exist in my mirror, it no longer exists in my veins. Perhaps that's why, when my children and I are out and about and I notice someone doing a double take in our direction, I never cease to feel some element of surprise: Isn't the bond my children and I share so rich and potent, the connection between us so obvious, so palpable, it speaks volumes, transcending all imagined racial assumptions?

Yet I recognize all too well, in my rational mind, that on the surface, there seems to be little resemblance between my children and me, and that fact can be confusing for those around us. There are times when I see a two-dimensional image—a photo—of Christian and it strikes me anew that he shares few physical features of mine other than the shape of his earlobes and the highlights his hair accrues in summertime.

Not surprisingly, this complex aspect of being a parent in a multiracial family—the fact that our children often do not resemble us, at least not at first blush—can be the source of not only endless awkward situations but complex reactions and emotions for both parent and child.

"Not matching" Mom or Dad now arises as a key issue for children as they enter kindergarten and/or grade school (especially as peers increasingly point this racial discrepancy out to them). We are best serving our child if *we* are conscious of our own thoughts and feelings regarding the disparity between our racial appearance and that of our child—and if *we* stand prepared for the way others react to that difference—before helping our child to do the same.

Frequently, for parents, these complex feelings are foreshadowed even in pregnancy. Consider Michelle Watson (Caucasian), who recalls that, when she was newly pregnant with her first daughter, Alex (African American/Caucasian), "I didn't think about the biracial part of having a child in a direct sense, but I do remember thinking that while all along I'd thought I would have this blond-haired, blue-eyed little girl one day, I wasn't going to actually ever have that blue-eyed blond-haired child who looked like me. It didn't bother me one bit—I was so excited about my baby in every way—but I was conscious that I had to let that specific image go."

Often, as we watch our biracial children grow, we can only muse at how little they resemble us. As Susan Fu (Caucasian), mother of Alex (13), Kayla (10), and Chloe (7) (Chinese/Caucasian) puts it, "I see so much of my friends in their children. A smile, a nose, a forehead . . . my children literally bear no resemblance to me whatsoever. I often wonder what it would be like to have a little person look like me . . . to see myself in my child. I will never experience that." Her musing is more matter of fact, however, than wistful. She and her kids have fun with their physical dissimilarity: "The kids and I goof around in front of the mirror sometimes. We put our faces right next to each other in the mirror and look really hard for some facial feature that we have in common. We laugh about silly things like a freckle or a nose hair, or Chloe's one strand of blond hair in an otherwise brown head of hair, but we never find anything similar. I tell them how beautiful they are—and how I wish I had *their* skin."

The idea that we might have once anticipated that our children would look something like us is hardly surprising; after all, most of us grew up hearing such comparisons made in our own families, whatever race they might be. "If you aren't the mirror image of your mother when she was your age!" or, "Isn't he a chip off the old block!" (Recently I opened up the local paper to see a full-page spread of photos showing the winners of the annual "Mother-Daughter Look-Alike Contest," with pairs of moms and daughters grinning from top to bottom.) In most families, we attach a certain pride—grandparent to parent to child—to bearing some resemblance to one another (that perfectly matched set of dimples, those dark comma-like eyebrows, that nose set just so) generation to generation. For years after my father passed away when I was 12, I felt a surge of pride and comfort whenever a family member or one of my dad's acquaintances commented, "Oh *you* must be Jay's daughter—I can *see* him in you," or, "You have that Jackson nose—it moves up and down when you laugh, the way *his* did!" Now, it isn't necessarily a *good* thing to have your nose move when you laugh, but I was proud of having inherited my dad's trademark nose all the same.

Similarly, I feel a small surge of pleasure when someone comments out of the blue that my daughter looks something like me, or that her coloring is like mine, or even that she looks like my mother, a physical affirmation that she comes from me, that she is mine. (I have sometimes wondered, does she feel a flutter of inner pleasure, too?) Even a friend of mine who is of mixed Asian descent, whose daughter is adopted from China, says she secretly revels in it when those not in the know comment on how she and her daughter share an identical profile. And I have often seen my son and husband turn and grin hugely at each other when people comment "You two look exactly alike!" The shared pleasure they feel is palpable.

My children and I will never be in a parent/child look-alike contest—and so what? To be sure, shifting from expecting to have children who resemble you to letting that assumption go is a minuscule moment in the overall scheme of parenting. But the point is this: Our society ascribes a certain pleasure value to family likenesses. In having a multiracial family we often have to wrestle with and set aside any value *we* might have unwittingly placed on our kids resembling us or our family of origin (as well as any guilt about having had those expectations in the first place.) Until we acknowledge and move past these complex feelings, we can't get to the much more important business at hand: how our *children* feel when others point out that they don't racially "match" Mom and Dad. Nor can we determine the best means of protecting them from any undue scrutiny they may endure, especially during this critical five- to eight-year-old phase, during which racial awareness about their own identity, their family's, and that of those around them, first dawns for them and their peers.

Meanwhile, navigating this often disconcerting public scrutiny and the attendant comments, which underscore parent/child differences, can be frustrating and daunting for parent and child alike. Because these scenes recur throughout the early school years, they heighten our child's awareness of physical differences between themselves and us as their parents, rapidly fueling a sense of feeling "other." Just think of it: When young monoracial children are told, "You're the spitting image of your dad!" (or a similar sentiment), they usually experience this parent/self comparison as positive and reassuring (one that implies other, deeper similarities and connections, e.g., "You're a lot *like* your dad"). The multiracial child, however, often receives a totally *opposite* type of scrutiny and commentary from others: "Your mom doesn't look like you at all!" "Is that *your* dad?" "What are you, adopted!? From where?" All these comments imply, "You look so little like your mom/dad—do you really belong to them?"

Consider this heart-rending story told by writer David Updike. While vacationing in London with his wife, Wambui, and son, Wesley, he was stopped by two policemen. Updike, who is white, and his eight-year-old biracial son were out strolling on the street together. The policemen insisted on first separating the two and then grilling each, alone, about what street they lived on, their names, their relationship. Satisfied that they were indeed father and son, the police explained that there were often runaway boys in the neighborhood, "begging and the like," and sometimes they fell in with the wrong men. Afterward, Wesley, uncertain of what had just transpired, told his father he wanted to go back home, to fly back to the United States, right away. "There is a sternness in his voice that I am not familiar with," writes Updike. Back at their hotel, Wesley curled up on the bed. "I can tell that he is not asleep." Updike continues, "He has pulled his shirt up to hide his tears. 'What's the matter?' I ask, panicking now. 'What is it?' I rub his small, strong back, but he does not—or cannot—answer: there are no words for what the matter is, for what has hurt him, and I, too, give up on words, on explanation. I lie down on the bed beside him, drape my arm around him, and he turns and pulls me fiercely to him . . . and then he cries in earnest, his hurt released in short, breathless sobs, tears flowing freely now as he weeps. . . ."[2]

Updike captures the feeling—"there are no words for what the matter is"—for what parents and children in multiracial families so often feel when onlookers (and in this case the police) assert that a parent and child can't possibly be just that.

Not surprisingly, explains psychologist Beverly Daniel Tatum, Ph.D. (African American), author of *"Why Are All the Black Kids Sitting Together in the Cafeteria?" And Other Conversations About Race,* "the more a child doesn't look like their parents—especially if they don't look like the parent they're with most of the time in public (often their mom)—the more attention they'll draw and the more others will tend to ask unwelcome questions."[3] And this attention being paid to the fact that a child doesn't seem to belong with his parent can be one of the major factors in determining how a multiracial child begins to construct his or her identity over time.

Because these moments of questioning are likely to occur most with the parent a child "matches" the least, it may fall more to one parent than the other to respond to these intrusions immediately and skillfully. Sometimes, even when parent and child *do* resemble each other in an interracial family, others can't see that resemblance because they have trouble seeing past skin color. As one Caucasian mom who has two light-skinned African-American/Caucasian sons put it, "I'm asked all the time, 'Isn't it difficult that your children don't look like you?'" But, she says, "My sons *do* look like me. The problem is that when white people see even a very light-skinned African-American person, they see something very, very different."[4]

Most times, it is the white parent who encounters the majority of stranger comments, since people generally don't question it as much when they see a "minority" parent with a child who also appears to be of an ethnic background.

Although mistaken identity incidents between Caucasian parents and their multiracial kids abound, incidents with minority parents and especially light-skinned multiracial children are often even more emotionally charged, especially when it's assumed that a dark-skinned parent can't possibly be the parent of a light-skinned, Caucasian-looking child. Indeed, African-American mothers of light-skinned babies sometimes report receiving suspicious stares when out in public with a child or even being asked directly, "Where did you get that baby?" as if they'd stolen their baby from its white mother.[5]

Kelley Kenny, Ed.D. (African American), coauthor of *Counseling Multiracial Families,* talks about one such disturbing incident when her African-American/Caucasian children—who are lighter in complexion than she—were young grade schoolers: "One day after she'd just started at a new school, Olivia was supposed to go home with a classmate and her dad to work on a project. I came to meet her at school because I needed to coordinate where and when to pick her up later. I was standing there with my younger daughter, Elena, along with Olivia and Olivia's classmate. Two teachers came up, looked at me, looked at my girls—who are not dark like me—looked at Olivia's classmate and asked all the girls, 'Are we *okay* here girls?' as if they were wondering if these three girls were safe in my presence.

"Just then Olivia's classmate said, 'My dad is here!' but the teachers still stood there, sussing out the situation.

"So I went into the street and said, loud enough for the teachers to hear, 'Hi. I'm Dr. Kenney, I'm Olivia's mom.' After that, the teachers went inside."

Although such incidents can be enormously confusing, *they provide critical opportunities to continue our ongoing dialogue regarding race and identity*—a dialogue we have, in a best-case scenario, already begun from the earliest stages and one that will serve as the essential foundation for our multiracial child's sense of self. But again, before launching into that conversation, it is important to know where our young children—now moving from preschool and into the early grade school years—are developmentally, so that we understand how to speak to them about race in an increasingly sophisticated yet age-appropriate way.

Understanding the Five- to Eight-Year-Old Multiracial Child

At this age young children are struggling to categorize the world around them in more sophisticated ways. Their rudimentary struggle to understand the world by categorizing everything in it grows more complex in the kindergarten and early grade school years as they develop and hone more sophisticated cognitive skills. Indeed, struggles to make clear-cut categorizations have been under way for years—starting long before grade school, at ages three and four—and are often quite comical to listen to because of the simplistic conclusions very young children draw. Nowhere are these efforts more evident than when very small children struggle to categorize their own family members, as illustrated in the following anecdotes.

Let's first consider these very young preschoolers efforts to categorize their own family members—long *before* the age of five.

One evening, as I was drying my daughter Claire—three at the time—after her bath, she announced, "Mommy! Do you know that Daddy and Christian are *Japanese?*"

"Ummmhmmm," I said, noncommittally, curious to hear more about what was going on in *her* mind.

"But you and I aren't," she added, shaking her head back and forth.

"We aren't?" I asked, wondering if she'd concluded that because we were both fairer in complexion we couldn't be.

"No," she said. "Because we don't have *penises.*"

Not long after that Claire returned to the subject, again out of the blue, "Mommy did you know that Daddy is Japanese?"

"I did know!" I said with a gleeful tone, echoing her own. "How about you?" I asked. "Are you Japanese?"

"Noooooo, Mommy," she said, shaking her head at me dubiously, as if unsure how I could even ponder such a question. Then, pulling a lock of her hair straight up into the air, she added, "Because look. I don't have Japanese *hair.*"

"Are you part Japanese?" I ventured.

"Ummhmmm," she said, casually, her eyes going back to her lunch. "*Part,*" she added, with the emphasis children add when they are trying to make something clear to themselves.

Mark Kenney (Caucasian) tells a story about his daughter, Olivia (African American/Caucasian). When she was four, she wanted to go to Africa but, he muses, "She announced to me that only Kelley [her mom] and she could go—I had to stay home because I wasn't black."

In her book, *Crossing the Color Line: Race, Parenting and Culture*, author Maureen Reddy tells a similar story about her son's efforts to categorize himself and others by race and gender at the age of three. Her son, she says, had noticed that he and his African-American dad both had penises but that his Caucasian mom did not. Deciding that the difference was due to race rather than gender he asked her, "Why do white people have vaginas?"[6]

Similarly, a two-and-a-half-year-old child with a black father and white mother, upon seeing several black women in a restaurant, comments, "I didn't know women were black."[7]

These toddlers' assumptions reflect the concerted effort they are already putting into making sense of the complex world around them by trying to create neat—if comically erroneous—categories based on basic physical cues: penis? vagina? black hair? brown hair? tan skin? white skin?

Between the ages of five and seven, kids are much more alert to the subtle differences between people's skin color and eye shape, and to grouping others accordingly (e.g., relating skin hue more to race than to, say, whether one is male or female, as they might have done only a year or two earlier). At age five, research shows, even children who have shown little interest in skin color or race (whether their own or other people's) suddenly become acutely interested in both.[8] Differences between a child's appearance and that of his or her mom or dad (especially if they have very different skin color and hair texture) may prompt all sorts of observations, questions and comments from our child—and their friends.

Consider this story Louise Lazare (Caucasian), mother of eight adopted children (six of whom are biracial), tells about her adopted son Tom (African American), whose skin is quite dark. When he was six, another black child said to Tom, "I know why your *real* mom gave you away—because you're so *dark*."

Erroneous as this boy's ideas were about what being darker meant, his efforts to create strict categories about racial differences—and to draw meaningful conclusions about what it might mean if a child's skin color is different from his mom's—are typical of children's efforts at this age to categorize family groups. Likewise his very concrete perception that skin color *should* match between parent and child.

Or, consider one little boy's announcement that "black and white kids can be friends with each other, if you're in the same class. But they can't get married, because they don't match. They can't have a kid together."[9]

Kids this age are tied to concrete perceptions of skin color as a way to "match" groups (white parent goes with white child; black parent with black child; *very* black child with *very* black parent; white parent with white parent, and so on). Between the ages of five and eight, early grade schoolers are also engaged in several major developmental tasks key to racial identity:

1. They are noting what makes one group different from another at a much more attuned level than when they were preschoolers. They are now learning to associate *racial* groups, in particular, with specific markers (the language one speaks or the food one eats, as well as one's physical characteristics). Children this age also show a much greater interest in other people's cultural characteristics, such as their rituals and customs, and are focusing their awareness on what goes into determining that an individual belongs in a particular group (e.g., What cultural markers determine that someone who is Japanese is a member of that country?).[10]

2. Children this age are much more curious about any group to which they feel *they* belong (e.g., What are the people in my family *like*? What do we have in common? What about my extended family? What about everyone who is part of my ethnic culture? And those in the country *I* live in?). For instance, when our son, Christian, was five, we were living in Japan. As a biracial American family, we incorporated the Japanese language, Japanese foods, Japanese videos, folktales, books, toys, artwork and traditional clothes into our day-to-day home life.

   One day, out of nowhere, Christian asked me, with a quizzical look on his face, "Mom, you're Japanese, too, right?"

   Struggling to understand where he was coming from, I asked, "Why am I Japanese?"

   "Well," he said, you eat Japanese food and you *live* in Japan. So you're Japanese, too."

   In his struggle to understand the world and the people within it, his criteria were clearly more complex than just looking at the shade of each family member's skin or our gender or the color of our hair.

3. Children of this age are increasingly interested in expressing the way in which *they share* the characteristics of members of their group, too. And, just as importantly, if helped by the adults around them to do so, they begin to develop a sense of pride in both their self-identity and in

belonging to their group. They are developing a *group* self-identity and a *group* self-esteem.

4. As their individual and group identities are evolving both cognitively and emotionally, they are beginning to realize that they are part of different groups *at the same time* (family, friends, school classroom or country) and that each of these groups has characteristics that make it distinct from other groups to which they belong.[11]

Because multiracial/transracially adopted children may have few others like them racially and phenotypically even within their immediate family, and because others may be quick to point out this fact, it is critical to help them realize that racial and facial characteristics are only one small—and insignificant—aspect of what contributes to "matching" as a family group. They need to absorb the unequivocal message from us that the power of family life surmounts differences of race or skin color. And the best way to do this is to show them that *we* do not categorize other families or groups by race.

Never will we have a better opportunity to impress this awareness upon them, for five- to eight-year-olds do not yet comprehend the rules *adults* use to determine racial group memberships. Nor do they comprehend racism or that certain privileges in society are given—or withheld—due to race.[12]

Even as our "little scientists"[13] are busily sorting out what makes people fall into different racial groupings, research shows that initially, children this age do not have schemata for categorizing others by race per se. According to psychologist Maria Root, Ph.D. (Filipino/Chinese/Spanish-Portuguese/German/Irish/Caucasian) and editor of *Racially Mixed People in America*, "Children are repeatedly *taught* [to label others racially] through . . . real and imagined physical features." To do so, they "must learn to *distort* the colors by which they perceive skin color in order to make accurate racial self-identification. This is a learned process."[14]

Because our children now stand at a crossroads of being racially curious and yet—for lack of a better way to state it—still racially naïve, these years provide a perfect opportunity to help guide them toward appropriate conclusions about what race does and doesn't mean. This requires educating and communicating with our multiracial children in such a way that they don't "learn to distort" their perception of themselves or others in order to make group societal labels of race "fit."

Talking About Race with the
Five- to Eight-Year-Old Child

One of the primary ways in which children in this age-group begin to gather more sophisticated information about their identity and that of their family is by asking curious questions about why they *don't* "match" their parents—questions that provide perfect opportunities for teaching moments.

Diana Finch (Hawaiian/Caucasian) recalls how her daughter, Emily (Haitian American/Hawaiian/Caucasian), began to ask a lot of questions at age five (having entered a larger grade school setting, kids begin to interact with more kids of varied racial backgrounds and hence have more questions about physical differences). Finch recalls, "Emily would come home from school and say, 'My friend came and told me that I'm not the same color as you. Why aren't I?' Or, 'My friend so-and-so is the same color as *her* mommy and *her* daddy.' or, 'If you're white and Daddy is black, did you know what color I was going to be?' or, 'Why am I not white like you?' or, 'Why am I not black like Daddy?' or, 'Why is my hair not like yours and not like my daddy's?' She had *so many* questions.

"I wanted to make sure that she liked the way she looked, so I said simple things to her like, 'Your skin is a beautiful color; yes it's different *and* it's very beautiful.' I also made sure to point out that she had some of me and some of her father; that her hair was not as kinky as his and not as smooth as mine. It was somewhere in between because she was a *combination* of both of us. The same with her skin color, which is right in the middle. I told her, 'You're you, you're combined. You're *both* of us.'"

Slightly different is the situation for adoptive multiracial families. One Caucasian mom of an adopted five-and-a-half-year-old Chinese daughter tells a story that echoes the experiences of many parents in multiracial families.

It was my daughter's first day of kindergarten. Lots of kids were filing in with their parents, holding on to them. One little boy saw that my husband and I were both white and that our daughter was Asian. He pointed to our family and said, in a loud voice, "Look Mom! They don't *match*!" My daughter looked up at me, confused and quizzical. The other mom was clearly embarrassed and pulled her son in the other direction. I leaned down and said to my daughter, "There are all different kinds of families in the world. You don't have to look *alike* to be a family. There are lots of families where kids and parents don't match and they are a family just like any family." Then I reminded her of all the different kids we knew—families from an adoptive support group we belong to—who didn't "match" their mom and dad. She grasped my hand tighter and drew up against my side. I whispered to her, "Whether moms and dads and their kids match or not, they are a family and family is for *always*. I'm your mom *forever*."

We need to remind our children, whether they are multiracial or transracially adopted, that there are many different types of families. Whether or not moms and dads and kids "match," family relationships are permanent. Pointing this out can help our children realize, and internalize, the essential truth that racial sameness doesn't define a family group: indelible love does.

Reacting to Strangers

We can send a clear message to our children that "normal" families do indeed come in all shapes, sizes and colors by the way we send that same message to inquisitive strangers.

Nancy Brown (Caucasian), president of the Association of MultiEthnic Americans (AMEA), says it's been helpful in dealing with such situations to start by assuming ignorance or mere curiosity on the part of the other person. "It isn't helpful to assume that they are being racist," she reflects. "My husband and I realized, early on, that if we responded to every comment with bitterness or anger, we'd go crazy." When her kids were very small, she recalls, "I made a conscious choice about what I wanted to model in front of them in terms of values and behavior. Just because kids are preverbal and don't talk doesn't mean they aren't soaking up all that is happening around them. They're like sponges. So if someone kept asking me inappropriate questions at the grocery store I took the route of education rather than being flippant or taking their lack of education personally. I would say, firmly, "Families can thrive even if everybody doesn't look alike." Or, I would simply say nothing and smile and move on. I learned that I didn't have to answer every single comment or question that comes our way. And that surprises some people because—especially if you are the white parent— strangers often expect you to collude with their unaware racism by getting you to talk about your child's racial difference *with* them. I chose not to do that because I would get that uncomfortable feeling on the inside that I didn't like what was going on."

Leceta Chisholm Guibault (Caucasian), mom of Kahleah (Mayan Indian/Guatemalan), age eleven, and Tristan (Latino/Colombian), age eight, tells this story of how she has dealt with supermarket strangers: "I remember one time a man in a shopping center took a long look at me, and then my children, then back to me. With Kahleah beside me, listening intently, he asked, 'Are they yours?' 'Yes,' I said. 'Are they brother and sister?' he asked. Kahleah put a protective hand on her brother's shoulder and replied, 'Yes, he's my baby brother.' The man looked at me and said, 'They don't look alike, they can't be *real* brother and sister.' I calmly stated, 'They are brother and sister.' He seemed puzzled and continued with, 'But they're not *blood* brother and sister, right?' Realizing at this point that what was truly important was what my children were getting from the conversation, it was time to end the interrogation. Smiling at my children, we proceeded to walk away."

Laura Rittenhouse (Caucasian) describes strangers looking at her daughter Lianne (Chinese) and asking her, "'Is she adopted?' I used to say, 'Yes,' as matter-of-factly as I could, but I felt diminished. That question *separates* Lianne and me. Now I answer, 'Yes, *we* are adopted.' That answer brings us together."

Susan Fu (Caucasian) says that in her family, where her blond hair and blue eyes contrast with the darker Chinese features of her husband, Dave, and their three children, "We've had many looks. When we're out or in a restaurant, people stare. I have a little saying I say in my head, 'Oh they must be talking about what a beautiful family we are.' They may actually be saying, 'Oh, look at that Chinese guy and that white girl.' But I still say my little saying to myself." Fu's positive spin on strangers' stares helps free her from feeling self-conscious or awkward or irritated. Instead, she emits a sense of pride about who her family is, pride that her children can't help but pick up on and assimilate.

There have been times, however, when she's had to speak back to intrusive strangers. "I have fielded endless questions. Once when I was with Chloe, a woman in line at the bagel store asked me, 'Is she one of the Children of China?' Recently, a man actually asked me, 'Does she speak English?' Another time a woman asked me where my children were from, and I told her 'they're mine,' and she said, 'I know they're *yours,* but where did they come *from?*' So I said, 'They're from my *uterus!*' I've developed a thicker skin over the years for dealing with these situations."

Cassandra McGowen (Chinese American, adopted) and Ty Kaul (Caucasian) talk about the important role humor has played in their family life, literally from the hour of their first child's birth. Cassandra had just delivered her daughter, Asia (Chinese American/Caucasian), when she asked Ty to accompany the baby to the hospital nursery. "He was following the nurse who was wheeling Asia in the bassinet," she says. "Suddenly the nurse turned to him, looked at him skeptically and said, 'Sir, I don't think this is your baby because this is a Chinese baby!' And he said, 'Well I certainly hope so because my wife is Chinese!'"

Sisters Jennifer and Samantha Franks (African American) relate how humor has helped them to deal with strangers who are confused by the fact that they have a white dad. (When they were quite small, their African-American father died, and their African-American mother later married their white stepdad). Growing up, says Jennifer, "Seeing who was going to react to our family was like a little game for us, one that united us." Sometimes, she recalls, she would tell people not in the know, "Oh, this is my dad," and they'd come out with something like, "'Oh, okay, I see the resemblance,' or, 'Oh, I see you have his nose.' My dad and I would just laugh," says Jennifer. "It was funny. Our family deals with all this by making it a kind of joke—sometimes we don't explain our family and then wait to see what people's reactions are."

Not that it's always been easy, or funny. Jennifer's sister, Samantha, remembers that when she was six or so, she went into stores with her dad and "the clerk would ask Dad if he needed anything. Then he'd ask me, separately, if I needed anything, as if I had come in to the store by myself. Why would anyone think that a six-year-old girl would come to the store alone? But they thought that was more likely than my being with a white man who was my dad."

Not that other people's surprise at their family constellation surprises her, reflects Jennifer: "It's kind of weird, because even though it seems so normal to me to have a white dad, I've only seen a few situations in my life where a white man is taking care of a young black girl. It even shocks *me* when I see it. That's my *normal situation* and it *feels* totally normal for me, and yet, when I see others in that situation I'm really surprised."

Sometimes people's reactions seem to have racist overtones, and that's what bothers Jennifer most. "There have definitely been some difficult experiences. Sometimes we've gone into a restaurant with my mom, and my dad, who is obviously with us, and the maître d' has looked straight at my dad and said, 'Ah . . . and who are *you* waiting for, sir?'"

Some families talk about inventing code words to help their children feel in control when they experience intrusive questioning—especially comments that ring with racial bias. As with any incident where a stranger's reaction is inappropriate—whether their commenting on our child's "exotic" appearance or expressing doubt that parent and child can be a unit—it's critical to take care of your child first, before worrying about hurting a stranger's feelings.

Gail Steinberg and Beth Hall, founders and codirectors of Pact, An Adoption Alliance, point out that one way to help shield our kids from strange comments is to have family members come up with an agreed upon code word that they can communicate privately in public settings. Such a code word "can be a quick device to halt the escalation of unpleasant situations without exposing your child to embarrassment in front of peers or other adults. A child armed with a repertoire of code words known by his parents and brothers and sisters is a child who feels in control and part of a unified family team."[15]

They relate how one family uses the word "spike" when anyone wants other family members to know he or she is feeling intensely uncomfortable and needs to exit a conversation. Or, parents might use the word when they surmise one of their *children* is having difficulty. On one shopping trip, for example, this same family talks about running into an acquaintance who decided to ask each transracially adopted child what they wanted to be when they grew up. She asked the older daughter, who is Asian, if she was planning to be an accountant; the youngest brother, who is of black and Asian heritage, if he wanted to be a golfer like Tiger Woods; and the third child, a Latino girl, if she wanted to be a gardener. At this point their dad interrupted in an apologetic tone of voice, "Oh dear, I seem to be having a *spike*. Sorry, but I just can't stay and chat . . . come on kids . . . say good-bye and we're out of here."[16]

The Suprising Comments *Our* Children Make

Strangers are not the only ones who come out with odd comments. Sometimes the strangest sentiments spring out of our child's own mouth. (Obviously our kid's comments are *not* laden with subtle racial innuendo;

our children are merely searching for a deeper understanding of their own—and their family's—racial identity.)

Often these comments run along the lines of a child expressing a wish to look more like one parent or the other (to "match" them) in terms of skin color or other features. But it would be a mistake to assume such comments mean a child bears a negative attitude toward themselves or their parents. During these years it is especially common for multiracial children to express a strong desire to look like their *same-sex* parent, or for their same-sex parent to look like them, as they struggle to identify more closely with their own gender. Consider this story of one little girl (African American/Caucasian) who was playing with a "magic wand." Her white mom asked her, "If you really had magic, what would you do?" Without hesitation her daughter replied, "I would turn your skin brown."[17]

Similarly, children may wish they could change the appearance of the parent they are most often with, if they clearly don't share a similar phenotype. When children bear little resemblance to one parent—to the degree that strangers and other kids are constantly reacting to that difference—it can cause confusing emotions for them when they are *with* that parent. This may be especially the case for biracial children who are assumed to be white, *except when* they're with their darker-skinned parent. Consider this example: "A biracial child with wiry blond hair and blue eyes is assumed to be white by his classmates and teachers, who have only had contact with his white mother. One day his African-American father picks him up from school and his best friend runs away from him, yelling, 'I played with a nigger.'"[18]

The shock that onlookers express when a white-appearing child's dark-skinned parent appears can cause the child to feel ambivalent about being seen, in some circumstances, in the presence of their darker-skinned parent. But this ambivalence is *not* a rejection of the parent. Nor is it a rejection of the child's own race or a sign of low self-esteem. It is a dearly held desire not to be singled out and made the center of *negative* attention because of what color one's parent is or is not.

Similarly, when a child who is light-skinned and biracial—say, African American/Caucasian—makes a comment such as "I'm white," it should not be seen as a rejection of her black racial identity. Rather, at this stage of development, it is still (as when she was younger) more likely to reflect her honest observation that her skin color seems closer to white than black.

It is of concern, however, when a child expresses a direct wish to not be of color or rejects any racial background other than white. Consider this biracial Chinese/Caucasian boy who confided to me his secret wish that his mom and/or he could be white: "Sometimes I remember wishing, when I was little, that I had a white mother. Or, I hate to say it, but sometimes I would hope that someone was going to tell me, just like in the fairy tales, that I was adopted and *I* was white. Looking back, I feel really guilty about my secret wish to be white, or for my mother to turn out to be my adopted Chinese mother." Because race was never discussed in this family, and because this young man grew up in a community where his was the "only" family like his, he erroneously assumed that he and his family were *not* normal. And that, he says, "didn't feel okay. I was always wishing it could change."

By reassuring children that families do come in all shapes, sizes, textures and combinations, we hope to send the clear message that our own particular family—that first, primary "group" to which our child belongs—*is* normal, 100 percent, no less.

Sandy Randall (Caucasian), married to Carol Franks-Randall, Ed.D. (African American), and stepdad for more than 15 years to daughters Jennifer and Samantha, says he and Carol have made the above concept something of a family creed. "We worked very hard to make it clear from day one that being a multiracial family was normal. That conversation about race is so important," Sandy Randall emphasizes. "We would always use the same little phrase so that they would forget about labeling people by color or race. We'd say, 'It really doesn't matter;' the color of someone's skin has no bearing on who they are or on who *you* are. At the same time, it was very important to us that they were very proud of their family heritage and of living in a multiracial family." As a result, says Sandy, "All over our walls we have photos of our extended family and half are black and half are white. The pictures are a statement to the world that we're proud of our family in all its forms. Those photos are as important as the dialogue."

Indeed, Samantha recalls the first time another child tried to tell her she didn't "match" her dad. "One day when my dad came over to school to drop something off for me, one white girl in the class said, 'That's your *dad*?!' I remember being so surprised she would even ask. I was like, 'Well, *yeah*. Why would you even *ask* me that?'"

Samantha was so clear that her dad was her dad—whether or not their skin color matched—that in her mind the other girl seemed crazy and strange rather than Samantha or her own family being the ones who were out of place. Building a strong foundation for our children so that they feel secure whenever a mistaken identity situation occurs is critical not only for the here and now but for the future as well.

Naomi Reed (African American/Russian Jewish/Caucasian), 20, relates, "I first realized I was biracial when I was about five years old. I started to notice when people would stare at me in the grocery store when I was with my mom. I remember I would always frown back at them. I recall a lot of stares and ridiculous questions that added up to my asking my parents what the deal was with all the weirdness I was feeling from other people. My parents always told me to just ignore people who stared at us, to keep in mind that they may not be staring out of disapproval and to remember that if they were, those people were just ignorant. It was *their* issue, not ours. My dad always told me not to hate people because of their comments . . . he made me realize that I didn't have time to hate other people because being hateful was much too self-destructive."

Even to this day, at the age of 20, Naomi deals with situations of mistaken identity, which irk her to no end. But the early foundation her parents laid—making it clear to her that the problem was not with her, but with the attitudes and assumptions of others, is one she still draws upon today, even when facing a frustrating scene such as this one: "Once I was watching my mom play tennis and this woman asked me who I was watching. There was only one black lady out there, so when I said I was watching my mom, she figured I meant that black woman, so she pointed to her and said, 'Is *that* your mom right there?' And I said, 'No, my mom's the lady in the pink skirt.' My mom was the only person out there wearing bright pink. And the woman said, 'Where? I don't see her!' After we'd been through this a few times I just said, 'how can you not see her? She's the only person out there wearing pink!' I don't cower in those situations at all and I don't see it as my problem; I let people know that I think *they're* close-minded."

Learning About Their Family Background

Because kids between five and eight are so interested in what characterizes their family "group," this is an excellent time to begin telling them details about their family background in all its rich variety—giving them a platform of pride to stand on which is so solid no one, and no comment, can shake its foundation. Indeed, says psychologist Maria Root, editor of *The Multiracial Experience: Racial Borders As the New Frontier,* a "sense of belonging and knowing to whom one is related gives [multiracial children] confidence [to] cope with the challenges" they may one day face.

Indran Amirthanayagam (Sri-Lankan American) talks about fostering this sense of family identity with his son, Anandan (Sri-Lankan American/Caucasian):

> It's so important to me that Anandan is proud of himself and of who his family is, and that he knows what to say when people comment about his background or are curious about his heritage. So I talk to him about his four names and what each of them signifies. I tell him: *Anandan* is an Indian name which means a wondrous reaction to the world, bliss and joy, just as we felt when he was born. *Guyomar* is my father's first name. *Andrew* is his mother's father's first name. And *Amirthanayagam* is my family name. So without saying it directly I explain to him that these are his various Sri Lankan and American names, and this is his history. I tell Anandan, racial differences spring up from the different corners and seas and islands of the world where these human beings have grown up. They don't signify that anyone is better or worse than anyone else is. They add color and variety in the world, which is pleasing. I have told him that if you were an artist you would want color, not a blank canvas, and people are the color on the canvas of the world. But I have also told him that these colors signify certain cultural histories and are attached to a variety of histories. And that if you put together these varied histories, these people, you have a richer world.

A multiracial child's name (which, as the expression goes, may seem to have "first and last names on a direct collision course")[19] can be a point of departure in and of itself for a conversation. I have, many times, gone over the meaning of my son Christian's names with him, as a way of articulating the rich texture of varied ancestries he claims. He knows quite well, at eight, that we chose the name Christian (a seemingly Anglican name) because it is a name rich with my mother's (and hence his) Scandinavian heritage, and it can also be spelled "Chris-chan," which, by adding the Japanese "chan" translates as "dear, beloved child Chris." We say Christian/Chris-chan, and it evokes Scandinavia and Japan and says you are dear and beloved to us all in the same breath.

His first middle name, Forrest, was chosen by his dad because nature connects us all.

His second middle name, Jackson, is my maiden name and my father's name. It links back, generation to generation, to the beginning of the country in which he lives. Christian's great-great-great-great-great-great-grandfather was American Western Territory explorer David Jackson, for whom Jackson Hole, Wyoming, is named. He opened the Oregon Trail for westward moving settlers and was a great-uncle of Confederate Civil War hero Stonewall Jackson—all of which is of outstanding interest to a young boy enthralled by stories of explorers and soldier heroes. In giving Christian this middle name, we gave him his tie to America itself.

And finally, his last name, Nakazawa, is his father and grandfather's name, and it links back in Japanese history to the small Samurai clan of the same name, which counts back eighteen generations. Translated, Nakazawa means "the valley between two mountains." And Christian is that—the connection between the "mountain" of the great land of America and the "mountain" of the great land of Japan. He is the fertile ground between, from which anything might spring.

In going over his names with Christian, and their multiple meanings and associations, I hope that he will gain a greater sense of his place in his family, and, moreover, his sense of place in the *world*.

I still recall how Christian (newly six at the time) once asked his Japanese grandfather, Ojiji, numerous questions about their Samurai history, what the castle his family once had in Japan looked like, once upon a time, oh so long ago. His grandfather drew him lots of pictures and told him that he, Christian, would be the eighteenth Lord Nakazawa if such a feudal system were still in place today. As Christian knows, that castle is now deep under water, its post–World War II rubble part of a dam.

Later, at bedtime, Christian peppered me with questions: "What would that have been like, to be a Samurai lord?" And we talked about the good things (meals delivered in your tatami room three times a day, an entourage of people to dress, bathe, tutor and entertain you, early training in Kendo— Japanese fencing—and horseback riding) and the bad (no heat, no medicine, a smelly hole in the ground for a toilet) and the ugly (warring feudal Samurai clans attacking your home in the night as you slept).

At that moment, he looked up at me and asked, "Mom? What do you think would happen if those two people ever *mixed*? Like if your blood from Davey and Stonewall and Daddy's blood from the Samurai lords ever got all *mixed?*" His hands stirred the air in front of him in a quick motion, as if working together finger paints on a page. "What would that be *like?*" His curiosity was palpable, his innocence complete. I had to laugh as I hugged him and said, "Well, Christian, that would be *you*. It's not that you're a mix of Davey and Stonewall and Lord Nakazawa, because those people all lived a long, long time ago, and you are you, completely special and not like anyone else now or in the past or in the future. But we each have a little bit of the genes of our ancestors and you have a mix of both of those genes. So you and your sister are what happened when both of these cultures "mixed" some 150 years after Davey Jackson and the last of the Samurai lords were laid to rest."

He was so surprised. "Oh! *Really?* I'm a *mix?*" he asked. His eyes widened. It was the first time he had ever verbalized being of "mixed" heritage and the first time that I could see the concept had really hit home.

Whereas preschoolers (ages three to five) can only categorize by one category, children in the early grade school years (five to eight) possess the cognitive ability to simultaneously categorize things by more than one characteristic—including *themselves*. As a result, they're better to understand the concept of being "mixed" or "multi" racial.[20] Providing our children with a concrete means by which to understand concepts like biracial, multiracial, multicultural or transracial, by starting to explain their ancestry, can help them immeasurably as they construct their multiracial identity.

For instance, a few months after Christian had that proverbial "lightbulb" moment (it really was as if I could see something switch on in his brain), our conversation came up again. We were at a swimming pool when two boys began to tease him, calling him "scaredy cat" because he didn't like being splashed in the face. He broke into tears. One of these boys had, on another occasion, teased Christian about his eyes.

Later that night, at bedtime, he told me, "You know Mom, today when they were teasing me, I felt all weird and little inside, like I wanted to cry but I didn't *want* to cry. But then I thought about my three selves and I felt really strong!"

"Wow!" I said, very curious. "What do you mean by your *three* selves?" I hadn't a clue and had some small vestige of concern at the concept, to be truthful.

"Well," he said, very matter-of-factly. "My Davey and Stonewall Jackson self, and then there's my Samurai self, and then my *third* self—the me that's both of them mixed together!" My heart leapt. The concept of being "mixed" had not only clicked, it had clicked *in* as a source of *strength*.

Samantha Franks (African American), an undergraduate at the University of Pennsylvania, talks about how, as she and her sister got older, "We were extremely aware of how proud my family was of themselves— and rightfully so. My mom (black), who grew up in a ghetto, got her master's and doctorate degrees at Columbia. My dad (white) grew up in a family of four kids that didn't have a lot of money and he had to take lots of loans to complete his education at MIT. My older brothers (white) went to Brown and Yale. My older sister (black) went to Harvard. One half of the family is black and they're incredibly accomplished. And one half of the family is white and they're incredibly accomplished. And that showed me that anyone of any race can accomplish whatever he or she wants. Race has absolutely nothing to *do* with it. The multiculturalism in my family makes me very proud. It's a matter of who we are regardless of race or the color of our skin."

One way to give kids this sense of who they are is to use the visual cue of a map itself—showing children the location of the countries that are part of their heritage, and how they interrelate in terms of their own identity.

One mom (Caucasian) talks about conversations she has had with her two adopted multiracial children, ages seven and two (both African American/Caucasian): "We look at books which talk about different regions of the world, and as we read them we talk about how groups of people who have lived for centuries on different continents have different shades of skin because they married each other for centuries, and because their skin adapted to the different climates and environments in which they lived. Many times I've gotten out the globe and shown them where Africa is and explained to my daughter that, in part because of slavery, African people have moved throughout the world, from continent to continent. Meanwhile, other people from other continents have moved to new continents, too. These people have all intermarried and their skin color has changed to become many, many different shades of skin. I tell my children that they *are* those shades."

Susan Fu (Caucasian) says that when her middle child, Kayla (Chinese/Caucasian), was five years old and in kindergarten, "She came home from school and said something about a little boy in her class and how she really liked his eyes. I knew the little boy, who is Korean. And, I said, 'Well, you know your eyes are a little bit like his. You're half Chinese.' And she said, 'No, I am *not!*'"

This was a good opportunity, says Fu, "to talk about not only the fact that Kayla *is* both Chinese and Irish, but to get out the globe and show her where her family is from. We discovered that Taiwan, where her dad's family is from, is *exactly* halfway around the globe from where we live in Maryland, and I remember how struck she was by that."

Giving a child this visual "map of the world"—one which highlights how, as people of different races increasingly traverse continental borders (through both modern transportation and via high speed communication) they are "mixing" races around the globe—can help them immensely in understanding not only who they are, but that their "mixedness" is natural and so is their mixed-race family.

Enhancing the Developing Sense of Self in Five- to Eight-Year-Olds

In shoring up our child's self-esteem, it is especially helpful if his or her "minority" parent possesses a clearly positive self-identity because that parent's attitude about his racial identity will manifest in how he addresses issues of culture and ethnicity with his children. Being comfortable with one's own ethnic background not only helps to give one's children an understanding and appreciation of that heritage with a personal depth of meaning that can't be provided by anyone else, it also affords a child a parent who understands, intrinsically and empathically, what that child might one day face because she is racially different. A minority parent who is comfortable with herself serves as the strongest and most natural role model imaginable for a child coming of age, showing how *she* can successfully emerge from her own experiences with a strong sense of self.

Ramona E. Douglass (African American/Native American/Sicilian/Scots-Irish/Caucasian), former president of the Association of MultiEthnic Americans, says, "It is my belief that children get their cues on celebrating their full ethnic/racial blends from their parents. If we are ambivalent about our own identities and worth in the world we cannot expect to instill confidence and pride in our children."

Indran Amirthanayagam feels that his own experiences as a Sri Lankan living in England when he was a boy may well have made him more attuned to incidents that may befall his biracial son, Anandan. "Before Anandan was born I thought a lot about my childhood in England and what occurred to me there," he recounts. "I remember we had just arrived in England from Sri Lanka when an old lady on a bike—dressed in black with a black hood—screamed at me, 'black Sambo Bitch Bastard!' I started to think about that black-cloaked cyclist when I thought of my own child's future." Although Amirthanayagam worried about what his child would encounter as the son of a Sri Lankan father and a white American mother, because he'd come through such experiences—in various different cultures—with a strong sense of self, he felt he could help Anandan do the same.

"Your child is your work," Amirthanayagam says resolutely. "As a parent one needs to provide tools and give assistance. When I was a child my father prepared me to deal with these encounters of racial prejudice from a position of strength. When I heard a racial slur in England, such as, 'You're a wog,' [an expression derived from a black golliwog doll that used to be popular in England], my father told me to just say to the person who was teasing me, 'Oh, yes, that means that I'm a western Oriental gentleman!' which deflected it back on that person.

"I want Anandan to know how to answer back with wit rather than with his fists. I'd rather he learn how to defuse a situation and not be ashamed of who he is, no matter what others might say or do," says Amirthanayagam. Having himself experienced that challenge as a child, he understands how difficult that task can be, and he has advance empathy for what his own son might one day experience.

In order to help his son build that inner strength, he says, "I have told Anandan that 'building bridges to other cultures—introducing your culture to those cultures and introducing yourself to other cultures is one of the great gifts you can give the world as you grow up. Through the parents you've already been given, and through living in different cultures, you've been given a head start on this bridge building.' I feel that when Anandan does meet the fist of intolerance or faces racial slurs he will face them with strength drawn from being a bridge between different cultures. That he will have a sense of self, a confidence, from having been part of these different cultures and having grown from that expanded sense of self."

A minority parent in an interracial marriage who understands what their child (who is, in part, of that minority background) may feel and face—and yet who has successfully dealt with these issues in their own psyche—can also help their white spouse to understand how their multiracial child may feel when they are viewed as being different. Not surprisingly, research shows that adult children in multiracial families often feel that their white parent was less well equipped to raise mixed children than their parent of color.[21]

If the parent of color is mixed, it can be even *more* helpful. Consider the recollections of Michelle Craig (African American/Japanese/Mexican/Dutch-German/Caucasian), age 17, whose mother is also mixed: "My dad is European American and he sometimes had trouble seeing where I was coming from—but my mom, being mixed, really got it. It also helped me to know that my [experiences] aren't as bad as what *she* experienced."

After the incident where Christian was told by another boy that he had "little black holes for eyes," my husband, Zenji, helped me understand the internal pain Christian must have felt by sharing some of his own experiences. That playground incident with the kindergartner had, for him, disturbing resonance. When he was growing up in Baltimore, he was routinely teased about his eyes. Once, he says, some kids were giving him a rough time ("chink eyes" and "Chinaman" were popular taunts) and he took them to the mirror because he wanted to prove to them that he was the same as anyone. He was certain that that was how the mirror would answer him. But the other boys pointed out how his eyes *were* slanted and theirs weren't. Right then, for the first time, he says, at age six, he saw for himself that he *did* look different. His eyes were not like theirs. He had never really seen it clearly before. Suddenly he understood that his eyes were different in shape and size and color, and because of that physical difference, they saw *him* as being different *inside*. He says he stood at that mirror and cried and cried, rubbing his eyes as if to rub that difference out. His own emotionally charged memories took my breath away and helped me to have a visceral sense of how affected my son might be over the long term by such incidents.

Even though a white parent may have to work harder to understand what it's like to encounter the raw sting and reeling injustice of racism, this is not to say that her passion for both preparing and protecting her child is any less intense than that of a minority parent. Because most white moms *didn't* have to deal with race issues when they were kids—and because the contrast between their life as a white child (and the racial privilege they experienced) and what they see their multiracial kids deal with may be vast—racial realities often come as a greater shock for them.

David Harris, Ph.D., professor of sociology at the University of Michigan, believes that "shock to a white mother's system when she sees what her multiracial *child* encounters is why white moms of multiracial kids get so outraged by what happens to their kids—it just hits them harder, whereas someone who is black has dealt with race issues all along." In fact, comments Harris, much of the current multiracial movement (to change race-related questions on the census and other government forms so respondents can check all races that apply, as well as to address other concerns particular to multiracial children and families) "is driven by outraged white women, and I think that's good. Society is more responsive to the whole movement because so many of the women driving it *are* white."

Whether a parent's desire for his child to develop a strong racial identity is rooted in the empathy he feels because of his own experiences as a person of color, or because, as a white person, she is shocked and outraged at the pivotal role race plays in how one is perceived in our society, the sum line remains the same: It is parents who set the tone for a home environment in which children feel wholly supported and loved for all of who they are and thus safe to share questions about race and identity as soon as they can begin to formulate them.

Protecting the Multiracial Child's Identity Development

Obviously, no matter what combination of races children may be, when their parents have established the cornerstone values of acceptance, love and support within their family, a healthy identity can flourish. And when that tone of acceptance and love is absent, it can be devastating for a child's burgeoning sense of self.

To be sure, parental dysfunction has devastating consequences for all children, but for the multiracial child there are often additional consequences. Consider again the work of clinical psychologist Maria Root, whose seminal study of 20 pairs of multiracial siblings documents how drastically parental dysfunction can derail the multiracial child's identity growth.

Because children between the ages of five and eight are becoming ever more cognizant of their environment and are also developing stronger categorization skills, if they are confronted by a parent's dysfunction (emotionally or physically cruel behavior), they tend to struggle hard to make sense of these events and explain to themselves why such hurtful and traumatic things are happening to *them.*

For this reason, points out Root, "repeated exposure to being told one is stupid, unwanted, bad, unworthy, or ugly may get 'color coded.'" Meaning that, in an attempt to make sense of her experience, a child may unconsciously assume that her parent is critical (or cruel or cold or distant or demeaning) *because* of that parent's *racial* makeup. This child may then distance herself from that parent's ethnic group "as a way of attempting to exorcise what went wrong." For example, several multiracial children who experienced a parent's emotional cruelty created a false sense of safety for themselves—telling themselves that they wouldn't encounter such cruelty again (later in life) by refusing to date anyone who was of the same racial or ethnic makeup as their cruel or cold parent.[22] Root tells an illustrative story of a set of multiracial siblings, who for years "distanced themselves from Filipinos because their Filipino mother had been so distant and self-centered." Similarly, when multiracial children are abandoned by a parent, they often "color code the abandonment and attach a negative feeling toward [people] of that parent's racial background."

This color "coding" may provide an alternative explanation for some racially mixed individuals who appear to hate themselves.[23] Their seeming self-hatred may stem not from being of mixed race but rather from an inability to differentiate themselves from the parent who was abusive. For example, if a biracial Mexican/white child is raised by a dysfunctional, Mexican father who is cruel, that boy may feel self-hatred for the part of himself that he fears may also be capable of cruelty; he equates cruelty with *being* Mexican. He may not completely trust that racial aspect of himself that he has "color coded" as having a propensity for betrayal and cruelty.[24]

As if all this weren't enough, when multiracial children are belittled, berated or emotionally abused by a parent before their own racial identity has been successfully formed, they spend significant mental energy sorting out why such abuse is occurring. This "sorting out" takes precedence over achieving the appropriate stages of normal racial identity development. As a result, the identity process is derailed.[25]

This is not to say that multiracial children who grow up with a dysfunctional parent can't or won't sort out their multiracial identity successfully. But it will take longer and be more difficult to do so over the long term.

The Benefits of a Strong Marriage

Although it's surely a given that a solid marriage is the cornerstone of a secure home setting for any child, it may be even more essential for a child in a mixed-race marriage to feel confident and assured of his or her parent's love for each other. Seeing two parents demonstrate affection and respect for one another, and witnessing their strong, enduring bond through good times and bad, answers a child's eventual query as to how Mom and Dad (seemingly so different) came together. It also reassures the child that interracial unity is natural and positive within the world, and within themselves. A mixed race marriage serves as a mirror for a child's own sense of how their two halves can successfully unite, for nowhere is their own racial mixedness better reflected than in their parents' marriage itself.

Meanwhile, the number of interracial marriages has skyrocketed. In 1990 the census reported 1.5 million interracial marriages. With the shift in the 2000 census—which allowed more accurate race-related questions—coupled with an increase in interracial marriages, that number has more than doubled to over 4 million.

One recent study by University of Maryland assistant professor Jaslean La Taillade (African American/Caucasian) on interracial couples found that

1. interracial couples were as happy in their relationships as same-race couples and reported using constructive communication skills
2. interracial couples were as accepting of their partners as same-race couples
3. interracial couples were as satisfied with their outside support networks (including family and friendships) as same-race couples
4. although interracial couples were more likely to experience subtle forms of discrimination, these experiences were unrelated to how happy and satisfied they were with their relationships[26]

This certainly resonates for me. When I first met my husband twelve years ago, my mind was occupied with passionate matters common to all new couples: luxuriating in getting to know this extraordinary person and negotiating the blending of two grown-up lives into one lifestyle. Our issues, as we brought our worlds together, had little to do with race and everything to do with exploring the other 99 percent of who we both are. Besides, it seemed to me that all couples were mixed couples: one woman and one man—how much more mixed can you get than that? In my heart, I didn't feel we were all that different from the dozens of other married couples I knew who were of mixed faith, mixed age, mixed life philosophy or mixed economic backgrounds.

Ask any interracial couple and they will tell you that from the inside, their marriage is no different from any other. Conflicts may certainly arise over finances, jobs, approaches to parenting, domestic responsibilities and communication issues, but rarely about racial differences. Conversations at home are far more often about what to have for dinner or how one's day went at work than they are about color or race. In one recent study, interracial couples reported sharing an especially high level of common values and beliefs, including respect, honesty, trust, faithfulness, appreciation of diversity, family (including family of origin) and religion or spirituality. A number of couples pointed out that these shared values were particularly helpful when it came to being consistent in their role as parents. Couples reported that in the everyday context of their relationships, their racial differences were a nonissue; indeed, they only became an issue when they were out in public where others reacted to the contrast in their skin color.[27]

Moreover, according to John Gottman, Ph.D., emeritus professor of psychology at the University of Washington and director of the Relationship Research Institute in Seattle (a marital research center), couples in marriages with significant differences—religious, cultural, racial, age-related, or political—may have a leg up on other couples. He explains, "All couples come from separate cultures; culture is about the meaning we ascribe to things, from how we act when someone we love is sick to how we like to celebrate birthdays. So even if two people are of the same race and grew up in the exact same town, they still come from two separate families, so they are each coming from their own individual culture." When we marry, Gottman explains, we often expect our mate to understand and meet our expectations. If that doesn't happen, we feel he or she must not love us enough. But because interracial couples "often enter marriage with a more conscious awareness of the cultural differences between them, they may be more likely to address these issues by talking openly about them, which helps to depersonalize the conflict and eliminate hurt feelings."

None of this is to say that embarking on a multiracial marriage isn't, in some arenas, difficult. Bringing two races together can make in-laws nervous and openly disapproving, putting enormous pressure on one or both partners to choose between their parents or the person they love. In one study, *two-thirds* of couples in black/white partnerships said at least one set of parents objected to their union at its start.[28]

Nancy Brown (Caucasian) recalls that although her husband Roosevelt (African American) and her father later became close friends, when she was dating her husband, she kept her relationship a secret for months, out of worry she'd be disowned. When she finally told her parents she wanted to move in with him, they tried to dissuade her. Two years later, when Nancy and Roosevelt announced their engagement, Nancy says, "my father said he didn't want this kind of alliance. He asked me, 'What are you going to do when he leaves you with black babies?' But I wouldn't succumb to that way of thinking."

Although Brown married her husband decades ago, even today nearly half of whites—more than any other racial group—do not feel it would be "fine with them" if a member of their family told them they were going to marry a black individual.[29]

This kind of societal resistance may be why other research suggests that people who marry interracially are more independent than those who do not and indicates that people willing to marry across racial barriers tend to be more secure about themselves and are able to make personal choices that are right for them, despite societal pressure.[30]

Still, as the number of interracial marriages skyrockets—as people of all races increasingly have natural, human interactions in meaningful ways in their communities and workplaces, often becoming friends, lovers and lifelong partners—the approval of interracial unions is increasing as well. A recent Washington Post/Kaiser Family Foundation/Harvard University study reported that although whites are divided (especially older whites) on whether it's better to marry someone of their own race, minorities report race largely doesn't matter to them when it comes to marriage. Nearly three-quarters of blacks, Latinos and Asians say, "it makes no difference."[31]

And today, nearly four out of ten Americans report having dated someone of another race—mostly in "serious dating relationships."[32] As Frank D. Bean, professor of sociology at the University of California at Irvine remarks, "If you have hang-ups about interracial marriage, get over it. The train's left the station."[33]

The Benefits of Having Siblings

For children who are biracial, the presence of siblings may have a remarkably positive effect on each child's self-esteem, giving each child a concrete sense that there are others like them, not only in their own home but within the greater world. Psychologist Beverly Daniel Tatum points out that "when a sibling comes along, the first child often has a great sense of relief in seeing someone like them in their family. It gives them a much bigger sense of seeing themselves reflected in the world around them."[34]

As Louise Lazare (Caucasian) puts it, after raising eight adopted children, six of whom are multiracial, one of the most important things parents in multiracial families can do is to "try not to have only one child of one race or racial mixture, whether they're adopted or your birth children. It's so important to try to make sure a child has siblings who look something like them, so they have another child who is different in the way they're different, a brother or sister they can talk to openly about what they're feeling; someone who understands and cares. It was always wonderful to see my children, as they were growing up, talk to each other about these issues, sometimes without me. I liked seeing that."

Still, siblings' experiences growing up may be very different from one another, causing them to develop very different racial identities. Each child is born with his or her own unique racial appearance, talents, gender and birth order, and each child is born into the family at a different time in the family's history (parents may be more or less affluent than they were when an older sibling was born or live in a more or less diverse neighborhood than when their older sibling was young, or attend a school in a different district with a different racial mix). Each child also has his or her own unique emotional experiences with each parent (one child may recall a parent as being depressed, whereas another, born years earlier, was off at college and never experienced that parent's depression).

Maria Root's research with siblings shows this clearly. For instance, she finds that while "name calling or 'authenticity testing' [are] common experiences for many persons of mixed heritage [they] are not experienced uniformly. Although these experiences may be initially unsettling to almost all children, some children will experience them as challenges they are able to constructively meet [whereas] a brother or sister may experience some of these same events as so hurtful that these experiences preclude them from joining in with the other children. Their way of coping or avoiding further incidents may steer their life course in a different direction than their siblings."[35]

For instance, consider the following siblings' very different experiences with racial identity (there is a 12-year difference in their ages): "The older sister, in her early 30s, grew up almost exclusively on and around military bases," writes Root. "Her father retired as she was entering her senior year of high school. She stayed in Germany to complete her senior year with her classmates. Meanwhile, as the family moved back to the United States, her sibling, the youngest of three girls, had just started school. She was exposed throughout her school years to the U.S. construction of race and the attitudes that stem from racial apartheid in this country. Although both siblings identified themselves as mixed race, the younger sister identified herself as ethnically black. Her older sister, also identifying herself as mixed, did not align herself with the black community in the same way. Culturally, she did not grow up in the United States. She speaks in a way that is labeled by her sister as white. The older sibling talked about a process of exploring being an "other" and exploring many different types of alternative identities in her search for finding herself once she returned to the United States. This search lasted for approximately 10 years, through her 20s."

Such differences among siblings' identities are not uncommon. In another family of three sisters, one identified herself as white, one as black and one as mixed.

In a best-case scenario, the one thing that siblings will have in common—regardless of the varied racial identities they might claim due to differences in age, appearance, temperament and coming-of-age experiences—is this: an understanding that racially "matching" Mom, Dad or their sisters(s) and brother(s) is of minuscule relevance compared to their bone-deep knowledge that their family is a port in a sometimes hard-to-navigate sea of racial complexity—a safe haven where they can be sure that their questions will be answered openly and lovingly, where their racial identity is never a taboo topic, and where all of who they are is supported and celebrated.

Jana Bender (African American/Vietnamese, adopted by Caucasian parents who adopted eight children, six of whom are multiracial), talks about the safety she felt within her very multiracial family environment, and how it helped her develop a deep feeling of inner security: "If I'd been in a home with all black people or all white people then it would have been different. But the very fact that my family was multiracial and we came from so many different mixed backgrounds—that helped my identity, my sense of being secure in who I am as a mixed race person. I thought that well, if being of different races and living together can work so well at my house, then it can work in the world outside too, wherever I might go."

Indeed.

CHAPTER THREE

"What Do I Do When Friends Say Hurtful Things?"

Navigating Friendships in the Middle Childhood Years

As CHILDREN BECOME IMMERSED in the playground politics of grade school, each interaction with their eight- to eleven-year-old peers becomes electrically charged with the paramount questions: "Can *I* play too? Do you want to play with *me*? Do you *like* me?" What seems to matter most now is who is friends with whom; who is included or not included in the group to join in fun, work and play.

It's not surprising, then, that so many of the young multiracial and transracially adopted adults with whom I've spoken—who viscerally recalled moments of taunting, teasing or being excluded—experienced these first shocking incidents during these grade school years. Often memories of peer teasing—which most recall happening between second and fifth grade—continue to be emotionally searing a decade or more down the road. Because of the immediate impact and lasting echo of these early encounters, I have found this time to be the first of two pivotal pressure points children in multiracial families face. Indeed, much depends on whether they successfully navigate this passage.

Although these years may seem latent when compared to the wonder and constant growth of early childhood or the drama of adolescence, nothing could be further from the truth. At this age, our children are carefully stuffing in—and watchfully recording—all the knowledge they can acquire about the world around them. Regardless of how they may appear on the surface, their minds are racing a mile a minute, busily formulating ever-expanding ideas that lay the foundation for what will soon be the vocal opinions they espouse as teens. They are busy forming opinions of themselves—who they are, their racial identity, what they are competent at and what they are not—at the same time that they are observing the same about others.

During this shift into the changing psychological landscape of middle childhood, as playground and social interactions become children's key focus, the question of whether their peers like and accept them becomes central to our children's sense of who *they* are. Their friends' opinions of them and desire to be with them (or lack thereof) is like a mirror in which they see reflected their own sense of self-worth. How can we help our children process these influences of peer opinion in the most healthy manner possible? How can we help them respond to any hurtful incidents or moments of exclusion from a position of *strength*?

As is true at each stage of our children's development, we first need to understand, through their eyes, the complex world they now inhabit—to peer with compassion into that emotional maelstrom where the newly garnered importance of friendship, a child's burgeoning awakening to his or her own identity and greatly increased social and racial awareness converge.

Pressure Point One: The Early Grade School Years

Although not all of my interviewees reported experiencing emotionally wounding incidents during these grade school years, the vast majority did. Consider the following stories told by young adults in multiracial families (or related by their parents) of moments when they were taunted in grade school—a time when they so desperately wanted to be accepted by all.

George Meyers (Japanese/Caucasian), now 24 years old and finishing medical school, recalls elementary school life as a multiracial youth with little fondness: "In grade school I went to a mostly white, Christian school during the week, where I was the only half-Japanese kid. On Saturdays I went to a Japanese school, where I was one of the only half-white kids. "I was 'different,' so I guess it was easier for kids to use me as a target. I remember in my Japanese school there was this huge rolling chair in our class. When the teacher wasn't in the room kids would take turns riding the chair around the class, and they'd punch me as they went by. I'd curl up in a ball or try to run away, but the other kids would hold me down." This scene repeated itself for several years. In fourth grade, it came to a head, says George: "I was trying to get out of the room. The other kids were trying to hold me. They wouldn't let me go. And I took one of the kid's heads and slammed it into the door. The teacher came racing back and yelled at me. I don't know what came over me, but I said to her, 'You've been watching them beat me up every week for years, and you say *nothing*. So how can you dare to say something *now*?' I don't know how I had that wherewithal to say that or where that inner resolve came from but I stood up to her."

Meanwhile, in George's almost entirely white, Christian grade school, though his exclusion by other kids was certainly more subtle, his school days were only marginally more bearable. "I was a very introverted kid at school. My mom [Japanese American] would go to parent–teacher conferences and she would know that I was having trouble making friends. So she'd ask the teacher about it and the teacher would say, 'Well, nobody doesn't *like* George, everyone *seems* to like him.' But the other kids held me at arm's length; I knew they didn't really want to be my friend."

"I didn't have a whole lot of friends so any friend was a 'good' friend," he recalls. "I remember I once went into my mother's room and said, 'Joe said I was his friend today!' This was so exciting to me because I never had any close friends in elementary school who came over to my house. I'd had birthday parties but whether I actually had *friends* is debatable. To me, a friend was someone who didn't single me out as *being different*. I was still—and not by choice—a pretty independent kid."

During those years, George recalls vividly, "I had this recurring nightmare—my mom remembers this too—this ominous dream where I'd be inside and outside of myself at the same time. I would see everything get further and further away to the point that I became very small and the earth began to move off into space, getting bigger and bigger. I could feel myself as *part* of the earth at the same time that I could see the earth moving further *away* from me. It was a terrifying feeling to watch myself moving away from *me*. I would run to get in bed with my parents but that wouldn't solve the problem. I'd concentrate on the light on their alarm clock until I fell back to sleep."

I couldn't help wondering, during my interview with George, if this nightmare, which recurred many times during his grade school years, might have reflected the way in which he felt alienated and apart from other people "on earth" because he was treated by other kids as if he *were* different, even alien. And if his feeling in his dream of being small and powerless might reflect his feelings of powerlessness in the face of those who teased, bullied or excluded him because he was multiracial. Not even his own teachers had stepped in to help him. And yet, as in his dream, at the same time that he felt different and apart he knew, intuitively, intrinsically, that he wasn't "different." That he was a part of humanity, like any human being on earth, and that being treated as if he *were* different due to his racial makeup was wrong.

Many parents of children in multiracial families also remember the hurtful incidents their children experienced in grade school (if they're aware of what occurred) with cinematic and emotional recall. Leceta Chisholm Guibault (Caucasian), adoptive mother of Kahleah (Mayan/Guatemalan), talks about the night eight-year-old Kahleah, then in third grade, "confided in me that she was being harassed at school by some of the older fourth and fifth graders who didn't know her. It started each morning after the bus picked her up. She's one of the last to be picked up and she has to make her way to the back seats, where all the third and fourth graders are supposed to sit. But whenever she would try to sit down, the other students wouldn't let her sit. When the bus arrived at school they wouldn't let her pass, so she would be the last child off the bus. In school, in the hallways, they would call her 'Chinese' and say she had lice in her hair. They made a point of walking around her. She told me she was so hurt and disappointed that her friends didn't rally around her as she felt she would have for them. She had been trying to deal with all this on her own. She told me, holding back tears, 'Mommy, at first they were just bugging me. I tried to ignore them. Then they were getting on my nerves. Now they hurt my heart.' I could not sleep that night," says Leceta. "All I could see were my beautiful daughter's sad eyes."

One young Japanese American/Caucasian woman relates that when she was about eight years old, "I went over to my friend's birthday party. Her male cousin who was about 13 said, 'Ooh, you're Chinese. You're Chinese. You eat stink-food.' Without missing a beat, my friend says to him [her cousin], 'You dummy, she's *Japanese*' . . . it just seemed so out of nowhere that this kid said this. And my friend actually knew I was half-Japanese . . . [but] she had already labeled me. I was really hurt. I thought I was just like them but . . . in this negative way my friend stated my race as Japanese, it really told me that my difference was always apparent to them."[1]

Whether a child's traumatic memories relate to an ongoing, chronic situation or a few isolated incidents, these experiences all too often define a child's *initial* realization that he or she is seen by friends as being different in some way.

Nicole Brown (African American/Caucasian), age 22, recalls an incident that occurred during these grade school years as "a wake-up call that not everybody was going to just accept who I was. Up to that point the only thing that had happened—for as long as I could remember—was kids being confused and asking, 'Is that your *mom?* or, 'Are you adopted?' But then, a friend I'd played with all through second and third grade—my 'pretend sister' at school—told me that I *had* to say whether I was black or white. She was adamant. She said I couldn't be both, I *had* to choose. It was a very strange experience to be so young and have this close friend care so much about the whole issue of my race, to negate my own experience, to deny who *I* said I was. I realized that if a good friend couldn't accept me for who I was, maybe it wasn't going to be such smooth sailing."

Although Nicole says she never *forgot* the above incident with her "pretend sister," she is also proud to recall that she responded to this friend with utter confidence—having been well prepared to do so by her parents. "I remember telling my friend that I *was* both," she says. "That I was mixed, like the chocolate and vanilla mixed together in chocolate milk. Maybe part of it is my nature, but I think I'm a very strong, confident person mainly because I was raised to embrace who I am."

Consider the insights of Matt Kelley, son of a first-generation Korean-American mother and a white father, and founder and publisher of *MAVIN*, the first magazine for multiracial young people. In reviewing the heartfelt letters and e-mails that stream in from readers, and in his experiences as he talks with multiracial young people around the country, Kelley finds "the bottom line with raising any multiracial child is how to raise a *confident* multiracial child. I see so many mixed kids. I see mixed kids who are so confident—maybe other kids make a comment to them about their slanty eyes or call them a banana or an Oreo or a zebra, but their response is really solid and simple and confident. Maybe their response is, 'My mom is this and my dad is that and I'm really proud of it,' or maybe their response is, 'That's none of your business,' but either way, they have a confidence in the way they respond that makes the topic dead in the water. The conversation is *over.* And then I might see another kid in a very similar situation who doesn't react that way and who doesn't have that confidence and they're really traumatized and the memory of that event stays with them. So to me, the question for parents is, 'How *do* you raise a confident multiracial kid?'"

The question, indeed.

Interestingly, when children do attain—with the help and guidance of mindful parenting and, of course, to some degree, temperament—that sense of confidence, they often barely remember events that another child may find so devastating. They may recall the incident, but it packs little emotional wallop.

Or they may not recall the incident at all. To wit, when I interviewed Nancy Brown (Caucasian), mother of Nicole, about what she recalled of her daughters' grade school experiences, she responded that one disturbing incident had stayed with her more than others. "It was around second, third and fourth grade that our girls started to have more incidents regarding being multiracial," she recalls. "I remember once, when Nicole was eleven, we were at Disneyland with a group. There was another girl her age in our group who clearly had a very negative reaction to Nicole having a black father and a white mother and being multiracial. When we explained to her that we were married, she began making gestures as if she were sickened by us, and all these comments like, 'Euwwwwww . . . *yuck* . . . '" It was a very discomforting and hurtful moment, and "Nicole picked up on it immediately," says Brown. They talked about the incident the way they always did when such things occurred, about "how silly it was that some people had difficulty with the idea that people of different races could be married." Although the incident occurred more than a decade ago, Nicole's mom can well recall the raw unpleasantness of the scene.

However, shortly after interviewing her mother, I asked Nicole about the Disneyland incident her mom had so vividly recalled. Nicole immediately responded, "I don't recall *that* incident at all." She didn't doubt that it had happened. But because race had been such an ongoing topic in her home, and because her parents had worked diligently to prepare her for what she might face as a multiracial child in a monoracial world—to shore up her self-confidence to withstand any such encounters (and to talk them through when they occurred)—the incident simply hadn't affected her enough to lock in as a significant childhood memory.

There can be no doubt that this is a critical time for us, as parents and caregivers, to find ways to make certain our child emerges from these years with a positive sense of self and an inherent confidence. But how?

Understanding the Eight- to Eleven-Year-Old Multiracial Child

Considering all that is occurring for kids during these years, it's easy to see why this is the first of two pivotal pressure points children in multiracial families must carefully navigate—and why they need judiciously delivered help from the adults in their lives.

Here are some of the rapid-fire changes kids this age are now experiencing.

The Importance of Peer Interactions

It's useful here to remember that children of this age have undergone a developmental sea change in a relatively short span of time. Usually by the age of seven or eight, children undergo a significant shift in the basic way in which they see the world around them. They have moved away from the egocentric concept that others see the world exactly as they do and that theirs is the only point of view imaginable. Children this age start to think more about how others—especially their friends—might view *them* ("What do they think of *me*?"). Social awareness comes in with a bang, and the spotlight shifts toward being accepted and liked by friends on the playground, in the schoolroom and in their neighborhood.

By seven or eight—now possessing the ability to recognize differences between themselves and others—their desire to figure out what *they* have in common with the various groups to which they belong (friends, family, cultural, racial) intensifies as they try to show the ways in which *they* share these group characteristics.[2] Groups of friends begin to form based not only on a sense of camaraderie and belonging, but on agreed on standards of behavior and perceived similarities. The group tends to agree on what is cool, what is uncool, what is boring, what is worth exploring, what sports are cool, what is acceptable to say and play—*and* who will be included or excluded in the game along the way.

As MacArthur Prize-winning educator Vivian Gussin Paley writes in *You Can't Say You Can't Play*, by this age, a structure "begins to be revealed [which] will soon be carved in stone. Certain children will have the right to limit the social experiences of their classmates. Henceforth a ruling class will notify others of their acceptability, and the outsiders will learn to anticipate the sting of rejection. Long after hitting and name-calling have been outlawed by the teachers a more damaging phenomenon is allowed to take root, spreading like a weed from grade to grade."[3]

As a result of this new group culture, interactions with friends reach a new intensity, foreshadowing what will occur so much more dramatically during the throes of adolescence.

Kids' Complex Understanding of Racial Differences, Cultural Differences and Racism

Although recognition of people's differences, and the effort to understand, categorize and label these differences, begins during early childhood, these efforts now take place on a higher cognitive level, building on and surpassing children's earlier understanding. Our kids' emerging social awareness cues them into a deeper understanding of what factors define racial identity. They now understand that we inherit some of our defining characteristics through our parentage and ancestry. They also comprehend that *they* are biracial because of the different racial heritages of their parents.[4] Increasingly during these middle childhood years, our children are gaining a mental "map of the world" and the capacity to understand where they and others are on that map due to their geographic, cultural, ethnic, racial, economic and family background. They are grasping the concept that while we are all simultaneously human beings and thus all similar in some ways, we are also members of specific subgroups,[5] meaning that there are differences between us, including our ascribed "races" and our complex ethnic cultures. They have the cognitive sophistication to grasp these differences in much of their complexity, though this ability to understand does not promise that they will have an open attitude toward such differences. Whether they do or don't largely depends on what we, as their parents, caregivers and teachers, have modeled for them in this regard.

Much of what kids this age are struggling to do is to understand and attach labels to these perceived differences of race, class, geography and ethnicity, all of which they are increasingly attuned to. Because children now understand that the color of their skin is related to their mixed-race heritage, and because they are carefully scrutinizing the world around them to understand the laws of nature, searching out what is absolutely true and what is not true ("The color of your skin is the color you are for *life*"), they understand that their skin color is permanent. Gone is their earlier fantasy thinking that it might change.[6] Now aware that they are more racially unique than most children around them, multiracial children between eight and eleven begin searching out and taking keener note of who is like them, and who is not.

At the same time, their friends, too, are revving up their efforts to understand and categorize others by race—and to ascribe value or lack of value to these racial and ethnic differences. Joe Bender (Caucasian), one of eight adopted children in his family (six of whom are multiracial), recalls, "I wasn't even aware that our family was different until I was in second and third grade—and then I became aware, for the first time, that the fact that we lived in a house where we were all of different races was a big deal. To me, it was just like, So what? It was as if other kids were saying, 'Oh, you have knees!' Well of course I have knees. But because of all those comments other kids would make I realized that people saw it as being such a big deal. I would hear it in the school yard all the time—one girl saying to another girl, as she pointed across the playground at one of my [biracial] siblings, 'See that boy over *there*, that's Joe's brother—can you *believe* that?' It became the thing that distinguished me from other kids. But I felt that there were other things about me that were a lot more interesting than that."

This kind of constant racial categorizing and the placing of social value, or lack thereof, on these differences can make for some searing moments for a multiracial child. Joe's sister, Jana (African American/Vietnamese), adopted at the age of four, says she recalls "at age eight I came to understand what it meant to be half black and half Vietnamese in America. I got it, all [of a] sudden, that because of that I was not considered to be 'of the best quality.' I wasn't old enough to understand that people in America related color to class. But I knew I wasn't thought of as beautiful by people around me. And I knew I wasn't really accepted by the other kids at school. I wasn't really included by them. It was at around that age that I realized that there were so many more white people than black or Asian people. I was *starting* to understand the role race plays in our society."

George Meyers had similar experiences. "During grade school I became aware that there was a deep racism out there. I didn't associate the *word* racism with what was happening at the time, but I associated what was happening with the fact that there was something out there that influenced people in such a way that if you looked different physically, they'd treat you in a certain way because of that."

Kids Become More Outspoken with Peers

Children this age have more complex verbal skills to articulate their recognition of the racial differences they see (and are beginning to attach greater or lesser societal value to), and they often do so in outspoken ways.

Louise Lazare (Caucasian), mother of eight adopted children (six of whom are biracial), tells a story that illustrates how grade schoolers tend to be verbally forthright: "I was volunteering at an inner-city Boston school, helping a table of African-American kids weave. My son Sam, who is white, my daughter Sarah, who is biracial [African American/Caucasian], and my son Tom, who is black and very dark were all with me," she recalls. "The boys at the table were whispering and looking at me and then at the kids. Then they pointed at Sam and said, 'He's your kid.' Next they pointed at Sarah and said, 'She's your kid.' Then they pointed to Tom, who is so dark, and said to me, right in front of him, 'But he's your boyfriend's kid.'"

Efforts by grade school children to differentiate, group and label others by racial cues and skin color go hand in hand with their willingness, however wrong, to fling these labels around with abandon—along with whatever pejorative perceptions of race these labels may reflect. Whether children's comments to a multiracial child are based in curiosity or due to a lack of greater societal and racial awareness (e.g., "What are you anyway?") or rehashed misinformation gleaned from racist views they've heard adults in their lives espouse, or from racially skewed media messages (e.g., "You eat stink food!") the delivery of the message can be devastating for the underprepared multiracial child.

The Heart of Cool

Kids this age form tightly knit peer groups, that, in a positive sense, help them develop key skills for social interaction and group cooperation, which will stand them in good stead in the future. But they are sometimes prone to unkind gestures toward any group their own group perceives as "uncool." This can spell playground distress for a child who is racially different. During the more malleable years of early childhood, children were curious to learn about people different from themselves, and open to embracing those differences without stereotypes; during the middle childhood years, this is less the case. Grade schoolers' attentiveness to differences in skin-color is often about confirming perceptions in keeping with society's racial stereotypes. Not surprisingly, some children and peer groups begin to use these perceptions as tacit societal permission to tease and exclude children whom they see as being racially different. Children are not cruel, but they are good at mindlessly copying cruelty and bias.

Because race in our country has long been a basis for exclusion, and because this is an age when wanting to be included becomes a central focus for kids, children who are racially unique all too often bear the brunt of this intersection between our propensity to socially divide by race and children's newfound tendency to shut out other children.

Given this confluence of factors—a shift toward buying into racial stereotypes, increased verbal acuity and a willingness to brazenly label (or exclude) others in verbally cutting ways, as well as the fact that peer inclusion suddenly matters much more than it did only a few years earlier—it's no surprise that when negative encounters do occur at this pivotal pressure point, they're much more wounding and intense than they were in early childhood.

Consider the recollections of Sara Moss (Korean), adopted by her Caucasian parents when she was an infant. "Between third and fourth grade we moved to San Diego. I remember the girls at my new school would pull their eyes up and say, 'Chinese.' They'd ignore me when I tried to talk to them. If I was walking by, they'd give me looks or stick their tongues out. I think kids that age are sometimes just looking for someone to poke fun at. But I didn't think about that then. I just felt I was basically worthless."

Some peer conversations that highlight differences because of being multiracial can be much more subtle but nevertheless have a disturbing ripple effect. Quite recently, for instance, I overheard my son, Christian, explaining to his Polish baby-sitter what the word "irritate" means. "It's when people do things that really *bug* you," he told her. "Like, for me, the thing that *irritates* me the most in the whole world is when kids always come up to me and say, '*What* are you—*Chinese*? Do you speak *Chinese*?' That really *irritates* me."

An Expanding Grasp of Fair and Unfair

Children between the ages of eight and eleven increasingly understand issues of fairness and right and wrong, and that racism *is* unfair, especially when they have had guidance in achieving this awareness. They now comprehend that unfairness and racism can exist on both the personal level (a hurtful comment from a friend) and the global level (societal/historical racism and negative stereotypes toward minorities). Although they do not yet grasp the politics of race, they are gaining a fuller picture of racism in all its dimensions.[7]

Let's consider all the factors that come into play for children at this age:

- Group friendships take on new and paramount importance. ("Am I included? Can I play too?")
- Children understand that inclusion in the group is based in part on how other kids perceive them. ("What do they think of me? Do they like me? Am *I* cool?")
- They understand that although we are all human beings (and therefore similar), we are different in terms of our racial, geographic and family backgrounds (we all belong to different, smaller groups). ("What makes *me* part of this group? How am I *different* from them?")
- They are searching for labels for these differences—both for themselves and for those around them, and they realize that positive and negative labels exist. ("She called me a 'mud puppy'!")
- Kids this age are much more vocal, often making their immediate thoughts and feelings known in unabashedly hurtful ways, even negatively labeling other children. ("He told me I run so slow because I'm just a banana and bananas only have one leg!")
- They now understand and are concerned with fairness and right and wrong, and usually they have (unless we have schooled them otherwise) a growing awareness that racism—and ill treatment in general—is unfair and wrong. ("Slavery was wrong; thinking that anyone with different skin is worth less is *wrong.*")
- They "get" the connection that being racially different may be a reason for being excluded and they realize how unfair this is. ("They think I'm different because of the way I look and that's why they say such stupid things. It's not *fair!*") And because children at this age tend to assume that their feelings are not just momentary but persist over

time and speak to who they are in general, they tend to think of any negative feedback or exclusion by others as indicative of an overall and persistent lacking within *themselves*, rather than as a momentary experience.[8]

All of these factors make taunting experiences even more hurtful for multiracial kids who, like all kids at this age, crave acceptance by their peers.

The Effects of Teasing on Multiracial Children

It is certainly not a given that kids at this age will be cruel to children who are multiracial or transracially adopted. Not in the least. But as parents, we need to be aware that as our children pass through these middle childhood years, they are more likely to encounter other children who have been schooled to adopt misinformation about race and pejorative racial biases and who will use these skewed perceptions as a reason to tease and exclude children of different ethnicities, especially those ethnicities that society (or their parents) have repeatedly devalued.

For all of these reasons, as children near the age of ten and eleven, approaching puberty, they may find themselves struggling within a social structure that psychologists term "a culture of cruelty."

As Dan Kindlon, Ph.D., and Michael Thompson, Ph.D., write in *Raising Cain: Protecting the Emotional Life of Boys*, "Beginning around ten, as a boy approaches puberty, normal cognitive development makes him more aware of himself and his place in the group and raises the stakes in the many diverse competitions that consume boys: who is stronger, who gets the better grades, who is a better basketball player, who is richer and has better things, and who can get the upper hand in teasing verbal combat. A boy's eagerness for autonomy, the fact that he now receives less teacher supervision, and his desire to cut loose from his parents' influence make him a willing recruit into the peer culture. At the same time, the group demands conformity and holds him up to ridicule for any failure to conform. Whether it is the TV shows he watches, the books he reads, the shoes he wears, the color of his socks . . . anything a boy says or does that's different can and will be used against him . . . Almost all boys hide their hurt because to admit it appears weak. And they all look to make preemptive strikes when possible—

to divert attention from themselves and onto others. In this psychological war no boys are truly protected. . . ."[9]

This insight into the emotional life of boys at this age sheds light on why multiracial boys, like George, who told of his own such experiences earlier in this chapter, often identify these years as yielding some of the most painful memories of their lives.

This is not to imply that the culture of cruelty at this age is limited to boys. Some girls are simultaneously developing their own culture of cruelty, though—as with boys—it is only beginning to rev up during these grade school years, in an opening act for the big show of adolescence. Girls tend to express their aggression more covertly through gossip mongering and ostrasizing girls they deem less popular. But the emotional damage done to the girl shunned can be devastating. As Rachel Simmons writes in her book, *Odd Girl Out: The Hidden Culture of Aggression in Girls*, "Unlike boys, who tend to bully acquaintances or strangers, girls frequently attack within tightly knit friendship networks, making aggression harder to identify and intensifying the damage to the victims. Within the hidden culture of aggression, girls fight with body language and relationships, instead of fists. . . . In this world, friendship is a weapon, and the sting of a shout pales in comparison to a day of someone's silence."[10]

Frequently, however, the emotional bruises our multiracial children brave do not involve taunts or acts of shunning aimed at their shoe brand, pants label or acumen at shooting hoops—all of which can be *changed*—but at the most fixed aspect of who they are: their genetic makeup. Often, mixed race children must work harder to be accepted by their peers. If they do not achieve that acceptance and are made fun of or excluded, feelings of deep unworthiness can ignite.

This is especially true for social neophytes such as grade schoolers. Developmentally, they are still trying to sort out reasons for *why* negative things, when they do happen, happen to *them*. All too often they assume that when bad things happen it's because of who *they* are. They are developmentally vulnerable to buying into the idea that you get what you deserve in this world instead of realizing that when others are cruel the problem lies within the *other* person, not you. For this reason, deeply hurtful teasing at this pivotal pressure point can wreak long-term psychic havoc, puncturing an underprepared child's expectations of what awaits him in life and derailing his optimism about how he will be treated by

to feel the need to protect us (no parent wants a child to bear the heavy responsibility of such a role reversal), they are nevertheless aware of what triggers our strong feelings and savvy enough at this age to try to keep from eliciting them. In some homes, children may even fear that if they tell their parents when something hurtful has happened their parents may, in part, blame *them* ("Well, what were *you* doing when he called you a 'Zebra?'").

All of this means that we often have to play the role of subtle detective in order to find out what's occurring in our kids' lives, how they're processing it, and what they feel. Often we have to be attuned to the nuances of even their silences, especially if we have reason to suspect something may be amiss.

Kelley Kenny, Ed.D. (African American), coauthor of *Counseling Multiracial Families,* explains, "If you have a child who is usually bubbly but they come in the door moping or extra quiet, you need to pay careful attention to that."

Whatever the signs particular to your child may be, when kids seem a little bit "off," bear in mind that, while it might be a million things (losing at Monopoly, not getting as big a slice of cake as her sister), it might also be the recollection of a moment of taunting that's caused them to shut down. The only way to find out is to subtly probe by telling them what you see: You might say, "I notice you're not smiling." Or, "I notice your homework seems to be taking you a lot longer today and I'm wondering what that's about." Or, if you suspect an incident occurred at a certain time or place, you might say, "I noticed that when I picked you up from John's party today you seemed very quiet . . ." And then see what they have to say. Every child is unique, every child has their own way of sharing painful feelings. As a parent, if we're attuned to these over time, we can begin to get a sense of when and how to jump-start a conversation to help get to the crux of the situation.

For instance, I'm often aware when something has upset my son, Christian, because of his quiet, serious expression, or the way he gazes out the car window on the way home from wherever we've been, a down-turned expression clouding his face. But if I ask him outright, "What's wrong?" the answer is inevitably, "*Nothing* . . . " No matter how I probe, the answer is the same. His insistence that "nothing!" is wrong only grows more resolute, as does his resentment at being prodded when he would rather retreat into his funk. However, if I give him control over how and when *he* chooses to share his experience (whatever it might be) with me, it seems to help him feel safer in sharing. After years of trial and error, I have learned to query gently when I sense something awry. For example, I'll say something along the lines of, "Well, I notice you seem kind of quiet. Maybe you're just super tired. But if you do have anything you want to talk to me about I'm here and ready to listen."

What a shift my shifting can make. Now, instead of "nothing," I'm likely to hear something like, "Okay Mom, but can I whisper it to you—later—in your ear? At B-E-D time? I just don't want to talk about it *now*." Once we've established that we will talk about it when *he's* ready, a visible relief settles over him. He seems less agitated just for the fact that I've *noticed* that something is wrong but relieved that I'm not pushing to find out what it is; I've given him the reigns as to when and where he'll share. Over the years we have developed a tacit understanding that he doesn't like to "talk about it" until the lights are out, until after family hugs and story hour, until we are lying side by side and all the world is silent. And then . . . he whispers into my ear. Then he feels safe.

Noticing when something is amiss—and ferreting out what it is—requires being mindful of a child's emotional world. "If you are a parent in a multiracial family, you know issues are going to come up. So you need to be very attentive," advises psychologist Maria Root. "It's when parents don't even go into this territory, or won't even open up the conversation, because they don't want to face what's going on, that children have the most difficulty."

Kelley Kenney (African American) says, "This conversation is so ongoing in our house that when I ask my kids, who have had their share of incidents as biracial children, questions like, 'What was school like?' or 'Has anybody questioned you?' ['What *are* you?'] they know *exactly* what I'm talking about. They know why I'm asking. I'm not *looking* to find something, but they know that if something comes up, it's an open forum and we can discuss it as much as they want to."

Sometimes you may gently probe only to discover there's nothing to find out. For instance, says Kelley Kenney, "A few weeks ago, my younger daughter, Elena, and I had this discussion where she said, 'Mommy, I was playing in the sandbox and this other little girl said, 'You're black!' and then this other little boy said, 'Yeah, you're black!'

"I didn't react; I didn't know if anything negative had happened or not. So I just said, 'What did *you* say?' And she said, 'I said I'm *brown*!' So I asked her, 'Was anything said after that?' And she said, 'No. We just went on and played some more.' And that was the end of our conversation. But I keep that conversation about race up front. It could be that next time something will happen. And because she's used to our discussing whatever happens it's easy and natural for her to talk about it either way. "

Provide Your Child with Identity Labels

Whether or not our children feel comfortable with explaining that they are mixed depends to a large degree on how well we have explained what being mixed means, from the early years on. If we have been engaging in an ongoing dialogue with our children regarding their full racial identity—and the racial mix of their family—since they were preschoolers, our children are well prepared to internalize these concepts. By this age children are easily able to simultaneously categorize by more than one characteristic at a time. That, combined with the fact that they are much clearer about the logical and essential role that heredity plays in determining their racial makeup, makes terms like biracial easy for them to grasp.

Educator Carol Franks-Randall, Ed.D. (African American), married to Sandy Randall (Caucasian), says, "If you give kids the words they need to explain their family being multiracial, it's not hard for them to do so. We have to make sure that kids understand who they are and give them the language so they can *articulate* who they are to their friends with *confidence*." With her own two girls—now young adults—Franks-Randall says that "from very early on Sandy and I were very proactive in giving our children words to help them communicate the multiracial constellation of their family, so it was easier for them when they had to speak up for themselves."

However, as we do provide possible labels, such as biracial (of two races) or multiracial (of more than one race), for our children, it's important not to *choose* one unilaterally for them. We would no more force a child to say "I'm biracial" than insist that she choose only one racial heritage. Instead, by providing children with an array of ways to articulate their identity, they can *choose* the way in which they want to describe *themselves*. For instance, if your child is African American/Korean, you might say, "You're African American and you're Korean American and in addition to being both of those you're also mixed. Some people may see you as black and some people may see you as Asian and some people are going to see you as mixed."[16] At this age, children understand the complex concept that their skin color does *not* necessarily determine how they are perceived or labeled racially, and that others may see them as one thing when they see themselves quite differently.

At the same time, our children need to know that other children may have difficulty in understanding their self-ascribed labels. It's not unusual for our children's monoracial friends to have trouble grasping the concept of multiracialness; it's very possible that racial identity—especially mixed racial identity—is not an ongoing conversation in their monoracial homes. Therefore even a school-age child who has learned to understand and embrace a multiracial label may find that when he explains his heritage to friends they question, misinterpret or even reject that view.

One mom describes her (African American/Caucasian) son's encounter at the beach with a white child who clearly had no framework for understanding that racial categories were not necessarily either/or: "I noticed eight-year-old Sean standing in waist-deep water with another boy and pointing toward the blanket where Doug and I sat," she writes. "When I asked him later what that was about, he explained that the (white) boy had asked him if he was African American or white—the other child's very first question, before name, age or invitation to play together! Sean went on, 'I said, both.' The kid said, 'You can't be *both*. Which one are you really?' So I said 'both' again, and told him to look at my parents for proof."[17]

Even if we have taught *our* child to use and to be proud of a biracial label, that biracial label (in Sean's case, "I'm both") may challenge a peer's view of the world, who in turn challenges our child when he tries to explain his identity and family makeup. The better we prepare our children with words to describe who they are, the more confident and resolute they will be, even in the face of such challenges.

These challenges can be tough indeed. Mixed children who are partially of Asian descent often talk about being called "bananas" (yellow on the outside, white on the inside); mixed children who are of part African-American heritage relate being called names like "zebra," "Oreo," "mud baby" or "mud people." Although terms like "half-breed" and "dust of life" (the latter used to refer to mixed Korean, Japanese or Vietnamese children "left behind" by American servicemen after wars in the Pacific Rim) are no longer common playground slang, having been replaced by other terms that sting just as severely because the intention to devalue a peer *because* she is racially mixed is no different than it was in the past.

Scripts That Help Your Child Speak with Confidence to Peers

If our children are underprepared for negative peer comments (e.g., "You're an Oreo!" or, "Your dad is black? You're kidding, right?" or, "What *are* you anyway?") they are likely to become so frozen with hurt and surprise when incidents occur that they're unable to respond effectively, making it unlikely they will emerge from such a scene with their self-esteem intact.

"Talking about the possibility of such situations is one way to inoculate children against the stress of this kind of racism," advises Beverly Daniel Tatum, Ph.D. (African American), author of *"Why Are All the Black Kids in the Cafeteria Sitting Together?" And Other Conversations About Race.*[18] As one young biracial adult—now a parent herself—says of her childhood, in which she felt she was left too much on her own to deal with racial identity issues and social interactions: "I thought my parents should have talked to me about it or tried to help me figure it out, but I don't think they knew themselves, so they just didn't try at all."[19]

By developing simple scripts, practicing useful phrases, and strategizing with our kids, we can help ensure that our children speak back to what's been said (and to who's said it) with a rock-sure self-assuredness.

A great deal of teaching comes through this sort of impromptu rehearsal. As we help our children role-play possible responses to unpleasant comments and peer questioning, we're simultaneously accomplishing several other important goals:

1. We are helping our children make their thoughts about their own racial identity more conscious.
2. When we ask key questions at appropriate moments in our conversations with our kids, we can gauge what information they lack in order to respond confidently to peers and fill in those blanks with them.
3. We are helping our kids learn to express their identity in ways other kids *their age* can understand and—hopefully—respect.
4. We are coaching our kids to hone their critical thinking skills by teaching them to question other individuals' misconceptions about race—helping to ensure they appropriately challenge these fallacies when they encounter them now, and as they come of age.
5. By offering many different scripts, we're allowing our children to *choose* responses that are true and authentic for them, which they will be that much more comfortable in articulating.

6. As we role-play varied scenarios, we are helping our kids understand that what matters most is *not* convincing another person of their point of view, but having authentic responses that deflect negative interactions and—ideally—stop inappropriate and hurtful comments in their tracks.

Here are some examples of small approaches to dialoguing about race and identity with our grade schoolers in our day-to-day lives—conversations that help prepare them to discuss their identity in their own right.[20]

A friend of mine has an eight-year-old son who is Indian American/ Caucasian. Although she was sure her son understood very well what being multiracial meant—they had been setting the groundwork for the concept for years through small conversations, exposure to characters in books, and others who were multiracial. Nevertheless, he recently came home from school and said in a hurt voice, "Joey asked me, 'What *are* you?' What is he *talking* about?" The question, she said, had never arisen from a friend before.

She was thoughtful for a moment before responding, "Well, maybe he doesn't know very many people who *are* multiracial. Did you tell him *you* were?"

"I don't think he'd even *know* what that means," her son replied. "I don't even know how to *describe* it."

Realizing that he was still unsure how to convey the concept of being multiracial to others—something he clearly needed help in doing—and that his frustration was getting in his way, she ventured, "Well, you know a lot of people in the world don't think about these things. They don't think about how people *can* be mixed. So we have to explain it to them. What do you think would be a *good* way?"

"Well I don't want to have to explain *anything*," her son said. "It just seems dumb people even have to *ask*!"

"I can understand how you might feel that way," she said, sitting down bedside him.

"But they ask me! All the time!"

"That must be frustrating . . . "

"So what am I supposed to say anyway?"

"Well, you might describe how *you* see yourself. Do you want to try that?"

"Well, Daddy is from India and your family came from Germany—so I'm both those things. I'm kind of double. Only I'm American too so I'm triple."

"Oh neat. That's neat that you think of yourself as double *and* triple. That's right, you're a mix of Indian American and German American. So you'd tell your friend . . . ?"

"I'm Indian and I'm German and I'm American?" her son asked.

"You sure could," she said.

"Or I can just say I'm *mixed*, right? That's what Mary [his older sister] says to people when they ask her all these annoying questions . . . "

"You could do that too. You have a couple of different ways you can describe exactly who you are, and you can choose whichever one you like best."

This type of casual, impromptu role-playing gives your child practice using specific phrases that will be easy for them to draw on later. It also lovingly encourages your child to be as brave and competent as they long to be, instead of as fearful and unsure as they often feel.

We can also find opportunities to help our child develop strategies and responses to the world around them by asking them what they're feeling when they seem awkward or unsure of themselves in situations when their identity comes into question.

For instance, let's say you (Chinese American) and your child (Chinese American/Caucasian) are walking through Chinatown, buying vegetables. Several Chinese Americans selling their goods address your daughter in Chinese (a language she doesn't speak), and she seems unsure of how to handle the situation. When she doesn't answer them they ask you, "Isn't she *Chinese?*" After twenty minutes or so of this, she burrows her head in your shoulder and says, "I'm *tired* of shopping!"

On the way home, you try to uncover more of what she's thinking:

MOM: What is it like for you when people mistake you for being full Chinese?

CHILD: I kind of like it. It's kind of neat. But then I hate it when they start talking to me and I can't understand them because they're talking so fast and then they think I'm a weirdo.

MOM: A weirdo?

CHILD: You know, like I look Chinese but when I open my mouth it's like all I am is stupid. And then they start jabbering at you and I don't have a clue what they're saying. I feel *stupid*.

MOM: Well, I don't think you're stupid. What would you like to do next time we go shopping?

CHILD: I want Chinese to come out of my mouth!

MOM: I'd like that too! I can see how it would make you feel better. I'd like to teach you but I only know how to *speak* Chinese; I never learned how to *write* it. So I can't teach you everything about the language I'd like you to know. Should we look into lessons?

CHILD: *Can* we?

MOM: We can . . . though it can take time to learn a new language. But I think this is a good time to start. Maybe we could study Chinese together?

CHILD: That would be fun. But you know, Mom, you'd have to do *homework* . . .

MOM (laughing): Oh no . . . Meanwhile, what should we do when we go shopping?

CHILD (thinking): Can you go over a couple of *little* phrases you know so I can answer people? Like, "I'm half Chinese" or "I'm still learning Chinese," or, "Ask my mom what she wants to buy . . . "

MOM: I think that's a *great* strategy.

Bear in mind too, that as children pass through the latter part of this developmental stage and approach the teen years, we can begin to introduce into our discussions with them the social, political and historical aspects of society's views of mixed race people. As eight- to twelve-year-olds increasingly gain a moral sensibility that helps them perceive the unfairness of racism toward themselves and others, this knowledge can provide a strong moral stance from which to deal with whatever might occur with peers. For example, your fourth grader says, as you're driving her home from school, "I'm never going back to school again!"

PARENT: Sounds like you had a really bad day.

CHILD: I hate school!

PARENT: You sound really upset.

CHILD (crying): This new girl Sarah, she's black, she was asking me, "What are you?" And I said, "I'm mixed, I'm black and I'm white," and she said, you're black or you're *not* black."

PARENT: Hmm. That must have made you feel pretty frustrated.

CHILD (mimicking other girl): "So are you black or *not?*" I told her, "I'm *mixed*," and she laughed and she and these other two girls walked away like they don't believe me.

PARENT: Well, maybe she got that idea from her parents because of the *history* of what it means to be black in America. You know, in the African American community many of us *are* mixed. A long time ago women slaves were sometimes forced to have children by white owners—completely against their will. It was very wrong. So even now if you say you're mixed in the black community, some people may get angry and tell you that's not the right identity, that you shouldn't identify with being *white* at all. You should only identify with being black, to help strengthen the black community after all the racism blacks have faced. But *you* aren't mixed because of our history of slavery. You were born because Daddy and I fell in love with each other and wanted you with all our hearts, just the way you are, a little bit of each of us. Like a lot of kids nowadays, *you're* mixed for all the *right* reasons. We chose to have you and we are very proud of you in every way.

CHILD: Well what if she says that to me again?

PARENT: Let's see. I'll pretend I'm her. And I say to you, "*What* are you?"

Child: I'm *mixed*.

PARENT (still playing role of other child): "No, you're not mixed, you're *black!*"

CHILD (sighs): How do I even explain it?

PARENT: You might say, "Yes, I *am* black. And I am white. I know that in the black community being mixed meant something different in the past than it means now. But I'm not a product of that time in America's history. I'm a product of now, of my parents, who are black and white. I'm *proud* to be mixed."

CHILD: Well what if she still says, "So either you're black or you're not!"

PARENT: You could turn it around and ask *her* a question.

CHILD: Like what?

PARENT: You could ask something like, "Tell me about why you care . . ." Or, "Tell me about why you don't think I can be both?"

CHILD: So then she has to answer *my* question!

PARENT: Well, it's a good way to deflect the attention off yourself—which it sounds like you'd like to do?
CHILD: Yeah, I'd like that.

Our gentle but probing queries can also nudge our children to become more conscious of their thoughts about their own racial identities:

CHILD (already immersed in a discussion about her cultural identity with her mom): I am American *and* white *and* Korean . . .
MOTHER: Are you more one than another?
CHILD: I'm more American than white or Korean because I live in America.
Mother: Are you more white or more Korean?
CHILD: Maybe I'm more Korean because there are more Korean people in my family.
MOTHER: Well, what about your friend Erin? He's black and white. Is he more black or more white?
CHILD: I don't know. That's up to him. It depends.
MOTHER: Depends on?
CHILD: Well, it depends on how much he is thinking about being all of those things. Maybe he feels like he's half of this and half of that.
MOTHER: When you think about being who *you* are, what do you think?
CHILD: I think, I guess, that I'm not really half of anything. I feel more like *all* of me is Korean and *all* of me is Irish. Because I'm not like, all cut up in pieces or anything.
MOTHER: So you are those two things mixed together?
CHILD: Yeah, but I'm just me. That's who I am. All of me is both of those things, kind of like when a lightbulb is all lit up. It's got the electricity and then it's got the lamp parts. And it's both those things but they work together. It wouldn't be a light if it didn't have *all* of those things.

Sometimes just a one-second conversation can help give our child phraseology he might never have thought of to respond to kids who may race-question him in the future. Linda Parker (African American/Native American/Czech/Irish/Caucasian), 22 years old, talks about how these teaching moments with her parents gave her ways of reframing the comments other kids made. "I remember the first time I heard the word 'nigger.' I asked my mom, 'What does it mean?' She explained to me very calmly that the original use of the word didn't have anything to do with being black, that the *Webster's* definition is 'ignorant.' She very clearly explained the history of the word and how it was misused and has nothing to do with being black." Armed with this information from her mom, Linda could speak back to other kids with more informed knowledge.

Leo (African American) and Diane Dillon (Caucasian) talk about how they helped reassure their son, Lee (African American/Caucasian), when other children called him names, by reframing the situation for him. "As parents we couldn't protect our child from everything but we could give him tools, armor to help him handle things when they came up. . . . we told him insults are words. Words can't control how he feels . . . *he* controls that and he doesn't have to accept what anyone says as truth."

Such exchanges are not long, drawn-out conversations (something many children rebel against at this age), but when they hit the mark the effect can be tantamount to giving our child a strong emotional shield.

Don't Overdramatize the Race Issue

Although it is just a matter of good, common sense, it nevertheless bears repeating here: Everything in moderation. Although much has been said here about the difficult hurdles that may arise for children in multiracial families, it is critical that, as we prepare our children for the reality of living in an overtly race-conscious world, we also instill in them an intrinsic faith in others—to assume the best about people—and help them avoid reading prejudice into situations where it doesn't exist. In other words, there is a point at which you can dialogue about race too much. By dwelling on how to handle potential peer altercations, you may unwittingly send your child the message that he is *destined* to be seen as "different," rather than the intended message that he is just right as he is and should feel utter confidence when and if he articulates who he is to the world.

Louise Lazare, like many parents of children in multiracial families, reports that "while we made a conscious effort to talk about race with our kids, we were careful to wait for things to come up first. We had a very open dialogue." But she and her husband didn't launch into discussions about race or about how to handle race-questioning unless something sparked that conversation: "When the kids were younger, sometimes we'd be out on our bikes and these adolescent boys riding by would make awful comments, like, 'Little niggers grow up to be big niggers' . . . Or they'd say to me, 'Does your husband know where *you've* been?' Awful moments like that would generate a big discussion about prejudice and how we might handle a situation. If I read something in the paper about civil rights, then we would all read it together and we'd talk about it. But we didn't just dwell on the topic. We let it come up naturally."

Talk with Your Children About Their Ancestry

We can also help our children defend themselves against childish taunts by talking with them about their cultural history, thus building on the conversation we began with them about their family history when they were younger. Helping our children actively read about and research their cultural history in general, and their family history in specific, helps promote a greater sense of personal rootedness.

Ramona E. Douglass, past president of the Association of MultiEthnic Americans and multiracial herself, says, "I encourage parents to read more themselves and to teach their children the importance of reading about their own history and roots. I come from Sicilian American, Oglala (Sioux) and blended African-American/Scots-Irish stock. When I was a kid we didn't get very accurate information from the textbooks of the 1960s. I made every attempt to seek what was real on my own, and the accurate portrayal of our history always fascinated me. I read up on the history of those ethnic entities early, discovering the good, the bad, and the ugly of it all. I reveled in the notion of the 'Negro cowboys.' My dad is from Denver and his background is the Native American/blended African-American Scot-Irish mix. Because I had done that reading and exploring of my own history early on, later on, when I was fifteen, I wrote a position paper called 'Death of A Sioux Nation: A Case of American Genocide.' Parents of multiracial children need to recognize the *power* that this knowledge of history can give their children."

Counselor Kelley Kenney (African American) talks about how she and her husband (Caucasian) attempted to help their older daughter, Olivia, understand more about the history of racism against blacks through the books she's reading for pleasure and then dialoguing about them. "We have a wide range of books that give Olivia a sense of the history of black people in this country. Olivia loves the American Girl series of books about girls from various different ethnicities at various times in history. They've provided her with a historical perspective about ethnic differences in a very perceptive way."

Sometimes, however, that conversation about our child's cultural history can be difficult. For instance, a summer ago, we took Christian and Claire to a Japanese-American museum in Los Angeles that is dedicated to the Japanese Americans who were interned during World War II. As Christian walked through the museum and saw the actual makeshift housing that Japanese Americans lived in for so long during World War II—all their rights stripped away—he stood dumbfounded.

"How could that *happen*?" he asked. A gray shadow settled on his face.

"The government was afraid they would spy against America for the Japanese," my husband told him.

"But they were *Americans!*" Christian said.

"They were," said his dad. "And what the government did was wrong. The government put them in camps against their will because of their race. But that was a long time ago. It wouldn't happen today. But a lot of races still have trouble understanding each other."

"Well, I know what would happen if someone tried to put us in a camp today!" Christian said firmly.

"What would happen?" I asked.

"They'd be *arrested!*" he said. "They'd be arrested *so* fast."

Although he saw this story as no longer applicable in *his* lifetime, understanding that it took place gave him some context for actual race issues in America, which may well affect him in his lifetime.

More recently, in an effort to understand both his mother and father's cultural history, Christian has become an avid explorer of his dual cultural pasts, probing more deeply into his Samurai family on his Japanese side, a history he has come, over time, to understand as a very rich tradition and also a tradition involving much bloodshed for wealth, titles, armies and land. Having lived in Japan, having visited many castles and having stood fascinated by their history, he is well aware that a Samurai's story is a violent one.

On my side, our distant relative General Thomas "Stonewall" Jackson, who fought for the South in the Civil War, is a figure who has intrigued Christian to no end. Too young to grasp that in Jackson's era slavery was an accepted Southern institution and that Jackson was in the mainstream in his time, Christian wondered how someone so revered in Southern cultural history as a great general could also have kept slaves.

Clearly disturbed, he asked me one day whether Stonewall Jackson fought for the South because it was his home or because he wanted to keep slaves and hold onto that terrible way of life.

"He didn't like owning slaves, did he Mom? He didn't, right?" He asked me.

"I suspect he fought for his home, the state of Virginia, and for his way of life, which *included* owning slaves," I said.

A few months later, during spring break, we took a road trip to Lexington, Virginia, home of Stonewall. On the tour, as we entered the kitchen, Christian asked the guide point-blank about slaves. "Did Stonewall Jackson keep slaves?" The tour guide explained to him that he had, commenting in a chipper tone that, however, Stonewall, quite unlike other gentlemen of his time, had treated his slaves almost as family members, often joining in when they were cooking in the kitchen, preparing meals with them, and so on.

He *had* kept slaves, the idea of which—the proof of which—was horrifying to Christian. He was quiet, his mind working a mile a minute. Though he didn't say anything about it during the tour, I could almost hear his mind racing: "Racism is wrong and if people are racist against the Japanese it's wrong, but here's this famous general who kept slaves and that was racist! But everyone thinks he's so great!"

At that moment, I had to wonder: If Christian were not multiracial, and if we were not involved in an ongoing dialogue about race, would he have been as intent on getting answers to these questions about racism—about what is right and what is wrong—or to contemplate their meaning in a larger context, as he was now? It is my hope that by introducing our son to varied aspects of his cultural history, we have sparked his *own* critical thinking about race.

Help Your Child Understand and Challenge Racial Stereotypes

In the process of figuring out why the world works the way it does, eight- to twelve-year-old children are shifting toward more solidified ideas of race.

They are testing out what they believe to be true ("black people always . . . white people always . . . ") and looking to confirm those beliefs. Because they are still young and these stereotypes are not yet solidified, this is also a time when inaccurate ideas can be challenged and *changed*.[21] This is the age of conscience, if you will, when the seeds of knowing what is right and wrong either take root or wither before they have a chance to grow.

If we want our children to develop antiracist thinking and behavior, we have to guide them. We can't protect our children from the reality of bigotry, prejudice and racism, but we can make certain they don't buy into any racial attitudes. This means that we have to help them distinguish between recognizing cultural patterns ("Japanese people eat a lot of rice in their diet") versus stereotypes and caricatures of these cultural patterns ("Japanese people eat stinky food with sticks!") by pointing out that difference to them. This means challenging all stereotypes we hear being espoused, whether they apply to our child's race or to *any* race.

When a child witnesses that stereotypes against any race are silently condoned—or, worse, *verbally* condoned—by their parents, they receive a message that when others use stereotypes to devalue *them* it *can't* be wrong. Putting *them* down must be okay, too. It can't be acceptable to stereotype people by race in one circumstance yet unacceptable in another.

Consider this example of a young man (Asian/Hispanic) adopted by Caucasian parents. His mother says that when they adopted their son, "We had no idea of what he looked like. We didn't care. They told us his mother was Spanish and probably Oriental too, but we do not know who his father was. It's something I don't talk about, because as far as I'm concerned, he's been with me from eight days old; he is an American and that's all that counts. I never worried about having him in this town; I felt like, because of me, they probably would treat him well. But they're very prejudiced in this town against anyone that does not fit in a redneck mold."

Now a teen, this young man talks about how his mother's own prejudice against minorities has, over time, become all too apparent to him and how devastating that awareness has been for him. "I think it's completely stupid when my parents are like, I don't care what he is, we'll love him anyway. . . . My mom's family, they use the word 'nigger' a bunch. You know, 'wetback.' Or my brother [Caucasian] unknowingly will say, 'that stupid Mexican.' But we always avoid the conversation. I wish I could just put it on the table, you know? I told my mom one time, when a Mexican pulls out in front of you or something, you scream that old stuff at them and you really expect me to be happy with what I am? You hear bad stuff about Mexicans so you automatically think Mexicans are bad. You kind of develop your own prejudice against your race. I'm really working hard—just to get out of here, do the best I can. I just can't wait to get out of here."[22]

In order to raise confident multiracial kids, we first must examine our own inner prejudices. Although none of us like to think we harbor any prejudices within our hearts and minds (after all, aren't we in a multiracial family? Doesn't that prove we bear no prejudices?), chances are, having been raised in a race-obsessed society, some of our small, unconscious actions convey negative messages to our own children. For instance, when we go to a cafeteria at the museum, do we sit only near people of our own race? If our uncle is over for dinner and makes a disparaging joke about another race, do we speak up or simply look down at our plates?

Mark Kenney, M.Ed., N.C.C. (Caucasian), parent of two multiracial girls and a psychologist in this field, says, "It's so important for us as parents to be conscious of the inner tapes playing in our *own* mind of stereotypes we've absorbed in our own lifetime. It's critical to be conscious of what we're saying and modeling, and that our words and behaviors match. And when we do make a mistake and make comments about differences that are *not* appropriate, it means admitting our mistake by talking about how we recognize what we've said is wrong, making that moment a teaching one."

Linda Parker (African American/Native American/Czech/Caucasian) feels that her parents were very successful in helping her to feel that she *wasn't* different—thus securing her self esteem—by carefully modeling non-racist behavior. She explains: "Our parents brought home very strongly to us that it was our actions, how we behaved, how we carried ourselves, our character, our values, our speech, all this determined who we were. It was hammered home to us that while yes, race is real, it's your demeanor, your character, your actions, your values that determine *who* you are, and who others are, too. And they brought that message home by modeling it for us. They never talked down to people. I can't remember ever hearing any racial slurs at all. We judged people by their actions. When it came to looking at other cultures we were only looking at the good things, we never focused on any negative stereotypes about any race."

Asking our kids questions about what *they* think when they witness prejudice can be instrumental as well. If we don't know what their thoughts are we can't help them shift their thinking before such thoughts become ingrained (e.g., do they see certain aspects of prejudice as justified because society implies they are?).

For instance, if your child is African American/Caucasian and together you see another black person being treated badly, in addition to perhaps commenting, "That was *wrong*," you might also probe to find out what your *child* is perceiving:

> PARENT: Why do you think that clerk followed that young black man wherever he went in the store?
>
> CHILD: Because he's black.
>
> PARENT: Why do you say it's because he's black?
>
> CHILD: Because black people steal things.
>
> PARENT: Really? Well, I'm black. You're black. Grandaddy is black. Grandma is black. Do *we* steal things?
>
> CHILD: *No!* I wouldn't steal anything.
>
> PARENT: No, we wouldn't. Very few people steal things. There are some people of *every* color—white, black, Native American, Asian, you name it—who don't respect the rule of not taking anything that doesn't belong to them. Luckily few people are like that, but it would be misinformed to think that people of one color are more honest than people of another color.

Handling Negative Encounters

Helping prepare our children for incidents that may occur is just half of the picture. Helping them process what happened in the *immediate* aftermath of any heart-crushing encounter is just as important. How do we begin to explain such experiences to our child in a way that minimizes their negative impact; how do we diffuse such incidents at the very moment that *our* heart is breaking in the face of our child's distress?

Devalue the Disparaging Remark

After a recent play date with a friend who has three older siblings, Christian came home and told me—as he took his hands and lifted up the corners of his eyes to make dramatic slants—"Carl's brother and sisters all said I have funny eyes that go *vroop*, up like this . . . and then they all did that with their eyes and laughed . . ." And with that he dropped his hands, shot me a glum, questioning look and collapsed his face into my chest like a Raggedy Andy doll. I felt his hurt and confusion grip my core. I thought for a moment and then told him, "I think that was a really silly thing for them to say. Remember that song—'Everyone comes from different places . . . everyone has different faces . . .' I guess they haven't had much experience with seeing all the different eyes that people in this world have. Just because they haven't seen a lot of Asian eyes doesn't mean Asian eyes are 'funny.' More than half the world has Asian-shaped eyes! Boy are they misinformed!"

The point here is not to make fun of the children who made the hurtful remark—not at all—but to diminish the power of their comment by letting your child know how surprising it is that these children don't have a broader or more educated world view.[23]

Here is another example:

CHILD: I told Greg I'm mixed but he doesn't believe me! He said I can't be mixed. He said maybe I'm just all mixed *up*!

PARENT: *Wow.* You mean Greg never knew someone could be Filipino and Caucasian at the same time? Gosh, I guess he hasn't been lucky enough to meet lots of other families like ours the way we have. I'm sorry he doesn't know more about the world!

Correct Any Misinformation

Another response to the above incident might be, "Asian eyes don't go up in slants like that, do they? Boy are *they* misinformed!" (Then head to the mirror to confirm what you've just said.)

Draw on Other Examples to Help Make Your Case

If you (African American) and your daughter (light-skinned biracial) witness another child commenting to your daughter, "That's really your mom! No way! Are you *kidding* me?" you might sit down with your child and first correct this misinformation. ("Did you hear what that little boy said? It sounds to me that he must think kids and moms have to match race by skin color.

Some people might think that, but it's *not* true. Moms and kids *don't* always match.") Then point out other examples that emphasize your point: "You know Tommy and his mother don't match. Susan and her mom don't match. We get a magazine every month that's full of kids and parents who are in families where their skin color isn't the same. How silly of him to have said that! I guess he doesn't know and see all the people we do!"

Invite Your Children to Voice Their Feelings

This is an obvious but easily forgotten step when it comes to soothing a child who has been the subject of hurtful jabs. Often we want so badly to jump in and fix the situation that we forget to stop and let our child simply *talk*. It's far more important to ask, "How did that make you feel?" than it is to spout philosophies about how wrong racism is or about how we think our child *should* feel. Any time a child is hurt, being silent and letting her voice her emotions—and then validating her feelings—can make a world of difference in how much she is willing to share with us. This, in turn, can make a world of difference in how much she is able to work through for herself. Instead of saying, "Oh, that's nothing, don't let it bug you," or, "Kids are just that way!" we will be more helpful to our kids if we say, "It sounds like you feel really hurt by that. I think I would be, too."

Being an active listener when our children share an incident involves focusing all our attention on them and on what they have to say, listening in a relaxed manner, asking key questions, not trying to fix the situation, not inserting our point of view and not making assumptions about what they may be feeling. When we listen carefully, we make certain that we understand exactly what our children are feeling and that all their feelings have a chance to come to the surface so that they express themselves fully. Sometimes, by "just listening," we can help our children the most.

However, we will not always understand what they are feeling. As counselor Mark Kenney puts it, "If you are a monoracial person you can't understand and you can't pretend to understand what a multiracial person is experiencing. As a white privileged male individual I try to understand what my daughters' experiences are. But I can't. And at this age our girls have a hard time articulating it. So my goal is to be available to listen to them and to talk to them about it whenever something arises, whenever they might need to tell me or ask me something."

Carrie Howard (Caucasian), adoptive mom of two girls (Chinese American), agrees. "As Caucasian parents in America we do not know what it is like to be a minority. I have some inkling of how it feels to be different when I look around a conference room at work and see that I am the only woman present, but in most of my daily life I am able to blend in. Members of racial minorities cannot do that. I will never be able to truly understand some of my daughters' experiences."

Build Your Child's Self-esteem

Build up your child's self-esteem as much as possible about the thing that has been most disparaged. For instance, after Christian came home from his playmate's house saying they'd made funny faces with their eyes, I told him, "One of the things I love about Daddy is the way *his* eyes look. And I'm so delighted that your eyes look a little like mine and a lot like his." In other words, draw on the dialogue you've already developed in the preschool years to reinforce the positive image that you have been sending your child about the feature that has just been devalued. One mom, Barbara Klein Moss (Caucasian), explains that since her adopted daughter Sara (Korean) was small, "I would tell her that her eyes were the shapes of bird wings and how beautiful that is."

Especially for multiracial girls, issues often arise around hair. Although the "hair issue" (as one teenager put it) intensifies in adolescence, many multiracial children say their hair started to become an issue for them in grade school. Nancy Brown recalls, "My older daughter's hair was thicker and kinkier than my younger daughter's hair. After I spent three hours with her washing and doing her hair she would still say, 'I wish my hair were straighter!' I would say, 'Well, we all have things about ourselves that we wish were a little different. We all have those thoughts, but you are perfect the way you are. Your hair is perfect the way it is.'"

Be Reassuring

Sometimes all a child needs to hear is that it's okay to be in the minority in her neighborhood or school. One little girl was upset at realizing that "there are only two students in the class who look like me." Her aunt, who is raising her, replied, "That's okay. There don't have to be any students in your class who look like you so long as your teacher is teaching everybody." Her niece then asked, "So it's okay that there's only three of us?" and her aunt said, "Yes it is."[24]

Reassure Yourself

If you have established an ongoing dialogue about being in a multiracial family, your child will not be scarred for life by incidents that occur. Although it can be devastating when your child's appearance, heritage or mixed background is questioned or made fun of, a child's feelings of hurt and frustration are *not* signs that he will be psychologically wounded for life. Through the ongoing conversation you've been having with your child since he was small, he has begun to internalize a voice of positive self-esteem that is stronger and more credible than the voice of the occasional, insensitive peer.

Building the Grade Schooler's Inner Confidence

In addition to knowing how to react when your child feels hurt or insecure there are other ancillary—yet very important—ways of helping them to feel confident about who they are at this age.

Solidify Positive Relationships

As you begin to get a sense of your child's friends, help her solidify her most positive friendships and relationships. According to Cynthia Erdley, associate professor of psychology at the University of Maine, "Parents often don't realize that good friendships don't just happen naturally for kids—parents need to take an *active* role." Indeed, studies show an association between parental involvement in helping to choose and arrange children's peer contacts and their social and academic adjustment. Parents who arrange play dates and monitor peer interactions appear to have more socially adept kids. And though direct parental involvement should taper off as children grow older, the need for monitoring remains. Erdley explains: "As kids enter the preteen years, they are more likely to set positive relationship trends in place if parents have been helping them to make good decisions along the way. By ages 10 or 11, patterns of acceptance, friendship and psychological adjustment begin to gel. Just making sure your child has chosen a few close friendships that are characterized by affection, a sense of reliable alliance and intimacy, and trust can be essential to your child's self-esteem, setting positive patterns in place that last until adulthood."[25]

For parents of children in multiracial families, paying keen attention to how our children are faring in social interactions with peers can matter greatly. According to Erdley, "We know that children who are rejected by their peer group are at risk for a variety of negative outcomes that have implications for their psychological adjustment as adults. [There are] similar risks for children who fail to develop close friendships. For instance, children without friends appear to be at increased risk for depression, anxiety, and low self-esteem."

How do we stay aware of our children's peer group interactions without being overly intrusive and while still fostering their sense of independence? How can we manage to "be there" for our kids and, at the same time, avoid the danger of micromanaging our children's social lives?

We cannot expect to know everything about our children's friendships or social travails; nor should we try. But we can make our home a welcome place for kids to play and gather on a regular basis (whether through play dates, sleepovers or visiting museums and the like with other kids and their parents) so that we can get some sense of peer interactions. We can develop close parent/teacher relationships and volunteer at school to get a keener sense of what's happening for our child not only in the classroom but on the playground. Having a mental map of our child's day-to-day world with friends will enable us to encourage their positive friendships and help them move away from relationships that may augur problems for our child's sense of who they are.

Develop Competencies

The importance of helping your child develop competence in different aspects of his or her life cannot be overstated. Developing a level of confidence and mastery that leads to success in a given area is what psychologists call *competence*. Different from performance (how many A's they bring home or how many soccer goals they score), competence is all about working hard to do something well and staying on top of it—not because you're going to be rated or graded but because you enjoy what you are doing and are absorbed in it.[26] For children in multiracial families, feeling competent and skilled in an area can act as a shield against hurtful messages peers may send them.

This feeling of mastery can take many forms. Ramona E. Douglass (African American/Native American/Sicilian/Scots-Irish/Caucasian) says that although she was initially "a timid child," she found her "voice and confidence through creative writing and through playing the violin and clarinet. . . . I knew that I was smart and I was unwilling to be treated as a second-class citizen anytime or anywhere."

Leo Dillon (African American) talks about how "as parents we wanted to protect our biracial son from being exposed to racism but that's impossible. It's there in so many ways and some are so subtle. We could give him love and support but we also wanted to counteract some of the messages he was getting from the outside world. We felt we had to go to the other extreme by trying to make him feel special, even superior, so that maybe he would come back to the middle. We tried to build his self-image by encouraging whatever he was interested in. If Lee wanted to draw we gave him art supplies and the best paper and told him a beautiful drawing deserved to be on good paper. Hopefully he would feel that what he did was important, too. Especially when he saw us drawing, too. When he showed an interest in jewelry we signed him up for a course when he was 11 years old and he learned to use a torch and work with metal. When he became interested in Lalique, we got books on his work and encouraged Lee to believe he could do work like that. The point was to value what he did."

Michelle Watson (Caucasian), mom of two African American/Caucasian children, agrees: "I think that part of one's self-esteem also comes from finding something which you have a passion for—something that you feel you're good at. I think, as parents, we need to find that something for our kids. That's important for my daughter. Music makes Alex feel a lot of self-confidence and so does swimming, so we do those things."

One important aside here concerning multiracial boys of this age: As children develop a sudden social awareness regarding how they are viewed by others, it can be helpful for them to be involved in sports. Because we are, rightly or wrongly, a sports-oriented culture, boys at this age who have little physical prowess may feel excluded as the playground divides between the soccer players and the basketball players, the kick ball team and junior striders. If a multiracial boy of this age feels different on these two fronts— because he's multiracial while almost everyone around him is monoracial and because he's non–sports oriented while everyone around him is strutting their stuff at recess—the grade school years may be a slightly trickier phase to navigate than they would be otherwise.

Still, sports are only one of many venues for helping a child develop a feeling of competence. Introduce your child to a wide range of activities and possibilities (over time, in moderation) so that he has the opportunity to develop competence (which emerges out of a pursuit one holds a passion for) in another area, such as art, music, mathematics, chess, acting, Lego building, rock collecting or some combination thereof.

Keep Up Your Effort

Although you won't always say or do the right thing, your continuing effort can make all the difference in the world. Even experts who deal with these issues, such as teachers or counselors, do not always know the right thing to say to their children when incidents occur or feelings erupt. "I struggle with whether you can always know what to say and when to say it," says Kelley Kenney (African American), who teaches about multiracialness as a college professor and counsels multiracial families. "Mark [my Caucasian husband] and I have been doing work in this area for a long time; yet even though we're immersed in this topic we don't always know the perfect way to react when something happens to one of our girls."

As you work to respond to your child's experiences in the most supportive way possible, remember you are involved in a process that produces cumulative, not immediate, effects.

It may help to keep your mind on the end goal, which, despite the complex issues that arise in parenting our children, is simple enough: to make certain our kids internalize a core belief—an unshakable faith—that emotionally cutting words (or actions) directed at them reflect something amiss with the person who delivered them, not something wrong with them or with *being* multiracial.

Overwhelmingly, in the course of my interviews, every optimistic, confident and emotionally healthy young adult I've spoke with seemed to have one thing in common: parents who—whether consciously or instinctively—helped them make this mental and emotional leap, which not only stood them in excellent stead throughout this pivotal grade school pressure point but helped center them for life.

CHAPTER FOUR

Facing the "What Are You?" Question

Moving Through the Turmoil of Adolescence

LIKE ALL TEENAGERS, OUR CHILDREN—now standing at the threshold of adolescence—are experiencing a mind-boggling set of physical changes: maturing reproductive organs, rushing hormones, and a heavier, taller (and barely recognizable) body staring back at them in the mirror. At the very same time, they are developing an excruciating awareness that how they look, what they say and what they do is now being scrutinized through a social microscope by their peers.

Against the backdrop of these rapid physical changes (which themselves pack a significant psychological wallop), early adolescents (ages 11–15) enter these tumultuous years with a deepened moral awareness, as well as a new-found capacity for complex thoughts and ideas. These thoughts now veer toward self-reflection about who they are, what they are competent in (and therefore what they have to offer the world), how (and whether) they fit in with friends and whether they are *normal*.[1] (The latter question is at the crux—as many of us recall from our own coming of age years—of many an hour of adolescent angst.) During this struggle to find out where they "fit in," young adolescents worry—and worry some more—about whether any-one else is like them: Is the way I look/act/think normal? Does anyone else feel the angst *I* feel? Does anyone else out there *understand* me?

As our teenagers wrestle with these questions, they embark on a seeming-ly overwhelming task: to know and understand themselves as individuals, as well as to discover their own unique place in society. By trying out and freely experimenting with different roles, they are struggling to find an identity that seems tailor-made for them, one that will reflect—amid friends and within society—their inner sense of who they believe themselves to be.[2] They seek a sense of self that will serve as a bridge between the childhood they have only recently left behind and their future as an adult, which awaits them.

But for multiracial adolescents, who by age 12 possess a deeper racial consciousness (a grasp of the factors that define racial identity, as well as a fuller awareness of racism in its historical and societal context), the questions "Is there anyone else out there just like *me*?" and "Where do *I* fit in?" which permeate this identity struggle begin to be increasingly informed by *race*. Because racial identity is such a key aspect of overall identity development, adolescents actively search for information about their racial heritages and try to understand what that ethnicity means to them.[3] All the while they are looking about for others who are *similar* to them. For teenagers, being *racially* like others is now a pivotal factor for assuming that they *do* fit in, that they are understood, that they are *normal*.

Which poses a pressing conundrum for the multiracial teenager. While monoracial adolescents can assuage some of the typical teen fear of not fitting in by befriending adolescents who seem to be "just like" them, for multiracial youth, this search is inherently more complex. Their fears of being different bear a heightened aspect: They often *are* racially unique in their school or neighborhood, or very nearly so. As they question whether they "fit in" with their peers, they often lack significant evidence to reassure them that indeed they do.

Not surprisingly, it is during this eight-year span (between the ages of 12 and 19)—years packed with intense changes and unrivaled self-growth—that my interviews reveal the second, and most intense, pressure point for multiracial and transracially adopted youth.

Between the ages of 12 and 15 multiracial children meet their most tremendous challenge, for this is where the most critical pressure point of their lives occurs.

Pressure Point Two: The Tumultuous Early Adolescent Years

Many of the young adults in multiracial families who shared their stories with me cited grade school as a time when they encountered their first disturbing interactions with peers—incidents that emphasized their multiracialness, as well as heightened their awareness that the world around them was not always comfortable with their mixed identity. However, it is during the middle school years, between the ages of 12 and 15 (sixth to eighth grade), that almost every single one of my interviewees encountered their most emotionally *traumatic* experiences.

Even when loving parents have worked hard to create a positive foundation for their child's identity, the adolescent's cognitive capacity for self-reflection and self-consciousness, the physical shifts that come with puberty, and their increasingly complex interactions with peers make it particularly challenging for them to gain a unified sense of self. Consider all that is occurring for them at this age.

Pressure to Choose One Racial Group over Another

Friendships are starting to shift in terms of racial groupings, and many biracial and transracially adopted children feel pressured to choose one racial group over another. As children enter middle school, they tend to form racially aligned cliques in a way they previously did not. Often plunged into a large middle school teeming with new students, young multiracial teenagers, like all teenagers, must struggle to find their place in an unfamiliar milieu. Suddenly social life is a far more heady and engrossing proposition than is their academic or family lives. Intense cliques quickly emerge based on shared interests (football, track, chess) and personal similarities (race, cultural background and socioeconomic status) as young teenagers hasten—for fear of being left out—to latch onto a group that feels familiar and where they feel they *do* fit. Quickly, they wrap themselves in that chosen cloak of identity. But in the process of trying to better identify and prove who they *are*, teenagers often reject all that they are *not*, including those who differ from them racially. Moreover, adolescents who are insecure about their own identities may exaggerate racial and other differences in order to help boost their own sense of self-worth, meanwhile demonstrating their solidarity to their own group.[4] For instance, a white teenager in a clique of white jocks may put down Asian Americans as a way of underscoring his place in his own group. But what of the Asian/white child who plays on the same sports team with said white jock? Where does this multiracial child find *his* social groove?

As these racial shifts occur, biracial and transracially adopted adolescents often experience unprecedented identity questions. Who does the biracial child join with? And what of the adopted child whose mom and dad (and even sister or brother) are of another race? As Beverly Daniel Tatum, Ph.D. (African American), psychologist and president of Spelman College, so aptly puts it: "As the school cafeteria becomes increasingly divided along racial lines, where does the biracial student choose to sit?"

How can our teenagers possibly choose to align with only one racial group when they are *both*?

Consider the recollection of Jana Bender (African American/ Vietnamese), age 31, regarding the racially based social splitting that took place at school during her early teenage years: "Being 12 and 13 in junior high was the toughest time in my *life*. We left elementary school and went into a bigger group in junior high. Everyone started dividing up and you had to choose which table you wanted to sit at in the cafeteria. All the kids were choosing where they wanted to be, so they wanted me to choose too—it was like, black, Asian or white, which is it? Black girls would come up and touch my hair and say 'What *are* you?' Both the black kids and white kids would say things like, 'You look like a door hit you in the face.' I think, because other kids were also struggling to develop *their* identities they want- ed me to choose mine. The black kids thought, 'If you're half black and yet you're not choosing to be only with the black kids, you must think there's something wrong with *being* black. Which means you must think there is something wrong with *me*.' They take it personally if you *don't* choose. The whole process was just weird and very hurtful. It made me feel awkward and different and ugly."

Being faced with this trend toward racial grouping—at the same time that they deeply desire to find acceptance among their peers—makes puberty par- ticularly challenging for the multiracial adolescent, especially given that feeling different for *any* reason in adolescence can be angst inducing enough. Indeed, in certain social settings the biracial child may feel different from *everyone*.

Nicole Brown (African American/Caucasian), age 22, says that eighth and ninth grade "was the hardest time for me. It's a time when you really want to belong and you need to have a group where you know you fit in. But I looked different. I felt torn. Because I hung out with the white kids at school, the black kids in my neighborhood felt I wasn't accepting of them and the black community. I spent half my time at school playing one role—as part of that white world—and half my time at home hanging out with the black kids. I felt that no one got me because I was more compli- cated. I fit into each world I was in, but then again I *didn't*, because no one understood me. Part of that is adolescence, sure, but part of that is being multiracial and being different things together—and yet the outside of you doesn't really show who you really are inside. There was a part of me that was very divided. The worst part is that I never got to be all of myself at the same time."

A young Asian/Mexican student talked about how kids divided by race at his Texas middle school. "At our school there's basically no mixing. You're white and you have all white friends; you're Mexican, you have Mexican friends; you're black, you have black friends. It's always on your mind; you're constantly aware that you're different."[5]

Because young biracial teenagers are so overtly confronted with the puzzle of where they fit in, they often have to consider the question of their identity in a more conscious way than monoracial teenagers do. Yet, even as they face extreme pressure to identify with only one racial heritage, they lack the developmental readiness to *choose* a racial identity.[6] This dilemma lies at the crux of why this is the most challenging crossroads in the lives of most multiracial individuals.

Making matters even more emotionally complex for multiracial teenagers is the fact that it is not just their casual acquaintances who are shifting cliques in this restructured social culture. Often, even one's *oldest* friendships and affiliations are suddenly subject to change.

George Meyers (Japanese/Caucasian), age 24, looks back at sixth grade and recalls, "I remember one time a group of boys tried to hang me on a coat rack. One of the boys was a quarter Japanese; I think he was trying to align with the white kids so he wouldn't be singled out for being part Japanese. He was turning against me as a way of making himself more white." Still, George reflects, while he had come to expect "that kind of thing" from kids he didn't know well, "When it happened with someone I considered a friend it really hurt me a lot more. I remember once I didn't catch what a group of kids were saying so I asked what was going on. And this one white 'friend' turned around and said in front of all these other kids, 'Shut up! Go over there—you're so *slow!*' That was the first time I'd ever had a supposed 'friend' turn on me—it had always been the enemy who had said those things. That was when I realized that some of my 'friends' thought of me as being different, too."

In early adolescence the seas of once dependable friendships are shifting. Jamie Mihoko Doyle (Japanese/Irish/Caucasian), now a 23-year-old graduate student, remembers how things intensified for her socially when "I was around thirteen. I just wasn't accepted by the white girls even though that's half of who I am. I hung out with one friend at school, but then she left and I had to try to make other friends. I made friends with one girl who was Mexican, but then, as the year went on, she started to ignore me and acted embarrassed to be around me. She just wanted to get chummy with the popular white kids in the class. There was a black group and an Asian group at school, too, and for a while I tried to hang out with the Asian kids. But even though they were more accepting I just didn't feel comfortable even *being* at that school by that point."

There were other issues occurring for Jamie around that time, too, she says. "A lot of other kids were from a higher socio-economic background than I was, and I felt overwhelmed trying to fit in with them." She also realized, she adds, "that all the boys at my school were only attracted to blue-eyed blonds." Jamie recalls feeling excruciatingly aware that she didn't mesh with her peers. As a result, she says, "my grades really fell. I hid under my bed because it was torturous to go to that school every day. I became an expert at finding ways *not* to go."

Mixed-race adolescents often feel more acutely than monoracial teenagers do that no one—not even parents or close friends—really understands the unique situations they face or the interpersonal conflict they experience. In her research on multiracial youth, Nancy J. Nishimura (Japanese American), associate professor in counselor education at The University of Memphis, and mother of three Japanese American/African American daughters, found that while each member of her focus group "was aware that identity development is a developmental task that represents a struggle for *all* young adults," they also felt "that their task was compounded by the fact that most people, including their parents, do not know what it is like to be multiracial."[7] Other research confirms this finding: many multiracial individuals who seek counseling as adults report that they have never expressed the depth of "aloneness, differentness, guilt, rejection, anger, disappointment, and/or despair with anyone before coming to counseling."[8] Of course, such intense emotions do not reflect the way all multiracial teenagers feel. Not all biracial young adults experience harsh social pressure to choose, and not all feel this kind of aloneness or angst as they come of age. But to some degree or another, most do.

As Matt Kelley (Korean/Caucasian), age 23, founder of *MAVIN*, the first magazine geared toward multiracial young people, explains, "there are some people who are multiracial who may never have an issue. But in my experience in talking to hundreds of mixed-race young people in this country, that's only one percent of the multiracial population. Sure, there are some people who will *say*, 'I never had an issue.' But when you talk to them in depth and ask, 'Have you ever had such and such an experience?' they say, 'Oh, yeah, I know exactly what you're talking about, that's happened to me and I hate it; it makes me so angry.'"

Other teenagers, like Rochelle Brown (African American/Caucasian), age 17, realize quite well what the issues facing them are. But, with the help of their parents, they have developed an inner muscle that enables them to exercise control over how much they let the confusion of the world around them affect *their* sense of self.

Rochelle recalls, "From time to time I had some issues, especially around dating when I was 14. Feelings of not wanting to be different would pop up—but they were never all-consuming. My parents always encouraged me to be proud of who I am and to identify with every aspect of who I am. There wasn't ever a time when I didn't know that I was multiracial—it was always really open and discussed in my house. My mom always tried to show me different races. I was five when she founded her group, MASC [Multiracial Americans of Southern California], so I was very conscious of being with lots of kids who were of different mixes and seeing lots of multiracial couples. I think that was very helpful to me as I made that transition through middle school and into upper school. It's a time when everything is so jumbled and confused; you're trying to find yourself and it is *so* hard."

This solid preparation by her parents stood Rochelle in good stead when she encountered peer pressure to act as if she were more one race than the other. For instance, she relates, "Once a girl told a good friend of mine—who told me—that I don't act black enough and that I'm too white. When I heard that I was crying. I was really hurt. I told my parents and my older sister about it and they said, 'How dare she say something like that? She doesn't know you as a person and she has no right to make judgments about you, *and* she's wrong.' Within a day or two I realized that what she'd said was so dumb. I remember thinking, 'Oh, you try being me, you don't know what it's like.' And I completely dismissed it. Whenever something hurtful happened my parents and my older sister would tell me, 'You don't have to look like anyone else to be happy with yourself. You're great the way you are.' By the time I was 15, I didn't really care that much about [being different] anymore. I shifted inside. I discovered that I'm happy with my race and with myself; I'm happy that I'm different from people; it's a good thing. I just feel like a complete individual. That I'm not in some kind of mold. Being multiracial is something I really like about myself."

Hearing such a story can't help but beg the critical question: How can we help our teenager to be one who passes through these enormously important years feeling so strongly that "being multiracial is something I really like about myself?" Who is so resilient that even the turmoil of the middle school years does not shake their positive self-perception?

Fortunately, learning what is happening developmentally in our adolescents' lives, and how these factors influence their racial self-concept, can make a tremendous difference in helping us to be a supportive and informed sounding board for them, whatever they may encounter, whatever feelings they may experience (feelings that hopefully they will articulate to us). Meanwhile, ensuring that our teenagers *do* confide in us, as any parent of an adolescent can tell you, is a tricky feat, especially given that teenagers are more independent from us than they were at 10 or 11—and more likely to internalize their hurtful experiences, which may only intensify their angst. As our children move away from us as their primary source of information and reassurance, and closer to their friends as their primary source of information and acceptance, they are, for the first time, paddling out alone—and straight into a sea of shifting emotions.

The Five Steps of Multiracial Identity Formation

During the teenage years, mixed-race adolescents embark on the demanding and consuming endeavor of successfully navigating their way through several distinct stages of multiracial identity development. It can be helpful, in trying to understand the complex emotions that multiracial teenagers often experience, to familiarize ourselves with what research tells us about how each of these stages impacts our children.

According to psychologist W. S. C. Poston, biracial identity development involves the following five basic stages.[9]

Personal Identity

Our child is merely that—a child—and his or her sense of self is, as we have already seen in the earlier chapters of this book, largely independent of his or her racial heritage.

Choice of Group Categorization

Despite the fact that they are of more than one race, biracial youth begin to face peer and societal pressure to choose a single racial orientation. But their immature cognitive skills—coupled with the fact that there are often few other mixed-race kids around them—makes it unlikely that they will be able to resist this pressure and choose an integrated, "biracial" identity.

Moreover, in their attempts to "fit in," multiracial teenagers may find that they aren't fully accepted by *either* of their racial groups and that, for them, there may be no racial "safe harbor."[10] Often a triggering event leads to this disturbing realization.

As one young Korean/Caucasian woman explains, "I always thought I looked white; I guess because my Korean [American] friends said I really looked white. They joked about my blondish-brown hair and green eyes. Then one day this white person called me a flat-faced slant eye. This was a blow to the image I had developed of myself from my mom and my [Korean] peers always telling me how much of a Caucasian I was. I always thought of myself as a white person who was part Korean. Most of my friends are all Korean. Most Koreans assume I'm white so they don't ask me, 'What are you?' I used to think Caucasians thought I was one of them, too, but now I'm not sure. Right now I'm going through this self-evaluation period in my life where I'm questioning my race. I feel like I'm going to have to choose one over the other, but no matter which one I choose, I'll never fit in because [that group will] think I'm of a different race."[11]

Enmeshment/Denial

In this difficult stage, multiracial adolescents most often feel a mixture of confusion, self-hatred and even guilt as they experience and deal with outside pressure to choose one identity and deny their other racial heritage.[12]

Often multiracial teenagers describe trying extra hard to fit into one racial group, even to the extent that they voluntarily undergo "authenticity testing" (being asked to do a hypercaricature of one racial side of themselves—conforming to certain tastes in music, wearing certain clothes and/or altering their speech—to convince peers they really are black or Asian or Native American or Latino enough). Some teenagers may even negate their sense of self to the extent they undergo hazing. This demeaning process, explains Maria Root, Ph.D. (Filipino/Chinese/Spanish-Portuguese/German/Irish/Caucasian), editor of *The Multiracial Experience: Racial Borders as the New Frontier,* may include being rejected or excluded merely for having white friends, being required to give up white childhood friends or act cruelly toward them in public, or compromising one's values (e.g., stealing, breaking the law, having sex or denigrating all white people, including one's parents).

This type of extreme hazing can lead to dire consequences. One expert who works with teenagers at risk on a daily basis revealed that 100 percent of the multiracial kids she interviewed in juvenile hall said they had committed the crime they were convicted of "in order to feel they belonged to someone, that they belonged somewhere" in a society that often makes them feel they just don't fit in anywhere.[13] (This may well factor into recent findings that a disproportionately large number of youth entering some state juvenile correctional facilities are multiracial. For instance, in 2001 the Kansas Juvenile Justice Authority reported that 10 percent of youth entering correctional facilities identified themselves as multiracial. Yet, according to the 2000 census, multiracial youth in Kansas compose only 3.9 percent of the state's under-18 population.)[14]

One Native American/Mexican/Italian/Caucasian young man says his struggle to prove to his peers that he really was of Mexican heritage made him "an easy target for gangs and drugs. . . . When you're mixed, you're caught in this middle ground [of] not being enough. You choose one side and try your hardest to be one side." He talks about how, as a teenager—aware of how his fair complexion and blue eyes stood out in his Mexican-American community—he wore clothes and copped an attitude to prove he was "the biggest, baddest Mexican." He explains: "When you looked at my face, you had to ask, 'Is he even Mexican?' . . . You would do anything to prove that you were part of that community. If someone came up to you and

told you to shoot that guy over there, you would do it [to have] that acceptance, and that's what gangs give you."[15]

Maria Root points out that among her interviewees, hazing was reported most frequently among respondents with an African-American biracial
heritage. But simply *being* biracial made teenagers of *any racial combination*
more likely to undergo extreme pressure to prove they fit in; a light-skinned
black teenager with two black parents was not as likely to face hazing as was
a light-skinned teenager of *mixed* black/white parentage.[16]

Not surprisingly, this type of hazing/authenticity testing, even if it does
not involve being coerced to break the law, often has far-reaching consequences for the teenagers subjected to it. A teenager subjected to any sort of
malicious hazing may emerge from the experience not only scathed but
having "color coded" the experience. According to Maria Root, "One
respondent concluded that black women were mean because some black
women had subjected her to cruel hazing experiences." As a result, this
young woman avoided black women altogether.[17]

Even mild forms of hazing experiences make it more difficult for an
adolescent to achieve a healthy mixed-race identity. Jana Bender (African
American/Vietnamese), age 32, recalls that at the age of 13 she temporar-
ily rejected one side of her own racial makeup: "The black kids made me
feel so awkward by touching my hair and asking questions and making
comments that I almost rejected *being* black. I think parents need to
acknowledge that these stages of racial identity development are totally
normal, and talk about them with their teenager and say, 'It's *okay* to hate
people of your own race sometimes if they behave badly, just the way you
don't like other people of other races when they behave badly.' Parents
need to reassure their teenagers that they *don't* have to choose one race. If
both racial groups you belong to don't get along you can still hang out
with both, and if you only hang out with one that's fine too. It's so important to talk about it *all*."

Mei Lin Kroll (Korean, adopted by Caucasian parents), age 27, talks about
how she rejected being Asian for years: "I figured the only way to get people to stop saying certain things to me because of the way my eyes looked,
or because of other Asian characteristics that people made fun of, was to *be*
white. So I only hung out with white friends and I only dated whites and
African Americans. I figured if I hung out with anyone who was Asian it

would only draw more attention to my being Asian and I didn't want to be categorized as 'FOB' [fresh off the boat]."

Although the stage of rejecting one's own race is often temporary, it is imperative that as parents we tune in to the possibility that our teenagers may secretly harbor such feelings. Only by being cognizant of what they may be experiencing can we succeed in helping them make sense of these confusing emotions and move past them. If they do not, they may become stuck in self-rejection and denial about who they really are.

Jason Sackett (Caucasian), a clinical social worker who frequently works with multiracial families and father of two Caribbean American/Caucasian children, points out the inherent consequences of getting stuck in denial about one's racial identity: "Identity development is a standard part of an adolescent's development: to know who you are, to have a relationship with others, and to be a successful working person, you have to develop a healthy, positive sense of yourself. And multiracial kids who possess a true, healthy, and authentic identity must inherently have a *multi*racial identity. If a teen feels pressured to reject one racial heritage, then he is going to be extremely confused about *who* he is as he struggles to develop this authentic identity."

So confused, in fact, that he is very likely to get stuck in the "enmeshment/denial" stage of racial identity development, which will render him unable to move on to the next critical stages of appreciation and integration of his heritages. All of his mental energy will be diverted into intense efforts to view himself one way (e.g., fully black, fully Asian), even though those around him clearly do *not* perceive him that way (e.g., "What are you?"). This dichotomy precipitates a core identity dilemma that can set a teenager up for all kinds of related life problems, as Sackett explains: "An adolescent who doesn't know who they are will very likely lack the ability to form intimate attachments to other adults. They are isolated from true intimacy with others because they're locked in this struggle to work out this core identity dilemma within. So here you have a relationship problem that's not directly tied to race—the issue is that they don't know how to form a healthy relationship—but it's based on the fact that they still don't know who they are in terms of their own racial identity."

These confusing and negative feelings regarding one or both racial backgrounds must be resolved in such a way that adolescents are able to move forward toward an *appreciation* of all their racial heritages. Only by making this leap will they be able to segue into the essential and final two stages of healthy multiracial identity development.

Appreciation

In this fourth stage of biracial identity development, mixed-race individuals might or might not be identifying with the racial group they "chose" in the second stage, but they are working now to learn more about and value the racial roots of *both* parents.[18]

Integration

In this final stage, multiracial individuals experience wholeness and integration, bringing together all their racial heritages in a healthy, authentic self-concept.[19] This is not to imply that such "integration" is easily achieved. Hardly so. But how well and how quickly our children are able to successfully pass through these stages (discussed at greater length later in this chapter) depends, to a large degree, on how attuned we, as parents, have been to identity issues for our children all along the way.

The Multiracial Adolescent and the Dating Game

Many mixed-race young adults report, looking back, that as dating became a key aspect of social life, being multiracial became a much bigger deal with their peers. Indeed, in this emotional maze of nascent sexual attraction, being mixed seems to emerge as a greater stumbling block, creating new social boundaries seemingly out of nowhere. Consider this anecdote told by psychologist Beverly Daniel Tatum, Ph.D. (African American), about a Korean boy (adopted by a Caucasian family) who had been best friends with a white girl from preschool to adolescence. When the children turned thirteen, she relates, the mother of the white girl called the adoptive mother and said, "I just want to talk to you before this becomes an issue and let you know that I'm not comfortable with our children dating." The white mom was shocked, first, at what her friend had said and, second, because she had assumed that racism would not be an issue in her son's life because thus far it hadn't been.[20]

Almost all of my interviewees related at least one emotionally scarring experience as they entered their dating years. Mental health counselor Kelley Kenney, Ed.D., (African American), coauthor of *Counseling Multiracial Families*, says, "As a college counselor, I see many multiracial college kids who are still hurt by dating incidents which occurred years earlier, when they were 14 or 15—and they are *still* coping with them."

Jana Bender (African American/Vietnamese) recalls: "Once we had this dance where the girls asked the boys. I asked this boy whom I liked and who liked me. He hung out with both black kids and white kids and we were really good friends. He said yes. But then he got so much flack about it; his white friends were all saying, 'Hey, she's black, she's not that cute.' *Two hours later* he came back and said no. That was the most devastating day of junior high for me. I didn't even ask him why. I didn't want to hear him say it."

Linda Parker (African American/Native American/Czech/Caucasian), age 22, emphasizes, "What bothers me most in terms of dating relationships is that I'll see a guy who is cute and I'll see him dismiss me right off hand. But later I might run into that same guy who dismissed me in a racial sense, and then he gets to know me and he's like, 'WOW!' And suddenly he's interested in me, when he wasn't before. And that hurts—the fact that initially I wasn't interesting because of the way I look."

Linda tells of one disturbing incident when "I was online with a guy I'd chatted with before. Earlier he had emailed me and said, 'You're too good to be true,' and he asked me to send him a picture. I said no, but I sent him this description: 'I'm 5 feet 8 inches tall, I have medium-length brown hair with gold highlights, high cheekbones, two dimples, almond-shaped brown eyes and caffe latte–colored skin.' And he said, 'Oh, so you're not white?' And I said, 'Yes.' And he wrote, 'Well, I'm a racist. I'm *really* a racist.' I wrote back, 'You must be joking.' And he said, 'Oh it's true. I don't like black people.' I couldn't believe he could think that—or *say* that to me. It makes me sick to think such people are even out there—and that one day he'll procreate and teach his children to be racist, too."

That was not Linda's only emotionally bruising experience during her adolescent/young adult dating years. She dated one boy for a while, she says, whose family "had a lot of issues regarding my color. His mother actually said to him, 'I hope you don't get too serious because I don't want little brown grandbabies.' That hurt a lot." But, she says, "I try to handle these experiences by making sure that no matter how others might react to me, I'm just *me*." Still, she adds, with a tone of hesitation, as a result of such experiences, "I'm at war with myself. Personally I hate society's norms and I hate even thinking of conforming to society's norms, but I don't want my kids to one day have to prove themselves the way I have. Because of the way society views people of color, I'd like my kids to be a little bit lighter than I am. I know it seems totally bizarre to say I hate it when people react to my race and then to say I don't want my kids to go through that, so I want them to have lighter skin. Personally I don't care what color my kids are. But the world cares. And if the world cares what color they are then I care."

An equally poignant dating story is one shared by Nina (African American/Jewish Caucasian/Japanese), age 19, who talks about the treatment she received from her (Caucasian) boyfriend's family. "My boyfriend's parents have prom pictures of their three kids all over their house, but even though he and I have been to a lot of proms together they have never put one up of us. One day I asked him why and he said, 'Well, it's pretty much that every-one else is white and they're more comfortable with that.'" Another time, says Nina, "I wore a Jewish star that my mom gave me to his house and after I left his mom said to him, 'Oh, she's not only black and Oriental, she's Jewish *too?*' I had always thought it was my boyfriend and me against his parents but then he said to me, 'Don't wear that when you're here.'"

Nina and her boyfriend briefly broke up after that. Later, when they got back together, Nina recalls, "I asked him, 'Look, what am I up against here?'

And he said, 'It's not just that you're black and white and Japanese, it's that you're multiracial. My parents disagree with what *your* parents did.' Basically, they told him, if he ever got back with me, they'd disown him."

Who Has a Harder Time, Multiracial Boys or Girls?

Divergent views on whether mixed-race boys or girls encounter more dif-ficulty during these emotionally laden years arose again and again in the course of my interviews. Many young women felt that boys of mixed-race coasted through the social/dating scene of the middle school and high school years.

"Biracial boys have it so much easier," reflects Rochelle Brown (African American/Caucasian), age 17. "Boys just naturally accept each other. With girls everything is much more complicated; girls are more concerned with appearance than boys. And girls are evil to each other. They gossip behind each other's backs. They are just cruel. And that really affects a multiracial girl—it makes it all the more difficult to find acceptance."

Psychologist Beverly Daniel Tatum agrees: "Biracial boys seem to have more social options than do girls, particularly if they are actively involved in sports." Participation in sports seems to help boys keep cross-racial friendships intact even if races divide socially during the teenage years. The camaraderie engendered by being part of a team not only helps solidify a teenager's sense of belonging but, because being involved in sports is also often a source of status in school, may help ameliorate some of the rejection many mixed-race teenagers encounter when they begin to date.[21]

Meanwhile, adds Tatum, although "biracial girls are often considered beautiful objects of curiosity because of their 'exotic' looks, this attention does not necessarily translate into dating partners."[22] Even as the "mixed look" becomes slightly more prevalent on billboards and fashion runways, some experts believe this trend is less reflective of overall progress toward embracing multiracial women for who they are, and more indicative of "equal opportunity objectification" of mixed-race women, reflecting society's desire to use polyracial females to fulfill fantasies in keeping with "the Jezebel phenomenon" of old.[23] (Even more disturbing to ponder—for *any* parent of a multiracial daughter and for *any* parent anywhere—are recent National Crime Victimization Survey [NAWS] figures from Bureau of Justice statistics, which show that multiracial women are significantly more likely to be victims of rape or attempted rape—at a rate nearly double that of Caucasian women and nearly five times that of monoracial Asian women.)[24]

Even setting this alarming finding aside, many girls experience difficulty during these years because they are exotified by society in a way that boys are not (the "exotic flower of the Orient;" the hypersensual Carmen-esque Latina and so on). Nevertheless, a number of multiracial adolescent girls—having grown up in a postfeminist age without the consciousness of female objectification that was part of the central dialogue of the feminist generation—report that they *enjoy* being valued for their exoticism. One young woman puts it this way: "I think it's much easier to be a mixed girl than a mixed guy. There is a positive stereotype that being mixed makes you exotic and beautiful and it plays into that fantasy men have. Guys don't have that beauty issue to help them. Everyone I hear talking about mixed girls always says, 'Oh, they're so hot!'"

Asked if she was disturbed by that objectification, she replied, "Is that objectification? It may be, but I'll take it!"

Being different in the sense of being exotic, however, may be a double-edged sword for mixed-race girls. If they are desired, they may feel that they are only being pursued for superficial reasons because they do look exotic; if they are not desired, they may feel they are *not* being pursued for superficial reasons because they look different. (It is usually later on, as young women mature, that they become more conscious of the way women in our society are often seen as sexual "objects.")

As the mother of a biracial daughter, I contemplate this possibility with near tears in my eyes. How will I help my daughter, Claire, through any dating heartbreak she may experience, when I can well recall having had a hard enough time handling the less overt rejections I reeled from when dating in high school as a monoracial individual? If being biracial does translate into being not only more objectified, but less "datable," how will I help my daughter, who is already so overtly exotified by every stranger who sees her?

This is not to imply that multiracial male teenagers skate effortlessly through these years. Consider one young man (African American/black/Indian), who, in Pearl Fuyo Gaskins's book, *What Are You? Voices of Mixed Race Young People*, relates the angst he experienced when merely trying to find a date for a party. "All these girls would not want to go with me or they'd make up some lie," he says. "For a really long time I didn't think of myself as someone who girls would go out with. I'd think, 'she probably doesn't think that I'm attractive.' I'd be at a party and people would be like, 'you have been talking to that girl all night long. Do you like her?' And I'd be like, 'No! Of course not' . . . lying half the time [because] I wouldn't have been allowed to date her [due to] pressure from friends and also a lot of friends' parents because in my family no one looks down on interracial stuff at all. . . . I wish I had had supportive friends in high school who did not look down on interracial dating and see it as a problem. I wish a friend could have said . . . 'Why wouldn't you go out with her? Both of you like soccer, and movies, and alfalfa sprouts.' I would have loved to find a group of people like that . . . but I don't think they existed."[25]

Additionally, research indicates that as young multiracial men enter the work place, they may have to work harder to prove themselves than do multiracial women. This might be particularly the case in work settings where women are, to any degree, viewed as less threatening or less competition for top positions than men are.[26]

Helping Multiracial Teenagers
Develop a Healthy Sense of Self

Naturally, the very thought of a child eschewing their appearance fills any parent with dread. It can be hard to imagine how or why our child *could* come to feel this way. After all, we remember her at two, at three, peering at her reflection with unbridled delight and abandon, enamored with each dramatic expression or goofy grin she gave the mirror. Each time I watch my four-year-old clown and curtsy for the mirror with sheer self-delight I wonder: How is it that our children lose that deep self-satisfaction?

Fast-forward ten years and you have a child with quite a different reaction to the image she encounters. Suddenly her hair is too kinky or too straight, her skin too brown or too tan, her eyes too narrow, her nose too wide, her face too flat. There is no self-glee now over her appearance, and, all too often, there is not even self-liking.

How can we gingerly step into our teenager's world—a world that becomes increasingly closed off to us in many ways—to help prevent her from undergoing this heart-wrenching transformation in self-perception?

The following insights come from many different multiracial teenagers and young adults, as well as their parents. They are both useful and inspiring.

Don't Solve Your Teenagers' Problems for Them

Although this may at first seem counterintuitive (why should we hold back on our opinions and advice when our children are facing their years of greatest emotional challenge?), our role in our child's life has changed. Now the question of "Who am I?" is not one we can address for him. He must address it head on, for himself. We will help him more if we encourage him to come to his own understanding of—and create his own solutions to—incidents that may arise. For instance, if your black/Italian-Caucasian teenager tells you that a friend's dad—driving her carpool for the first time—insisted that she *couldn't* be Italian, you might express to her that you understand how that would be hurtful, and then ask *her,* "Well, *why* do you think he would say something like that? What do you think his experiences have been that he would come to such a conclusion?" Rather than step in to fix the problem ("Well, when *he's* driving car pool, I'll drive you myself!") ask her: "How do *you* want to handle this? Do you *want* to do anything about this? If so, what can I do to help you?" If we have successfully prepared our child thus far, her competence in such instances might very well surprise us.

Naturally, there are more weighted circumstances that require us to be an integral part of our child's decision-making process—to either make a joint decision with her or make a parental decision *for* her (certainly when hazing or harassment or any situation occurs which may put them in emotional or physical danger). But, in these final shaping years—before our teenagers leave home—we are helping them more if we are now less their *guide,* and more a resource from which they can seek *guidance,* as needed.

Help Your Teenagers Name the Problem at Hand

When incidents do arise, as you listen to your child, it can be useful to help him name the problem for what it is. Because so much that surrounds being of mixed race is *implied* by the actions of others (e.g., a girl says yes to a prom invitation but changes her mind after coming back to school the next day, saying only "my parents don't think it is a good idea, that's all") but *unspoken,* it can be a great relief to our teenager to hear an adult simply state outright what is likely going on, thereby validating his experience. For instance, we might say, on seeing our son's glum face, "Yes, there are certain families who prefer their child doesn't date anyone whose racial heritage differs from their own. But just imagine how sad it is that they cut so many people out whom they could have gotten to know. I think that's really, really unfortunate."

Prepare Them to Fill Out Forms

Help your child prepare for the school, organizational, and government forms she will be filling out—forms that may imply she doesn't exist. Census 2000, for the first time, allowed individuals to "check all races that apply" when designating their racial heritage(s). Prior to that, census and other organizational forms required multiracial individuals to choose one race ("check only one") or "other." Although all federal forms (including forms for all state agencies, organizations and schools that receive federal funding) must include "check all that apply," by fall 2004 very few state agencies (e.g., schools) have made this change (for more on this issue see Chapter 5).

Matt Kelley (Korean/Caucasian) talks about how this invisibility on institutional forms—as well as in school curricula—impacted him as he came of age: "Until I was thirteen I was aware that I was half white, half Korean. All my projects at school were always about being Korean. If we had to study a country, I studied Korea. If we had to do a flag project, I chose the Korean flag. I didn't really see how I was different from my friends who had two parents who were, say, both Norwegian. I had some idea as to what race was, sure, but I didn't understand what *racism* was. So I didn't judge anything that happened to me based on my race."

In eighth grade, Kelley switched schools. He suddenly had to field endless "What are you?" questions from his new group of peers. In this unfamiliar setting, he recalls: "I felt hyperexposed." At the same time, he was now old enough to fill out his own forms for school (e.g., for standardized testing as well as for other organizations). Yet there was never a space provided for having a mixed-race background. Kelley had to either check "other" or choose whether to say he was Korean or white. He could not *be* both. But, he posits, "identity is based on how you see yourself and how *others* see you. And when every form you fill out tells you that how you identify yourself is not an identity you *can* have, how can that not affect how you see yourself? It fosters that feeling of 'I don't exist. I'm a freak.'"

Indeed, he points out, "a really dominant experience of being multiracial is facing this jarring contradiction between being hyper-*exposed*—reflected in all the 'What are you?' questions and confusion people express over not *who* you are but *what* you are—contrasted by being hyper-*invisible* in all the 'check only one' directives on forms, and unacknowledged by teachers and in school curricula. It doesn't make any sense. And, as adolescents, whether we should or not, we assume everything *should* make sense. So if we don't get it, we just assume that everyone else but us does understand why this conflict exists, and that there must be a valid reason."

In the course of his work as editor of *MAVIN* magazine, Kelley says that more than a few times he has talked to young adults who recall "actually thinking they *were* aliens—they thought they *had* to be." And why wouldn't they? he asks. "It's as if the world is moving on apparently oblivious to this dilemma that's earth-shattering for you—the person in the middle of it. '*Do I exist or do I not exist?*' Meanwhile society hasn't even noticed that you're having to ask this question or *why* you're asking this question. That's where the alien component comes from. If no one else is bothered by this contradiction, if they don't think it's weird, you feel like *you* must be an alien. If there's something about the way you look that compels total strangers to stop you on the street and ask, 'What are you?' then that must be happening for a reason. You *are* alien."

This dichotomy—being hyperexposed due to intrusive questions yet invisible on institutional forms and in school curricula—is one that hopefully will be lessened, to some small degree, by the "check all that apply" directives that are soon to be government mandated. Because this change is only slowly (if at all) trickling down through most state governments and school systems, some parents and teenagers have devised their own alternative answers to the "check only one" race question. Several teenagers talk about writing in "human race" under "other." One young adult talks about how she changes the "check one race" directive to "check one's races" (by adding two "s" letters) and then circles all that apply. Other parents cite going to school boards with their teenagers to demand forms be changed and, using the 2000 federal mandate to back them up, help effect that change. This activism also sends a strong message of personal empowerment to their kids.

Whatever tack you and your teenager choose to take when you face antiquated red tape state-your-race forms, come up with your plan together. Moreover, use the issue as a jumping-off point to see if your teenager wants to vent any feelings he may have about being overquestioned and overexposed in our society, and at the same time undervalidated. Sometimes just listening—at the same time that we help them to name and frame the problem for what it is—can be our most important job.

Help Your Teenagers Understand the "What Are You?" Question

As children mature through the teenage years, they become increasingly capable of understanding the multiple layers of what's transpiring when race-questioning occurs. For instance, if your adolescent comes home after a party feeling frustrated because several new kids he met barraged him with the "What are you?" question, you can remind him that "What are you?" is often posed to people of mixed race out of a lack of awareness that our society is becoming increasingly—and quite rapidly—multiracial and conveys that person's out-of-date, stereotypical way of organizing our society. Sociologist Teresa Kay Williams (Japanese/Irish/Welsh/Caucasian) says that we all have "what might be called a 'compass' for navigating race relations. But, when that racial compass fails—when people feel that someone's facial and physical features are unfamiliar and don't fit into the rigid categories they use to categorize people—the *What Are You?* question is prompted." Williams believes this question unveils "the racial and social disorientation of the person asking the question as much as it potentially dislocates the person *being* asked. The racially mixed person may feel doubly othered by such constant interrogation because the interrogator seems to be saying, 'In my construction of the world, your look, your speech, your behavior, your mannerisms, your name, and your overall presence do not have a place. You defy my limited understanding and social application of race. I have no label to fit you, to pigeonhole you, and therefore to make assumptions about you. I need to know what you are so I can ease this discomfort *I* feel for being unable to peg you.'"[27]

By helping our kids understand the errant psychology that prompts race questioning, we bring home the motto, The ill lies with society, not within them.

Help Your Teenagers Explore More Responses to the "What Are You?" Question

Along with reiterating to our teenagers that it is not their duty to accommodate society's label-prone approach to race, we also need to encourage them to come up with their own creative answers to race-related questions, affirming for them that a wide array of responses to race questioning are legitimate. For instance, they may choose to answer such questions by asking those who query them why they care to know or how such information, once gleaned, will be of any use to them. Or they may feel the most effective and comfortable response for them is to simply refuse to answer or just walk away.

Matt Kelley (Korean/Caucasian) confesses he is still learning to deal with the "What are you?" question. "If there is anything about other people in our society that we assume we can easily determine it's gender, but soon after that it's race," he explains. "We assume people can be put into five basic racial groups: black/white/Asian/Native American/Latino. It's not something we think about doing; it's like a reflex of our eyes. It's profiling. So, when someone is confronted by a racially ambiguous person and all of a sudden one of the most important things on their list of ways to identify that person can't be filled in, it's such an unfamiliar and jarring hiccup it's almost as if they can't move on until they fill in that missing piece of information." For that moment, says Kelley, "It's as if all the rules of respecting another's privacy don't apply." While Kelley realizes "you can't be angry because people are programmed to look and ask," that doesn't mean it isn't frustrating. "If someone asks me, 'What are you?' and I try answering, 'I'm American,' they'll just persist with, 'No what *are* you?' until they get a label that works for *them*."

Because it can be harmful to multiracial youth to face such insistent questioning over and over, Kelley believes "you have to protect yourself." On this front, he is still struggling. "I'm not a person who's going to say, 'I'm 100 percent Korean and I'm 100 percent white.' I feel many times that it's more like I'm 49 percent white and 49 percent Korean. I feel connected to white culture because I grew up with my [white] dad. But I *don't* feel connected to white privilege. I feel very connected to my Korean culture because of growing up around my mom's family. But I *know* that I won't ever be fully accepted by the Korean-American community. I am *not* Korean to most Korean Americans. I'm not Korean to my own family. If you look like me, you're not *Korean.*"

Sometimes, says Kelley, "my way of dealing with the 'What are you?' question—how I find empowerment—is to tell other people I'm something *other* than half Korean and half white, because to me it really doesn't matter what they think. Having a label only matters to the person who is trying to give you one." For instance, Kelley relates, he is often perceived by people to be Latino or Filipino. "If someone comes up to me on the street and asks, 'What are you, Mexican?' I might say yes, even thought I'm not, not as a *defense* but as an *offense*—as a way of regaining some control. Because if someone comes up and asks 'What are you?' they are contributing nothing and they are asking me to give them something. I feel kind of like how *dare* you compound that trauma I've already had? If I respond by saying 'I'm half Korean and half white,' I feel defeated: I feel the person asking the question has tried to take something from me and I've given it to them."

Kelley admits he thinks that "it would be better to educate people by being generous with our time and telling strangers, 'Well, my dad is X and my mom is Y and I'm multiracial,' and to always remember that not everyone is asking you the question for the wrong reason." But for now, like so many multiracial youth, he is currently more concerned with empowering *himself*—and appropriately so.

Ramona E. Douglass (Native American/African American/Sicilian/Scots-Irish/Caucasian), past president of the Association of MultiEthnic Americans, similarly recalls that, growing up, she often sensed that people felt she owed them some kind of explanation about her racial heritage. "I made many whites and blacks uneasy because I wasn't easily classifiable at first glance. Many people mistook me for Hispanic, some thought I was Jewish." Douglass says she let everyone assume what they liked. But "when people learned that I had any African ancestry they were annoyed that I hadn't announced it in advance." It was as if, she says, "they wanted me to wear a *sign*. I kid you not. But it was *their* problem, not mine."

Still, when mixed-race youth are together, the context of race questioning is quite different. Kelley points out that multiracial youth love to tell their own stories to each other. "They talk about being sick of being asked, 'What are you?' but at the first opportunity we want to know what each other's background is."[28]

Some multiracial youth view the "What are you?" question as little more than an annoying fact of life. Jamie Doyle (Japanese/Irish/Caucasian), now age 23, believes that "although a lot of young people talk about how angry it makes them when people ask 'What are you?' I think that if you understand it's not meant to be an insult, then you can handle that question in a very nonconfrontational way. People are just trying to find out."

When asked how she handles such queries, Jamie says she often takes a moment to "explain being biracial" by painting a two-minute family portrait: "Sometimes I say, sort of jokingly, 'My mom is a 5 foot tall first-generation Japanese American, and my dad is a 6 foot 3 Irishman. We're a kind of Japanese *and* American family. We'll have natto (a Japanese dish of fermented soybeans) with steak, and enjoy them together. My dad doesn't speak much Japanese. He speaks to my mom in English, she speaks to him in English/Japanese, she speaks me in Japanese, and I speak to her in English/Japanese.'"

Whatever artful means your teenager arrives at (or wants to experiment with) for interfacing with the curious, lend your support. After all, we who are monoracial really can't understand what it is like, day in and day out, to have our public self probed and prodded at, or our appearance constantly evaluated. But we can reassure our teenagers that they do have a multitude of possible, empowering responses to choose from when strangers ask them to explain "what" they are.

Accept a Teenager's Fluid Racial Identity

It's okay if your teenager's racial identity is "fluid" during these adolescent years, even changing from one primary racial affiliation to another. Many multiracial teenagers report that as they become more secure about who they are, they are able to adopt a fluid racial identity. For example, a black/Asian teenager may very well describe herself as biracial in some situations and with some groups, and as black or Asian in other settings.

This concept of fluidity might, however, initially seem suspect. How can it be emotionally healthy for a biracial teenager to sometimes define himself as only one of his races, when we know that children who are pressured to "pass" as monoracial (present themselves as being of only one racial background when they are multiracial) cannot emerge successfully from the critical task of developing an authentic self-concept?

In truth, achieving fluidity of race is quite different from being pressured to choose one race while *rejecting* the other. Having a healthy racial identity—one that is adaptable depending on the situational context—is a skill that emerges only as a result of reaching the goal of racial integration and appreciation of all of one's racial heritages.

As mental health counselor Kelley Kenney (African American) says, "It is so important that multiracial teenagers develop this sense of adaptability, so that they are able to function in a positive way in a number of different environments." This skill is an asset not only for them, but for the community and the world they live in.

"Many biracial and multiracial people identify themselves differently in varied situations, depending on what aspects of identity are salient," psychologist Maria Root explains. She uses the example of the mixed-blood Native American character Vivian, portrayed in *The Crown of Columbus,* a novel by Louise Erdrich and Michael Dorris. Vivian describes this process as "watering whatever set of her ethnic roots needs it most."[29] Often this "situational ethnicity," Root points out, is misinterpreted by others as a sign of a multiracial person's inner confusion when in fact it represents a young adult's increasing *comfort* level with all of who they are. Still, it may confuse others by challenging *their* illusions of racial boundaries.

David Harris, Ph.D. (African American), professor of sociology at the University of Michigan and parent of two biracial children (African American/Caucasian), has developed what he refers to as a "matrix of race." It beautifully illustrates why a mixed-race individual's identity so often becomes fluid. Harris explains that when people are asked, "What's your race?" or "What are you?" their "answer is dependent upon a range of variables that may change at any given moment in time." According to Harris, one's racial identity shifts according to three factors:

1. *Based on what?* On what criteria is the asker making their assumptions about a mixed-race individual's identity? Based upon their ancestry, phenotype, or culture? For instance, an African American/Caucasian child who is very light-skinned might be considered biracial or Black by people who know his ancestry but white by those who only know him by his physical appearance.

2. *According to whom?* According to what other people think I am when they see me? Or how I define *myself?* Or do you want to know what I *look* like? For instance, says Harris, while you might assume your Fedex person is one race, your neighbor might assume the same Fedex person is of another race. And yet, if you ask your Fedex person, he may tell you he is of yet a different race.

3. *Depending on what and where?* In this aspect of Harris's racial matrix, "if someone is half-black and half-white, their racial identity will depend, in part, on *where* you see them. If you see them at a Hip Hop club in Chicago, you may see them as black, but if you see them eating at a University club at Princeton, you might see them as Mediterranean-European."

Harris emphasizes that for the majority of Americans the question of race is an easy one—they're white and everyone around them thinks they're white. However, "there is this growing group of multiracial people with a discrepancy between what they perceive themselves to be and how others see them." And yet, he explains, when multiracial people shift their answers—given the context of their situation—"we think that the problem is with them; that they have some inner ambiguity about which they are. But the problem isn't within them or with their answer. Their *answer* isn't flawed." Rather, it's the logic of the *question*—which assumes that a single-race identity fits all people and that a person's answer will be uniform to all situations—that is flawed.

"Lived race is very complex," emphasizes Harris. "People can move in and out of overlapping groups depending upon what the context is and who the observers are. And yet we try to measure race in very simplistic ways."

Bethany Fry (Native American/Italian/Caucasian), age 24, reveals how she experiences this fluidity of race in her life. For example, when she visits her mom's Native American relatives in Montana for two weeks every summer and she's in a store, "people will say, 'Oh Indian—look at this.'" But, she adds, "when I'm with my dad (Caucasian) during the winter and I'm not tan, people just assume I'm Italian. Yet if I'm in Miami or Mexico everyone assumes I'm Spanish. How I'm perceived depends on where I am and who I'm with."

Matt Kelley nudges this fluidity of race concept one step further. "What's fascinating about growing up in the U.S. is that because my mom is Korean and my dad is white, I'm half Korean and half white. But that's not my *experience*. My *experience* is based on what I am perceived to be. And what I am most often perceived to be is Latino or Filipino. And if a person's identity is based on a combination of how they perceive themselves *and* how others perceive them, then in some small way I do know what it's like to be Latino or Filipino." "Think about it," Kelley says. "If someone comes up to me on the street and assumes during our encounter that I am Latino, then, for those ten seconds, I have experienced some small aspect of what it's like to *be* Latino. I don't know what it's like to be Latino every day, but I do know what it's like to be perceived to be Latino." Kelley emphasizes: "We take for granted the idea that you are born with your race and that your race doesn't change. That might be true for 90 percent of people, but it's not true for those of us who have an ambiguous phenotype—those of us who are multiracial."

There are limits, however, to the concept of fluid race. It is very rare, for instance, that multiracial individuals with some white heritage (except those who are very light-skinned) are considered white in our society. Any ethnic aspect of one's appearance automatically causes people to label that individual as of a minority race, an assumption that lingers on, echoing the antiquated and racist concept of the "one-drop rule."[30]

Stacy Bell (Caucasian), executive director of the K & F Baxter Family Foundation (which supports research on biracial children) shares her take on how this limit to fluidity of race has had an impact on her two biracial (African American/Caucasian) children. "From the time they were very little I would say to my kids, 'You can identify as being biracial or you can identify with being black. But you can't say you're white.' It's not that they wanted to be white, but they see the white side of their family much more than the black side, and they couldn't understand why, if they could say they were biracial or black, they couldn't say they were white, too." Bell feels, looking back, that it helped her kids (now 11 and 14) to realize that this limit to their identity *wasn't* just about being black. "I explained to them, 'I know it's hard to understand but that's the way things are in this country. If you look to be of *any* race other than white and you have a parent who isn't white, you can't *say* you're white.' As they got older and they understood the way race works in our society, they understood that this wasn't just a black/white issue. It was a *societal* issue."

How Do Multiracial Teenagers Develop into Confident Young Adults?

Weaving one's way through this labyrinth of identity, friendships and emotions—and integrating one's experiences into a positive sense of identity—is a task faced by all adolescents in mixed-race families. Fortunately, despite the psychological and developmental pressures converging on the multiracial teenager during these years, many adolescents successfully attain a strong and healthy multiracial self-concept. For these adolescents, attempts to align with only one racial group begin to feel artificial and inappropriate—a complete denial of who they know themselves to be. They simply *must* stretch toward a more whole sense of self. In so doing, they begin to achieve the critical fourth and fifth stages of successful multiracial identity development: *appreciation* of all of their racial backgrounds and *integration* of these heritages into a resolute and cohesive self. As a result, they are able to make being biracial work for them rather than against them.

Jana Bender (African American/Vietnamese) talks about how this was the case for her. After a slew of difficult years in junior high and high school, she says, "I just got this mentality that I wasn't going to be pressured into choosing one race over another. Something in me said, I'm *not* going to play this game. If I liked someone I was going to be friends with them—no matter what race they were or what clique they were in. I thought, 'I don't care if you don't like me if I hang out with the black kids—and I don't care if you don't like me if I hang out with white kids.' I don't know where I got that strength that I just wanted to be me, to be friends with whomever I liked, but it gave me a lot of sense of self. By twelfth grade I realized that all my friends were getting along great. I was very conscious that these were two races hanging out together and I sometimes had to remind one person of one race of the humanity of the person of the other race. I felt this role was very important, to be a bridge between two racial groups in that way. I'm sure that it strengthened my sense of who I am today."

What allowed Jana to have what she calls "that strength" of self to not reject either of her racial heritages despite enormous peer pressure? It certainly made an important difference that, like all of the multiracial young adults I've interviewed who have achieved a healthy mixed-race identity, Jana's parents laid a strong foundation for her to embrace her full identity. Consequently, the extreme pressure to identify with only one of her racial heritages felt inherently wrong to her. Less fortunate are kids whose parents do not prepare them from the earliest ages with an open dialogue regarding being multiracial; these kids are left vulnerable as they enter adolescence.

To wit, we might remind ourselves of the University of Memphis study on multiracial college students (briefly discussed in Chapter 1), which found that young multiracial adults who were raised in homes in which their multiracialness was not talked about—and whose parents did not openly address the issues their children might one day face—feel somewhat betrayed by their parents later on in life. As one college student put it, "I don't think [my parents] understood what it was like to be me. When I said, 'I'm different,' they just kind of dismissed it. It was almost denial, or maybe they didn't know how to deal with it."[31] Another student voiced a similar regret: "If someone had been there to guide me through, encouraging me to accept being biracial, it would have been easier."[32] Moreover, these underprepared kids tended to see the problem as partly within themselves, rather than within people around them and society, making it much more difficult for them to emerge from adolescence with their self-esteem intact. Meanwhile, most young adults who were successfully prepared for life as multiracial individuals report that as they exited the turmoil of middle school and turned sixteen, seventeen and eighteen, they began to feel much more comfortable with themselves *and* their surroundings.

Nicole Brown (African American/Caucasian), now 22, says, "For a long time I only dated black guys because I didn't want to offend anybody. I worried that if I did date white guys the black community would look down on me." But, she says, by the end of high school, "I just felt that I wasn't going to date anyone for anyone's reasons but my own. I began to enjoy who I am and to revel in it. Now I can be in a group and, because of my multiracial background, I can relate to and connect with and make relationships with so many different types of people. It's something extra that I have that others don't have."

Many other well-prepared multiracial teenagers report that during their latter years of high school (ages 16–18) they began to work through many of their identity issues. As they moved closer toward appreciating and integrating all of who they were racially, they were better able to negotiate race issues amid their peers and thus settle into a peer group that was both accepting and comfortable for them.

The College Years: Unexpected Challenges

For multiracial teenagers, the fragile process of reaching a unified sense of self is often only truly achieved during the early college years (ages 18–19). Indeed the social atmosphere during the first year or two of college often echoes that of middle school, only with more mature (yet no less needy) players. Suddenly insecure again in this collegiate sea of new faces, personalities and possibilities—and away from family and friends for the first time—most college freshmen quickly segregate, once again, into racially differentiated student groups as a means of finding their place and announcing their identities.

Meanwhile, mixed-race teenagers must also "announce" their identity in this wholly unfamiliar environment, a setting in which *they* lack social and familial support from family and friends—those who already know and love them for who they are in all their depth and complexity.

Naomi Reed (African American/Russian Jewish/Caucasian), age 20, relates, "When I came to college I attempted to maintain a multicultural group of friends, but at the University of Texas everything is racially divided. At first I decided, okay, I'll conform to that racial division and make some friends, so I basically immersed myself in the black community, which was awesome. But I was still feeling a little bit not complete in that my pursuance of a biracial identity made some black people feel like I was trying to make myself less black, and I mean that's absurd because I love my people and I look black. If I wanted to embrace my other half that should have nothing to do with being black enough."

Naomi recalls that as time went by she began to feel more strongly that it was essential for her to bridge out to her other cultures, too. "Now, basically I'm friends with whomever wants to be open-minded and accept me as a black, Jewish, biracial American woman."

"During the college years race seems like it is more of an issue again," agrees Samantha Franks (African American), a 22-year-old whose stepfather is white. "I feel like a lot of people put their race on parade—it's suddenly a much bigger part of how people identify who they are. I don't like it. I'm well aware of and extremely proud of the fact that I'm black but I'm not going to parade it all around. It doesn't define me and I don't define others by race."

Other multiracial college students report that this racial segregating by peers shocked and disturbed them during their first year of college. Linda Parker (Native American/African American/Czech/Caucasian), 22, says that it was during her "freshman year at college when I first realized that people saw me as different because of the way I looked. [One guy] said that I was going out with white guys because I was denying the fact that I was black and because I was ashamed of being black. And I said, no I'm not, are you crazy? *I'm just me.* That was a very hard time for me. Not only did I realize that I was different but I realized, in a larger sense, there were not just two categories—white or nonwhite—there was this third race which was *mixed.* And I was in this third group. That had never occurred to me before."

Suddenly, she says, "I started looking in the mirror with a complete sense of alienation. It was the first time that I started not liking how I looked and saw my complexion and my looks as a big handicap. Growing up, people had often complimented me on the way I looked. I'm not saying that I agreed with them, but that was how people responded to me my whole life. And suddenly I didn't like what I saw. I would look into the mirror and I'd say to myself, I wish I *weren't* this color."

If, however, we have helped equip our teenagers all along the way for challenges to their sense of self, such experiences will not defeat them but rather ignite in them a desire to reaffirm and strengthen their biracial identity.

Jamie Doyle (Japanese/Irish/Caucasian), 23, talks about how this was the case for her: "When I began college, finding my niche was problematic. Students separated by rigid racial lines, and since I was biracial, finding my place at the university was difficult. Once my roommate and I went to a party for girls interested in joining this Asian sorority. I wasn't sure if I should go because I don't really look that Asian. But my roommate said, 'Oh yeah, of course, you're Asian!' I went but it was really uncomfortable. The girls were all giving me dirty looks and exchanging little whispers. They were really clear they didn't want me there. They elucidated for me that I was *not* Asian enough to be part of their organization." So, Jamie says, "I chose a diverse group of friends instead; they encompass just about every shade in the racial spectrum. I just decided I wasn't going to try to prove anything to *anybody.*"

College students' consciousness about their mixed identity is much greater than it was at 13 or 14. Consequently, if and when their identity is challenged by college peers, they are able to make much more conscious choices about how to respond to those challenges, and the choices they make to express their individuality as a multiracial person are that much more intentional.

Although these college years may present a final challenge to our children's efforts to integrate their self-concept, they also provide new and fertile ground for self-exploration. Because 18- and 19-year-olds are often trying on a whole new sense of identity at this phase of life, and because college is a laboratory for self-discovery in general, these years provide a watershed opportunity for older multiracial teenagers to explore their mixed-race heritage in what is often a more diverse setting than they have had access to previously. They may join different ethnic groups to explore their ethnic background (e.g., becoming involved in the Black Student Alliance), take ethnic studies classes, learn a foreign language that pertains to their minority culture and so on. Although our child may arrive at college with one primary racial identity (usually reflecting the prevalent racial identity in our home), in the process of exploring his other racial heritages more fully, he may change his dominant racial identity.

Consider Tracy Scholl's (African American/Caribbean American/German/Caucasian) experience. At age 29, she recalls that, having grown up in a white suburb, once she reached college, "I became immersed in African-American history. All my courses were African-American courses. I learned the black kids' language—their slang—even though at first I couldn't understand a word of it. I was raised practically as a white person. But in college I became an African-American person."

Having experienced this opportunity to engage in full-fledged racial examination and personal inquiry, many students begin to integrate that new identity into a more fully biracial or multiracial identity.[33] This proved to be precisely Tracy Scholl's experience. After immersing herself in black culture in college, she says, "Now I'm *both*. I think I really wanted my friends back from high school. I was in a crisis. Although I loved my black culture, I wanted to be myself foremost and I didn't really want to give up all of my [white culture]; I thought 'I want to keep some of this.' At about age 21 I assimilated into more broad stream society. I wanted to have a multicultural life. I had learned the black culture and I thought, 'Well, now that I have that I want to be able to choose and have all kinds of friends.'" Later on, says Tracy, in her life as a young professional in New York City at age 25, "Monday to Friday I lived like a white person and even my white friends would jokingly call me 'the black wasp.' They could not believe that I lived in Harlem on 110th Street. Then, on the weekends, I'd hang out with my friends from the neighborhood; I'd go home and be black."

Tracy found acceptance in college in an all-minority student group, which helped her develop an appreciation of being black, which in turn led to a more authentic and confident biracial identity. However, some multiracial college students, like Jamie, report that for them, traditional university-sponsored minority student groups are problematic because (not having the "typical" features of that ethnic group) they are questioned about why they are interested in joining or even asked to prove their ethnic membership. Echoing the authenticity testing that mixed-race teenagers may experience in adolescence, multicultural college students may find that once again, in order to belong, they must repress important aspects of who they are.[34]

As a result, many mixed-race students on university campuses are increasingly forming their *own* mixed-race student groups. These groups, emphasizes Professor Nancy J. Nishimura (Japanese American), "are like 'family' to the extent that they [are] with people with whom they [share] a common bond." Students who form and join multiracial college organizations often report "feeling a sense of comfort and acceptance as 'whole' persons" for the first time. As one interviewee put it, "Just in talking to other members of SHADES [a mixed-race student group], there was that common bond [of sharing] a lot of experiences I had gone through that I thought were unique to me."[35]

Jamie Doyle (Japanese/Irish/Caucasian) says she had similar feelings about helping create a mixed-race student group on her university campus: "Helping to form and strengthen Neapolitan was an important chapter in my life as a multiracial individual. I've seen our organization grow slowly each year, and new faces coming out to meetings. I feel lucky to have been able to bring awareness of multiracial issues to campus—and to help bring together a group of people with the same interests regardless of their racial background. I've learned that there are similarities amongst all of us who are biracial, regardless of our racial composition." Furthermore, says Jamie, involvement with so many other mixed-race students has helped her integrate all of *her* heritages more fully: "It's allowed me to be all that I am—a whole person. When I was growing up, I'd often have to explain myself to other people in parts, especially at school. And those parts weren't consolidated into one person. Now I don't have to talk about myself in a fragmented manner—I feel I'm a whole and complete person when talking about myself as someone who is biracial."

This is not to imply that multiracial teenagers and young adults who have succeeded at developing a healthy multiracial identity during these years want to limit their social interactions to mixed-race groups. Not in the least. Nishimura points out that in the course of her interviews, mixed-race group members emphasized that the value of their mixed-race student group was that it was "a support group, a touchstone from which they could draw strength and reaffirmation as they moved out to participate in other campus activities. One of the clearest and strongest themes to emerge . . . was that the multiracial students had no desire to isolate themselves from other students or promote multiracial exclusivity."

Indeed, many of my young adult interviewees reported feeling quite good about their tendency to *not* affiliate with only one group—be it monoracial or multiracial. Many reported feeling especially good about having become a bridge between different groups of people who might not otherwise have come together. Often they expressed great pride and confidence about this role. Looking back from their twenties, some even reported a feeling of moral achievement at now being able to stand in a place where they are able to have empathy for all. As Bethany Fry (Native American/Italian/Caucasian) puts it, "In a way I'm inside both groups and I'm able to help both sides to understand the other's point of view." Others report feeling an enhanced authenticity as individuals as they choose to be surrounded by people they like for who they are—and who like them for who they are, too. They talk about having emerged from adolescence with a greater sense of what makes for a genuine friendship or a love relationship. They have arrived at self-appreciation; they have achieved self-integration.

Naomi Reed (African American/Russian Jewish/Caucasian) sums up this feeling—shared by many multiracial youth—eloquently: "I think being multiracial has allowed me to see things from both sides of the color line, opening my mind to differences of all types so that I don't prejudge anything or anyone. It has allowed me to see love for what it really is, which is something I think a lot of people miss out on."

There is little more that we as parents can ask for but to have our teenagers emerge from adolescence with not only an appreciation for all of their cultural backgrounds and an integrated multiracial identity, but also with a deepened awareness of each person's humanity. This awakening will enrich their own life experiences, as well as the communities we all live in.

CHAPTER FIVE

The Big Picture

My Community, My School, My Culture

THE MOST PRESSING CHALLENGE that confronts our children—feeling authentic, confident and comfortable in their multiracial identity—is impacted not just by each age-related developmental stage, but also by the diversity (or lack of it) in their community, sensitivity (or lack of it) to cultural/multiracial issues in their school environment, and how well we, as their parents, make sure they are both exposed to and immersed in their varied cultural heritages as they come of age.

Consider, for instance, these examples of how home and community setting directly affect a multiracial child's emotional well-being, at any age:

Even when my older son hears a comment that singles him out in some way—"Austin's mommy is black and his daddy is white!"—he doesn't pay any attention because he's in a community and a school where so many kids come from different-race parents. He just thinks, 'So, what's your point? And . . . ?' To him, being mixed is just *normal* because everyone around him is mixed.
—Jason Sackett (Caucasian), clinical social worker
and father of two Caribbean American/Jewish/Caucasian boys

My middle school was *not* diverse, but I grew up in Southern California, which was very multicultural. We not only had all the races, there were also a lot of other multiracial Japanese/Caucasian families. Living there, being half Japanese and half white was *not* something really different. That really helped to keep me from feeling like I was really weird, despite all the difficult things that were happening to me at school.

—Jamie Doyle (Japanese/Irish/Caucasian)

Perhaps it is obvious to say that when multiracial children are able to see themselves reflected in their own community, they have a broader array of positive multiracial role models, a greater comfort level with their own identity and a strong, internalized sense that it's okay to be racially "different." Conversely, when such diversity is lacking (as in many American communities and schools), it can impact our child in myriad ways.

Consider this transracially adopted young person's reflections on growing up as the only person of Latino heritage in the neighborhood: "I've often wondered why we didn't move to an area where I wasn't the only Latino kid around who wasn't a farm worker or somebody's maid. I don't know how it would have been if there had been other kids who looked like me around while I was growing up, but I think many things would have been easier. I never knew what it felt like not to be different . . . until I went to college and found other Latinos. My life is so different now, and I am much happier. If you really care so much about me, why didn't you move?"[1]

Psychologist Beverly Daniel Tatum, Ph.D., author of *"Why Are All the Black Kids Sitting Together in the Cafeteria?" And Other Conversations About Race,* points out that if a mixed-race black child grows up without "positive ties to a black community it will be very difficult for the child to value his or her heritage. There will be no buffer against the negative messages about blackness in the wider society, posing a threat to the child's developing self-esteem."[2]

Several studies bear out how a feeling of disconnect from one's minority culture impacts a child. For instance, one study examined extensive data from the 1990 Census (which provided parents with a "check only one race" choice) to determine what influenced parents to identify their biracial Asian/Caucasian children as Asian *or* Caucasian. It found that the presence of other Asian families in the community played a significant role in how parents identified their children, *especially* among third-generation Asian families whose parents had immigrated several generations ago, and whose links to Asian culture were thus more diluted. Indeed, the longer an Asian family had lived in America, the *less* likely parents were to identify their biracial children as Asian *unless* they resided in an area with a significant Asian

American population.³ (However, this finding can be extrapolated only so far. Because the 1990 Census directed parents to choose *one* race for their child, we can't assume that parents who chose a "white" label for their children didn't, in day to day life, actually encourage their children to identify as biracial.)

The lack of a diverse community has quantifiable effects on multiracial children. According to psychologist Maria Root (Filipino/Chinese/Spanish-Portuguese/German/Irish/Caucasian), Ph.D., editor of *The Multiracial Experience: Racial Borders As the New Frontier*, children are more likely to color code negative behavior in others "if the family is isolated from other interracial families or lives in a homogeneous community." (If, for example, their mom, who is Native American, is emotionally unstable, they "color code" her behavior by telling themselves the *reason* she can be cruel is *because* she's Native American.) Biracial children who grow up in largely white communities or attend largely white schools are more likely to identify *themselves* as solely white. Indeed, living in an area—and engaging in a lifestyle—that does not reflect or incorporate a child's ethnic heritage is "akin to the exposure biracial children [have] had who were cut off from white families and primarily exposed to the extended family of color and a community of color."⁴

Beverly Daniel Tatum stresses how important it is that all multiracial children—regardless of their mixed heritage—see other children who are *like them*. She points out, "White parents, especially, may tend to undervalue the importance of being able to see oneself reflected in one's environment. You simply can't underestimate the value of that for your multiracial child." Clearly, raising our children in a fully diverse area provides them with an intrinsic sense of being "normal," which is instrumental to their inherent sense of self-worth.

And If You *Don't* Live in a Diverse Community?

Although the civil rights movement of the 1960s helped integrate communities and schools across America, many multiracial families—although diverse within their own homes—do not live in highly diverse areas. Our family is, alas, one of them. Well aware of the benefits of being in an integrated neighborhood and community, I struggle every day with the fact that, after having lived as a family in the highly multiracial (and international) Tokyo, we are now settled in a lovely small city outside the suburbs of Washington, D.C. Although this town provides every other factor we value in community life, it is hardly a Mecca of multiculturalism, much less multiracialism.

Long before we had children—and after college and work experiences that took us each to many other states and countries—my husband, Zenji, and I (not yet acquainted with each other) both settled in our town. We met and married here and began to make a life—in my hometown and near his—near extended family and treasured friends. We became entrenched in community life. We had one child and then another. Each of them, in turn, began to make their own deep ties to grandparents, aunts and uncles and, for my son, who is, at this writing, eight, his own treasured friends.

Still, having immersed myself in the emerging research and having experienced the multiracial wonder of the ex-pat community of Tokyo, where so many families *were* multiracial, I miss living "a multiracial life" outside the four walls of our own home. And we worry over the cost our kids will pay for missing that influence. Shortly after we returned from Japan a few years back, my son, Christian, and I began to have a series of small conversations that brought home to me how deep *his* feeling of longing was for a more culturally diverse setting.

The first conversation (one of many I've recorded in our family journal) occurred when he was five, shortly after our move stateside:

"I wish I could control the world!" he told me one night at bedtime, his tone wistful.

"If you could control the world, what would you do?" I asked.

His answer was immediate, his eyes brimming: "I'd crash Japan into Annapolis!"

Another time, at six, his best Japanese friend—with whom he'd played since infancy—moved back to Japan. The morning after our good-bye party for his friend's family, I went in to wake Christian for school. As I gently shook his shoulder, before he even wakened, he broke into ceaseless, wordless sobs. Immediately I knew the cause. I sat with him, rocking his body as he clung to me.

"Is it Ken-chan's leaving?" I asked. He nodded his head and I wiped his tears with my hand. I had never seen my son engulfed by such sadness before, as if his heart were flooding forth a feeling of loss he could not name or contain.

Some months later, I gently broached the topic: "Is it ever hard not having many other families around like ours? Or kids who look a lot like you?" I asked.

"Pretty hard, Mom," he said. "I have friends like me who live in other places but I never get to see them."

"Is it hard because you miss seeing *your* Japanese/American friends, or because there aren't many kids around us who look a lot like you?"

"Both, Mom," he told me. "Both."

More recently, at seven and a half, knowing that I had interviewed dozens of people for this book, he asked me if *he* was going to be in my book, too.

"Do you want to be?" I asked.

"Okay, I guess," he said. "Are you going to *interview* me?"

"Sure!" I said, sitting him in my interview chair. "So, Mr. Nakazawa," I began, "how do you feel about being multiracial?"

"Do you mean being Japanese and Caucasian?" he asked.

"Umhumm," I said.

"Well," he started, as I typed to keep up: "I feel like any other kid except I feel a little different. It seems like I'm the only one at school that's like that, and it doesn't really matter to me—all that matters is that I'm healthy and it seems like everything is normal. But I feel like there needs to be more multiracial kids around me. I feel like nothing is different except the little stuff like I'm Japanese and it's kind of cool to be Japanese. I don't have my friend's brains so I don't know what they think. I see lots of multiracial families at festivals and church and when we're with my cousins. And every time we go to the baseball game and see the Orioles play Seattle and see the Japanese hitter Ichiro, I see lots of multiracial families in the seats near our seats and I feel good when I see them. I feel so good, I feel great. And I feel so great about it I'm going to explode because it means there *are* lots of other kids like me."

A few weeks ago, he came home from school noticeably glum, his lunch untouched. In a snuggle-up conversation he confided that his "boring" packed lunches (which avoid heavily processed and packaged foods that seem to worsen his asthma) were bugging him to no end. Suddenly he burst into tears. "I just don't want the other kids to think I'm different *in a really big way,* Mom!" he cried, holding me tight. As I held him, I was both startled and newly concerned—did his fear of being different really revolve around asthma and his lunch box? Or was the truer source the fact that he is one of the few multiracial kids in his grade? *Lunches* I could fix. But how could I fix the latter?

These conversations weigh heavily on me. We are entrenched in our community and we feel our familial roots have an intangible benefit we are loath to abandon. We also know that diversity (not just having all races but other multiracial children and individuals whose phenotype mirrors that of our son and our daughter) in our community is equally essential for our child's emotional-well being. Where to from here?

This conundrum has led me to closely examine the issue of community, diversity and parenting the multiracial child. If a major move is not in the best interest of our family, what other factors can we set in place to ameliorate the negative effects of having our kids grow up in a less than ideally diverse setting? And can these other factors make up for what a child is missing by not being immersed in a diverse community? I wanted to know. I *needed* to know.

And so I began to ask interviewees about their experiences with growing up in diverse versus nondiverse cities, towns, neighborhoods, communities and schools. To be sure, while many of my interviewees cited the diversity of their hometown or neighborhood as a salient factor in helping them or their children feel comfortable with who they were, it also became apparent that many seemingly well-adjusted and confident multiracial young adults with whom I spoke were *not* raised in a highly diverse setting. Indeed, some of my most well-adjusted interviewees—confident, secure and self-realized young people—reported being the only person of mixed race (and often one of very few people of color, period) in their immediate community. How, I wondered, could it be simultaneously true that although one of the most important factors for ensuring our child's well-being is community/school diversity, many children who grew up being phenotypically "different" in their immediate surroundings did not *at all feel* different?

Over time, a kind of pattern began to emerge among my interviewees that shed important light on this question. It became clear that both of these sets of kids who were thriving so beautifully had one thing in common: parents who willingly accepted and met the challenge of carefully, thoughtfully preparing their multiracial children to grow up emotionally healthy in a world that all too often projects its confusion and awkward feelings about mixed race individuals onto them. These were *not* parents who "hushed up" racial/multiracial issues. They understood that this preparation meant establishing a wide-open forum for discussing their children's multiracial identity from the get-go; providing their children with appropriate possible labels for their identity without forcing a label on them; practicing well thought out answers to tough stranger/peer questions to help their children confidently defend themselves in a society that makes gross assumptions based on physical appearance; helping their children understand the dynamics of race in America while at the same time *protecting* them from being wounded by racism; and exposing their kids to others of mixed-race heritage through as many means as possible, which for some kids, but certainly not all, included living in a diverse environment.

Kids who reported having had such parental concern, involvement and support talked passionately about their parents having given them these "gifts." They overwhelmingly seemed to feel that this process of highly aware, informed and interactive parenting made the biggest difference in their lives as multiracial youths.

This is not to say it is wholly apparent that such mindful parenting is sufficient in and of itself to overcome the clear disadvantage of not living in a highly diverse setting among people who are racially similar. But I have interviewed many, many multiracial youth who seem to prove that very aware parenting can ameliorate—to a surprisingly *large* degree—the negative effects of not growing up in a specifically multicultural/multiracial community.

But, not surprisingly, there are more pieces to the puzzle than this. In the course of my talks with multiracial teens and young adults, one seemingly ancillary factor emerged so repeatedly that it began to seem a *central* element in helping our multiracial kids grow up with a secure sense of self.

The Benefits of One Familiar Locale

In discussing how some interviewees did quite well growing up in nondiverse environments, a number of young people felt it had been enormously helpful to them that they had known their neighborhood friends from when they were quite small (e.g., preschool friends they had moved on to grade school with; sons and daughters of parents' close friends with whom they had grown up—friends who had totally accepted them for who they were from the sandbox onward). When interviewees reported having bonded with a small group of friends (even if these friends were not racially diverse) *before* the age at which real racial awareness dawned, the natural spillover of security garnered from such familiarity (this unquestioned acceptance from one's peer group regardless of racial makeup) seemed to have a protective effect on that multiracial child's sense of normalcy and belonging to that peer group and also contributed to a feeling of naturally "fitting in" with peers in general.

On the other hand, when that long-term familiarity with friends and community was missing because a family frequently moved or changed schools, multiracial children experienced more difficulties.

George Meyers (Japanese/Caucasian), age 24, reveals that "to this day I regret I didn't go to the same elementary school my neighborhood friends went to. It would have been a totally different experience for me. Even though it wasn't a diverse group, being half Japanese was not an issue in the slightest with them and it wasn't an issue with their parents. We had all known each other since we were very young. We had always been great friends and I always felt totally accepted by them. I was very close to those kids."

Once George did go off to a different elementary school, as well as to a Japanese school on Saturdays, he recalls, "I could gradually feel myself losing touch with the kids in my neighborhood—and yet that had been my base. Losing that base hurt. As those friendships disappeared all I had left were the kids at my schools who didn't know me and who kept me at arm's length and that was not a fun time."

Similarly, Matt Kelley (Korean/Caucasian), age 23, recalls, "In eighth grade, I switched to a private school in Seattle, where I didn't have my same small community where I was already known. I didn't have my old peer group. People didn't know anything about me and so they began to make associations about me based on what I looked like. And I didn't look like the black kids or the white kids or the Asian kids." Kelley says that as he was quickly inundated with "What are you?" questions, he felt suddenly set adrift in this unfamiliar peer group. His sense of himself began to shift from feeling, "I was no different from any of my neighborhood friends," to feeling "I'd been plucked up and put somewhere totally new where I was completely hyperexposed and the weird one."

On the other hand, for multiracial children whose families stayed in one familiar locale and built and maintained emotional connections to a few friends they made quite early on in life, another picture emerges entirely.

Rochelle Brown (African American/Caucasian), age 17, says, "I think I have the most friendly street. There are so many kids running around all over the place. And even though it's not very mixed, we're all friends. I've known all these kids since I was two—I *really* know these kids—and race is really secondary. We're *friends.*"

Carol Franks-Randall, Ed.D. (African American), a school superintendent in New York State, whose Caucasian husband is stepdad to her two black daughters, talks about how their girls grew up in "a very nondiverse neighborhood area. But we never moved. Our kids never had to move from their house or change their groups of friends. There were no new neighborhoods, no new towns. We wanted them to have that stability. I think giving them the stability of staying in one place helped compensate for the fact that we were in a nondiverse locale."

Carol's daughter, Jennifer Franks (African American), age 22, talks about how meaningful this stability was for her. "I can't think of any more than one interracial couple, other than my mom and dad, in our area. And yet we just made one connection at a time with other families in our community, just as any other family would. People liked us for who we were. We *knew* them, and they *knew* us."

Still, this comfort of being *known* in one's community and the feeling of security it provides our child with—because it sends a clear message that emotional ties supercede racial differences—only benefits a child if we as parents have also worked to bring diversity and a deep consciousness of our child's heritages into their life through other active means. The first without the second is hardly enough to give our children the strong emotional legs they will need to stand on in life. Indeed, children *particularly* need to be involved in a dialogue about their multiracialness—and be actively involved with *all* their cultures in an *intentional* way—when they reside in a nondiverse environment. Otherwise, our children are likely to face a devastating shock when and if they move and leave the protective, familiar environment of their safe-haven enclave and enter the world at large.

Moving from one community to another often forces racially mixed individuals to renegotiate their racial identity amid peers and neighbors, as the way people view *them* changes. Especially if, as they grew up, their racial identity was negotiated for them—even if indirectly—by their families (e.g., everyone knew their dad, the doctor, so, as kids, they never faced race questions because of their dad's elevated status in the community). However, if that family moves to a new community, or if the child enters a new school or later leaves home for a job or college, she may have to negotiate her identity in that new environment on her own[5]—something she sorely lacks practice in doing. Having lost that familiar group who sees her for who she is, regardless of race, it is suddenly doubly important that she has been immersed in both of her cultures and has been prepared by her parents to articulate her identity confidently, competently and comfortably to others.

Linda Parker (African American/Native American/Czech/Caucasian), age 22, reveals how she experienced just such a shock when leaving her "almost entirely white community in Vermont." Growing up, she says, "there were maybe only three nonwhite people in my school. It was *not* a racially diverse place. Still, I never felt that anyone viewed me as different. It was like, 'Oh, you're Catholic, you're like everyone else.' There was such a great advantage to living in that small community. It was so personal and intimate; the sense of *being* a community was so strong. I joke that my mom was so active in everything that she was the untitled mayoress of our town. We knew *everyone*."

However, when Linda went on to college, she had to negotiate her racial identity for herself—and she was not at all prepared for the shock that race seemed to suddenly inform everything. She talks about going for one potential job interview with a supervisor for a summer position. Although they had spoken for two hours on the phone prior to meeting, once they met his immediate response was, "I had no idea this is what you looked like! I wasn't expecting that."

Linda admits she sometimes finds herself wishing she "could go back to being blissfully ignorant of any racial barriers. Sometimes it seems that all people see is color. It seems like the more aware I am of how big an issue my appearance is, the less confident I am in my abilities as a person, a female and a professional." The sudden jolt she experienced when moving out of her protected environment—one in which her racial identity had been negotiated for her by her family—and into "the real world" took a toll on her self-identity as a multiracial individual.

But when our children have been immersed in an ongoing conversation about being mixed and exposed to their diverse cultures, even a drastic move does not shatter their sense of self. Such a move may present new information that helps shape and inform their view of the world, but it does not *shatter* their worldview.

Carol Franks-Randall's daughter, Jennifer Franks (African American), age 22, says, "It's startling when I look back on how homogeneous and nondiverse the community I grew up in was. In our area only 4 percent of people were black. I was very accepted by everyone growing up so it was fine. But it was a big transition from high school to college. My university, Harvard, is a very diverse place. And I enjoy that. It seems very natural for there to be a lot of different races of people together in one place. I'd love to settle in a place where there is as much diversity as there is here."

Asked what helped her achieve such a deep comfort level when she moved into a diverse college milieu—despite having grown up amid a nondiverse group of people—she says, "My *parents*. The fact that my parents, [black and white] were married was just very indicative of their having a very open nature. Growing up, I would watch my dad responding to people's questions and the way he dealt with it helped us deal with those questions. When questions came up he let everyone know, 'Yeah, I'm their dad. So what?' Our aura as a family was that 'We're *not* weird. We're a mixed-race family *and* we're a completely normal family,' and that's how we felt and that's how we are. My parents made it clear to us that not only was that our perception of ourselves, it was the perception we *expected* others to have of us. If they didn't, we just assumed there was something wrong with *their* view of the world."

In a *best-case* scenario, multiracial kids will have the following critical elements in their lives:

1. A diverse neighborhood/community environment that includes a significant number of people of all races and widespread acceptance of all races, as well as multiracial families and individuals similar to our child.
2. Aware, informed and involved parents who know how to talk to their children and imbue them with confidence about being multiracial and about their family constellation, instilling in them a core belief that any incidents that may occur reflect something askew with society, not with them. As Carol Franks-Randall (African American), puts it, "Parenting children in a multiracial family takes another level of attention compared to what you'd need to give in a nonmultiracial family.

If you want to be successful as a parent and as a family then you have to be sure to give it the care and attention it deserves."

3. A familiar, consistent group of friends with whom a child develops strong emotional bonds, before racial awareness and a playground culture of cruelty—which all too often single out children who are racially different—converge. In this sense, parents encourage their children to establish rich friendships in their community setting from preschool onward with peers who know them for *who* they are and with whom they feel understood and appreciated as an individual, regardless of race, over the long term.

Still, we cannot always, in every family situation, provide all three of these elements. Parents sometimes have to take or keep jobs in nondiverse settings for the economic well-being of the family. As Mark Kenney, Ed.D., N.C.C., coauthor of *Counseling Multiracial Families,* puts it, "You have to work with the best you can under the circumstances. It's not a matter of having every perfect factor in place as much as it is about how well you compensate for what you *don't* have."

The factor that may fall farthest outside of our control is whether we live in a diverse neighborhood/community. Which begs the question once more: In what other ways can we augment our children's understanding of diversity and self-appreciation of their multiracial identity if such diversity is not apparent on the sidewalks of their community?

Bringing Children's Culture into Their Day-to-Day Lives

To say that it is critical for mixed-race families to put themselves and their kids in situations where they have interactions with those of other races would be a gross understatement. Without such exposure, our children can't help but feel "alien"—*especially* if they reside in a nonculturally diverse area.

Because it is essential to our children's self-esteem to have a dual cultural identity that integrates all of their genetic and cultural heritages and because we know that mature mental health depends on *accurate* self-knowledge,[6] we must do whatever extra legwork is necessary to expose our kids to their varied cultures, and to the world's diversified cultures in general, as well as fully support them in their exploration of these cultures.

Researchers suggest that multiracial children whose parents help them achieve this "bicultural competence" demonstrate greater creativity and flexibility of thought because they're able to use their knowledge of more than one cultural approach to life's challenges when they face demanding situations. Children who are raised in two cultures, research suggests, can also be expected to have higher levels of self-esteem, have greater understanding of others, and attain a higher level of achievement than multiracial or trans-racially adopted children in monoracial cultures.[7]

Nancy Brown (Caucasian), president of the Association of MultiEthnic Americans and mother of Nicole and Rochelle (African American/ Caucasian), explains how this rings true for her: "My girls have gained so much by being part of two unique cultures and heritages. They have experienced all the ethnic foods and cultural events that are part of being German and Jewish—including having had a Jewish education and having been Bat Mitzvahed. *And* they have experienced all that goes with being black Baptist and Methodist and rural down-home Texan, from their father's culture. They've had so much exposure to so many diverse environments that they're now completely comfortable in many different arenas."

At the other extreme, a 24-year-old African American/Caucasian young adult reveals her anxiety about not possessing the cultural knowledge of black or biracial individuals who've grown up having been exposed to their black culture: "I'm 24 years old. I feel like I ought to know more [about African American history and culture] than I do now . . . even in social situations where we're having discussions, I'm afraid [a monoracial black] will find out that I don't know about black history and say that I'm not really black. I feel all the time that I'm scrambling to catch up—to get up to speed with everybody else, in terms of what I should know."[8]

Or, take Cassandra McGowen (Chinese, adopted by Caucasian parents, and mom of two Chinese/Caucasian daughters), who expresses deep regret that, "culturally, I have no Chinese history. It's one of these things where I don't even see myself as Chinese unless I look at myself in the mirror. There is literally nothing to clue me in to who I am unless I look at myself, and then it's like, 'Oh, Whoops!'" Now, as a mom, Cassandra feels, her kids "are at a disadvantage because I don't have any Chinese culture to pass on to them. It's the one big thing I'm missing. I do Chinese New Year and cook some Chinese food, but that's not enough. I even went to China to try to explore the culture but it wasn't fun at all; it only made me more conscious that I don't know anything about it; that I don't have a sense of history there; that there is no tangible background for me to give to my kids, and I regret that. I think I'm going to have to go on my own bicultural journey before I can take my children on one."

In some cases, because a child's cultural past is not fully explored and supported, biracial children may feel the need to overcompensate for not being fully one race by "acting more black" (or white) depending on which group's acceptance they are seeking, cautions psychologist Beverly Daniel Tatum. Tatum tells the story of one biracial nine-year-old who lived in a black community. Not having ties to her white culture, she acted "blacker than black" in order to prove she had a *nonwhite* identity. "She lived with more pressure than any child should have to deal with," emphasizes Tatum.[9]

All of which adds up to this: one of *our* achievements, as parents, must be to provide our kids with substantial positive exposure to all their cultural heritages. Here is a roadmap for helping to secure bicultural competence for your child—and your family.

Embrace Your Family's Ethnic Culture(s) as a Whole Family

Inclusion of our children's varied cultural backgrounds should not be for their sake alone. Helping your children become bicultural means integrating their ethnic culture into your *family's* lifestyle and culture. "It's important to make your whole family bicultural," advises psychologist Willie B. Garrett. "If 'cultural education' is focused on your child alone, and made something unique to them, it may have a distancing effect." Garrett gives the example of families who "don't talk about cultural issues at all and then send their kids to Korean camp for a few days once a year." If it is a child's sole exposure, and if she is the only family member exposed, she will feel singled out for being different from the rest of her *family*. A child who is singled out for special cultural attention in a way that others in the home are not— dressed in silk Chinese pajamas, sent to special cultural camps and so on— may feel objectified in her own home. Far better to send the message, "*we* are a bicultural family," making certain our children know, not only are they multiracial, so is their whole family.

A number of individuals in multiracial families shared with me how their family had succeeded in sending that message. Susan Fu (Caucasian), mother of three biracial Chinese/Caucasian children, says, "Having my children has made me interested in everything Chinese. I have developed a love of another culture. I read everything I can about China—from the cultural revolution to modern-day events. I just can't get enough of it. It's been mind-expanding, world-expanding and personally broadening for me—and I think it makes me a better mom to my kids to be able to teach them and explain to them where they've come from."

Fu adds that she and her husband have traveled to China four times. On their last trip, they took along their eldest child, Alex, who was then eight years old. "We got to make Chinese pottery with this famous Chinese potter, and we looked at so much history in the museums. Just *being there* with all the Chinese people helped Alex to identify himself with both his cultures."

Bethany Fry (Native American/Italian/Caucasian), age 24, explains that "because I grew up in a nondiverse area, I didn't really have any friends nearby who were Native Americans. But we spent part of each summer in Montana. We'd have pow wows and dances and we'd go to as many art festivals and cultural events on the reservations as we could. I liked being out there with my Native American family; it felt good. At home, the rest of the year, we did a lot of Italian stuff. I feel like by having two cultures I get twice as much culture. I have broader experiences in life. It feels like a richer self."

Kelley Kenney (African American), coauthor of *Counseling Multiracial Families,* says she and her husband (Caucasian) provide "lots of cultural opportunities for our family. Last weekend my daughters and I went to a festival where a woman was teaching African heritage dancing, drumming and the whole bit. I was able to tell my girls how their grandma had involved me in African dance when I was a little girl and that I had performed. They asked how old I was when I danced and did Grandma know African dance, too. . . . Later we each got up during dinner to show some of the steps we'd learned. The whole experience was so rich." Kenney explains that their approach to being a bicultural family is to "put it all out there on the table that Mommy is of African-American heritage and Daddy is of Italian heritage and as a family we're made up of all of these heritages, though at various times we might celebrate one thing at one time, and another culture at another time. We are trying to widen their knowledge base to help our girls possess that fluidity of racial identity that is so critical to their success in life."

Again, living a bicultural life is a more challenging endeavor when we don't live in a diverse environment. (Indeed, says Garrett, for some families who live in nondiverse areas, he has had to "work out diversity plans" for exposing them to more ethnic influences.) For my own family, this "plan" involves scouting out in advance what events are coming where and when—musical festivals, cultural fairs, craft workshops or special exhibits— and traveling the hour or two necessary to nearby metropolitan cities to attend them. My kids consider it a given in their lives that once or twice a month we pack the car with snacks and lunches and head as a family into Washington, D.C., or Baltimore for a special Japanese festival or concert or play or craft workshop. These special adventures coupled with time spent having ethnic family dinners and celebrations, as well as family get-togethers with our children's multiracial cousins—and always having books, videos, costumes and toys in our home that reflect Japanese culture and their biracial heritage in particular—have, we hope, helped create a strong yet fluid bicultural environment for our son and daughter.

This is not to imply that casting our cultural net as a family should begin and end with exploring only our ethnic cultures. Encouraging our children to celebrate their own ethnic heritage necessitates that they internalize the importance of valuing *all* cultures. Teaching kids to value their cultural identity has to reach, as one mom puts it, "beyond simply giving a brown doll to a brown child, or teaching her only about the wonders of her historical country . . . to me, adding only [our daughter's ethnic culture would be] just as bad as having only 'white' culture. We want to communicate embracing people of all colors."[10]

Redundant as the idea might at first seem—given the overwhelmingly white culture in which we live—this embracing of all cultures includes one's white culture. Willie B. Garrett expressly points out that too often "white parents ignore the *white* side of their kid's heritage. Because *they* feel a sense of shame about the history of racism in America they send their child the message that they shouldn't feel good about *being* white. It's so important for the white parent to know it's okay to feel good about *being* white. If their child is white, too, that child should be encouraged to feel good about that side of them and to know that there are many, many good white people, too." This means also exploring the white European ethnic culture in your family—be it Polish, Danish, German, Sicilian—to help your child have a rich sense of all their cultural backgrounds.

Look into Special Camps and Other Programs for Kids

While it is important that the entire family partake in any cultural exploration as a unit, this does not preclude *also* having your child attend a special camp or summer program that further enriches her understanding of her cultural heritage. Also, consider an immersion experience for your child such as living or visiting abroad in a cultural exchange program or hosting a cultural exchange student from one of your child's ethnic cultures.

Consider Giving Your Children a Culturally Meaningful Name or Nickname

Although we named our son Christian, which speaks to both his British and Scandinavian backgrounds as well as his Japanese heritage (Chris-*chan* means "dear beloved child Chris" in Japanese), and although his last name (Nakazawa) is certainly ethnic (meaning the valley between two mountains), we did not provide him with a Japanese middle name. Now that he is eight, and I am so much more aware of how integral our Japanese culture is to our family life and identity, I regret this. When we lived in Tokyo, we discovered that many interracial families had given both English and Japanese first names to their children. When they spoke to their child in Japanese, they addressed him with his Japanese name; when they spoke to him in English, they used his English name. Some moms felt this helped their bilingual child cue into "switching" languages more smoothly in their brain.

Jamie Mihoko Doyle (Japanese/Irish/Caucasian), age 23, discusses how integral her name has been to her biracial self-concept over the years. "When I was a child I was nicknamed 'Mimi'—from the 'mi' in my first name, 'Jamie,' and for the 'mi' in my middle name, 'Mihoko.' By calling me 'Mimi' my parents emphasized that I shared both heritages. Later, in high school, I decided I only wanted to be called Jamie. But when I got to college, I realized how important having my Japanese name was to me. It's something from my Japanese culture that I can *never* lose."

Give Your Children an Opportunity to Learn Their "Second" Language

Many multiracial individuals express deep regret regarding *not* being bilingual to the extent that they are bicultural. Cassandra McGowen (transracially adopted Chinese parent of two Chinese/Caucasian girls) relates how her "biggest regret is that I don't know Chinese. I feel so stupid in Chinatown when I don't understand a word they say and they keep talking to me. I would have liked to have learned Chinese."

Even very young children may express the desire to learn the language that accompanies their bicultural identity. Agnes Horowitz (Caucasian) discusses how her transracially adopted daughter (Chinese), at the age of three, heard another girl in her nursery school speaking fluent Mandarin. Agnes recalls: "Maggie asked me, 'What is she talking about?' We talked about how Mandarin is another language. Then, a few days later, Maggie said, 'I want to speak Chinese, too.' At first, I thought, she's just a baby, she doesn't mean it. But she kept asking and asking. So we started taking Chinese classes. When I saw how motivated she was, I just jumped in there. Now I go to classes with her."

Gather Regularly with Both Sides of Your Extended Interracial Family

If children primarily see only one side of their multiracial family and have little to no contact with extended family members (grandparents, aunts, uncles, cousins) of their other racial background, the lens through which they view their racial identity may become skewed, making it more difficult for them to attain a healthy biracial identity as they come of age.[11] Just as importantly, they may miss out on the rich, intimate experience of learning about their cultural past from grandparents and other family members who can share memories, holiday traditions, folk tales and the like, all of which paint a rich, visual portrait of faraway lands that intrigue and educate our children about their ethnic heritage all the more. In our home, we are so grateful for our semimonthly dinners with my husband's parents. My husband's father, born in Japan seventy-odd years ago, made his way through medical school in Japan after World War II, triumphing through the difficult transition from catered-to eldest son of a distinguished family to penniless medical student who emigrated to America on a scholarship to finish his education. His tales of long-lost family castles, Samurai clans and survival in the mountains during the war entrance my children, drawing them closer to their Japanese heritage. After the dinner dishes are cleared, he draws kanji (Japanese characters) and does calligraphy with our kids, regaling them with stories of his youth. What might seem an intangible cultural past becomes visceral through their grandfather's eyes. Meanwhile, their grandmother, actively involved in Japanese/American cultural exchange programs, organizes Japanese dance and musical concerts, which they adore.

Involve Your Family in Interracial Family Organizations

Counselors Mark Kenney, M.Ed., N.C.C. (Caucasian), and Kelley Kenney, Ed.D. (African American), talk about how important their involvement in a local group of multiracial families has been to their daughters, providing their two biracial girls an opportunity to be around and socialize with other kids and families who resemble them, especially given that they do not live in a diverse area. "They need that time with other kids to create a frame of reference of acceptance," emphasizes Mark Kenney. "That way, when and if they are in an environment that is nonaccepting, or if someone says or does something that is rejecting, they have a positive frame of reference—a place inside which they can point to and know it *can't* be about them because they have this other setting in which they *are* completely accepted. And that can help to decrease the hurt."

Louise Lazare (Caucasian), mother of eight adopted children, six of whom are multiracial, advises, "The most important thing you can give your kids is access to other families like yours."

Nancy Brown (Caucasian), president of the Association of MultiEthnic Americans (AMEA) and cofounder of a local group, Multiracial Americans of Southern California (MASC), couldn't agree more. She recalls how she started MASC to help provide this normalcy—this frame of acceptance—for her biracial African American/Caucasian daughters. "We started the group because we felt it was important not only to help dispel the myths about interracial families but to raise our kids so they could own all parts of their background. We wanted to share the comfort of talking about the issues that come with being in a multiracial family—whether you're transracially adopted, multiracial yourself, or a parent in a multiracial family."

Brown says when people first came to her group, "the most frequent comment I heard was, 'I feel as if I've just come home.'"

Her involvement in starting and running multiracial organizations had an immeasurable effect on her daughters as well. Nicole, age 22, recalls, "We always had all these wonderful families and friends—through my mom's group—coming in and out our door; families who were all kinds of crazy combinations. So even though my girlfriends at school weren't mixed I grew up in a very mixed world. I never felt I was the only one." Her younger sister Rochelle, age 17, expresses a similar sentiment: "My mom's involvement with MASC made me conscious of a community like me, of *my* community."

In a sense, children whose parents make the effort to be involved in—or even found—multiracial organizations seem to absorb not only what it means to be multiracial but, moreover, to grasp, as if by osmosis, that being in a multiracial family is as normal as not being in one.

Does School Meet Your Children's Needs?

Among the most crushing experiences related to me by young multiracial individuals involved not only their struggle to feel "normal" within nondiverse school environments, but also to be understood and not rigidly categorized by teachers, whose positions of authority gave their actions added weight. Several interviewees reported interfacing with teachers who emphatically told them they could not have an ethnicity in addition to their heritage of color (e.g., they could not be of white heritage if they were "black"). Some teachers held stereotypical assumptions that black/white multiracial kids would underperform or that Asian/white kids would outperform because of gross stereotypes attached to students of those minority heritages.

Nancy Brown (Caucasian) feels too little is said about "the level of anxiety and fear that parents in multiracial families experience about school environment. We have to ask ourselves: 'what is the environment going to be like for my kids? Is their biracial heritage going to be respected and acknowledged? And what do I have to do to make that happen?' It's a very significant issue and it's not something monoracial families have to go through." Brown recalls that when her younger daughter (African

American/Caucasian) entered school more than a decade ago, "Although I knew the school did a great job paying attention to diversity issues, there was a new teacher and I was concerned. We went in on the first day and saw that this teacher had put a banner around the room with different sign language signs on it—and all of the hands were of different subtle shades. I knew, when I saw that, my daughter was in good hands." Nevertheless, Nancy says, "I always made sure, no matter what, to inform every elementary school teacher that my child was being raised to claim both her heritages and considered herself multiracial."

Ensuring that our children are in good hands in their school setting requires choosing, wherever possible, a school that offers not only diversity among its students but a multicultural curriculum that is attuned to the issues multiracial children face. But making an informed school choice means first educating ourselves about what a strong diversity program should offer, and what a culturally sensitive classroom should look like.

This can be tricky, especially given that the current widespread push toward a more "multicultural" classroom often has little or nothing to do with being more culturally aware of multiracialness and—in fact—may even make multiracial students feel they are even more the odd birds out in class. Why is this? All too often diversity and "multicultural" programs *confuse* the valid concept of "culture" with the artificial construct of "race." By dividing "cultures" into strict racial categories they teach students that human beings come in five basic flavors, so to speak: Caucasian, African American, Native American, Asian and Latino, thus reinforcing the erroneous idea that we are all genetically different according to race, and therefore being divided into rigid racial categories is natural.

According to psychologist Maria Root, the fact that "multiculturalism in the classroom is still framed within a monoracial paradigm" points to the fact that the very different concepts of culture, ethnicity, nationality and race are often no better understood by teachers and school psychologists than they are by the average person.[12]

How, then, do we begin to ascertain how a school's "diversity program" is taught and determine whether or not it acknowledges and addresses mixed-racialness in its approach to cultural diversity? We can start by asking administrators whether their school works toward meeting certain objectives.

Objectives for Preschool and Elementary School Children

Look closely at a prospective school to examine whether:

- The school has a strong life skills curriculum that shows children through role-playing and discussion sessions how to handle conflict and incidents when they occur.
- Teachers enforce a nonexclusionary policy ("You can't say you can't play") during recess and other free play periods.
- Pictures of students' families, including interracial families, are displayed in the classroom or nearby, reflecting this variety of family compositions. Students see these and other visual images of multiracial people and interracial families in their daily school setting.
- Children are encouraged to learn through artistic play about their own realistic physical characteristics by drawing, painting and making collages with a variety of flesh-tone colors to help illuminate natural differences in a positive manner. By using paints or food coloring, for example, students might mix colors to match the true shades they see around them in skin color, hair, eyes, etc. Or they might experiment with different shades of the color red to illustrate the tremendous varieties that exist within categories.[13]
- Teachers and administrators welcome parental input and involvement on issues of concern to parents—whether it's making sure there are pictures on the wall that reflect their child's unique identity, having parents teach about their child's unique customs, country or heritage, or suggesting teachers bring children together to talk through any negative incidents that may occur.

Objectives for Every School: Elementary, Middle or High

It is important to know that your child will benefit greatly if the administration has set, and met, the following goals:

- Teachers and administrators support biracial children in attaining a multiracial identity and respect the interracial fabric of their families.
- Students are exposed—through stories, photos, books, films and discussions—to how people in this country have, through marriage, suc-

cessfully mixed religions, national heritages and ethnic, racial, political and linguistic differences throughout history; these myriad family constellations are both common and acceptable. Students may work on (and display) their family trees, going as far back as possible and noting the differences of each child's ancestors by nation, language, culture, etc., and showing *each* child's multiple *cultural* heritages (not just African American/Caucasian or Chinese/Caucasian, but also Czech/Norwegian and so on).[14] Such a program not only helps multiracial students see that they are not "different" but helps white children better identify and feel comfortable within our increasingly multicultural society by realizing that they too are of more than one culture, thus eliminating any disconnect Caucasian children may feel with those of multiracial heritage.

One interviewee, Katie Lasso-Gordoa (Chicana/Caucasian), age 28, explained how useful this exercise had been for her. "The idea of others saying I was 'multiracial' used to make me feel angry. But once it was explained to me that all that really meant was 'you are one person with different cultures,' I wasn't angry." Rather than feel that being multiracial made her "different," Katie was able to grasp how *common* being a person of mixed culture was. Although being of a mixed "race" heritage brought up more issues for her when interacting with others than it might have for a person of, say, mixed European heritage, she was able to internalize the reassuring knowledge that, in essence, we *are* all multicultural beings.

- Students are exposed to successful biracial heroes and individuals (e.g., Frederick Douglas, Alexander Dumas, Maria Tallchief, etc.).[15]
- A discussion of genetics introduces the concept that the mixing of genes is a natural, positive and dynamic process (see the discussion of the genetics of race later in this chapter). Ideally, the notion that purity can be very limiting is explored (e.g., 100 percent purebred animals are often subject to disease, and limiting artistic endeavors to only primary colors can reduce creativity).[16]

As one young woman (Japanese/Caucasian) explained, the realization that gene mixing is dynamic in nature helped her revel in her multiracial identity, especially after having struggled through some particularly difficult stages in her racial identity development. (When she was small, she thought "there was a physical line that divided the

Japanese me from the Caucasian me" and quizzed her mom and dad about which half of her was white and which half was Japanese. Later, at her mostly white elementary school, she viewed herself as a white person "who happened to eat a lot of sticky rice," until another student in her diverse middle school called her a "cheating Jap." It hit hard, she says, and caused her to "focus on primarily my Japanese side, completely ignoring my white side." In what is a familiar story among multiracial youth, however, she didn't feel she quite belonged at the Asian students' club, either. Finally, when she came to the realization that she was "neither Japanese nor white, but *both*," she was, she says, invigorated by "the theory of hybrid vigor, [that] a specimen derived from two different species has the strongest traits of both sides."[17]

- Discussions about individual differences are encouraged and supported, and children are exposed to the concept that "different" does not mean "abnormal." For instance, the questions and comments children inevitably make about physical differences among their classmates are used as a segue into a discussion of possible family compositions (adoptive, single parent, interracial, grandparents as caregivers and so on). All children of mixed race heritage are encouraged to share their family stories.[18]
- Children engage in discussions that help them understand the ways in which all children are the same, as well as the commonalties that unite all children, worldwide.[19]
- The school's administration and teachers recognize the need to move beyond conventional diversity curriculum materials, discussions and activities that divide the world into neat, distinct racial and ethnic groups. They recognize that while "multicultural" education is structured to accommodate *all* students in schools, it relies greatly on the notion that there are specific, static racial groups that must be addressed and fails to address multiracial children who cross racial borders by having family from *two or more different* ethnic backgrounds.[20] Students are therefore encouraged to think beyond these five racial groups (Caucasian, Asian, African American, Native American, and Latino), and to consider the richness and diversity within humanity and within the classroom. For this reason, students are never divided into groups based on physical characteristics. Likewise, the school *avoids* curricu-

lum materials that show one child or person representing each standard racial group.

- Family members are encouraged to come into the classroom to share their family culture, celebrations and history.
- Teachers are encouraged, through diversity training workshops and the like, to carefully examine their own attitudes about interracial marriage and biracial children and to consider how these attitudes may affect their interactions with their biracial students.
- The school works to *heterogeneously* group students and encourages heterogeneous socializing, discouraging groups formed exclusively by race. Teachers are conscious of helping students develop a strong personal identity *without* having to put down other groups or develop a them-versus-us mentality. When racially divided social groups do form, teachers recognize the difficult situation the biracial student faces when confronted with choosing only one racial group. Teachers are cognizant of the need to support biracial students as they learn the emotional tools necessary to bridge the gap between racial groups—and to choose friends based on like interests rather than shared physical characteristics.[21]

As one young multiracial woman put it, "Sometimes it seems like teachers are just 'there' and oblivious to what's going on. It means a lot when a *teacher* says to you, 'Hey, I'd really like to know about your experience—about what it's like to be multiracial,' or when they acknowledge the pressures you face."

- And finally, it is critical to find out if the school has updated its registration, application and other forms to include a "check one or more races" directive and no longer uses a directive that instructs parents and students to "check only one race." Ideally, administrators and teachers recognize the psychological validation inherent in being able to define oneself accurately as a multiracial individual—and have worked to institute this change at their school. (The federal government issued guidelines that accompanied the "check one or more races" change to Census 2000, stating that all federal and state agencies that receive federal funding must make this form change prior to January 1, 2003. The Department of Education requested an extension to the deadline to ensure that there would be a uniform means of reporting this data, not only among its 84,000 public schools but also by other Federal agencies and institutions.

By fall 2004 *all* public school districts will be required to allow students to check multiple races to identify themselves.[22] Meanwhile, the race of all multiracial students is still reported by the National Center for Education Statistics (NCES) according to the standard five racial categories. Indeed, according to data conducted in 1995 (the most recent available) by the NCES, although 41 percent of schools report that they *do have* students for whom the five standard federal categories of race are *not* accurate, nearly three-quarters of schools report only using the five standard federal classifications of race.[23]

If your child's school receives federal dollars (e.g., any public school) and if the forms at your child's school do not allow respondents to check more than one race, ask that they be changed immediately. If your child attends an independent school, ask that these federal guidelines be used as a benchmark for its own approach to the "race question." As psychologist Maria Root explains, "School districts that have made changes on these forms and allow for more than one designation demonstrate a willingness to consider that the child's experience may be more complex than has traditionally been recognized for children of mixed heritages. Having a registration form that allows a parent to accurately identify a child is a step toward a different racial dialogue on a microlevel and macrolevel. Something as minor as this form is a reminder to some teachers to try to think differently about race and ethnicity."[24]

Of course, the above guidelines may have you gulping—and feeling that your child's school falls woefully short of the mark in meeting many of these ideal goals. If so, you are hardly alone. Despite the fact that we are speeding—in evolutionary terms—toward an increasingly multiracial society, institutional change is slow and often hard won.

In the final analysis, you may need to be the one who spearheads the necessary change in your child's school, by working with administrators and teachers toward common goals. This might involve volunteering (if you are an artist) to teach an art class about the hues of the color palette with grade schoolers, volunteering to assist students in a family tree project, or arranging for speakers on mulltiracial issues. In sum, it means advocating for the type of learning environment that best serves your child and, ultimately, all children.

In circumstances where a school meets very few (or none) of the above guidelines and administrators remain inflexible to change, it may be time to consider changing schools, even if it means driving farther or making the financial sacrifices to attend an independent school that pays better attention to these issues.

Inoculating Kids Against Racism

Part of being culturally aware means being aware of the racism that exists toward those of "minority" ethnic heritages—as well as the specific racism that exists toward *mixed* race individuals. To successfully prepare our kids for the potential drama and complexity of life as multiracial individuals, we have to prepare them for the reality of this racism and the impact it may have on their lives.

But first we need to set the groundwork for this endeavor by educating them (and ourselves) about how artificial the concept of race actually is. Perhaps we can best understand what race is by elucidating what it is *not*. Over the last several years geneticists have reported that the standard five racial categories into which human beings are typically lumped—Caucasian, African American, Asian, Native American and Latino—do *not* match up to corresponding genetic differences. According to Joseph L. Graves Jr., Ph.D. (African American), author of *The Emperor's New Clothes: Biological Theories of Race at the Millennium,* "Neat categories of race simply do not exist, and there is little to no genetic variation between different races.'" Indeed, genetic researchers recently reported that sub-Saharan Africans are the source of *all* human life (and their genes the source from which all of our genes originate),[25] a finding that sends many people's concept of race into a tailspin. "Race" itself is revealed as merely a social construction that makes use of human variations to create artificial boundaries—boundaries that are then used to place people in rigid categories. Graves emphasizes that "despite the unambiguous character of the recent studies of human genetic diversity . . . the fact that no races exist in our species has not been adequately communicated to the lay public."[26]

Meanwhile, these arbitrary distinctions are used in turn, says University of Texas professor Peter Jensen, to place some in dominant positions and others in subordinate ones—a dynamic that is naturalized so that it *seems* to lie outside human choice, allowing the "dominant group" to uphold these distinctions.[27]

Enter an increasingly multiracial generation of children, who, in the very fact of their makeup, defy this dominant/subordinate dynamic. It's little wonder, then, that multiracial people meet such challenges from every quarter. Even as people struggle to place them into one of five narrow categories, they prove how mythological these racial differences truly are.

All of this is knowledge that can spark fear in the heart of any parent of a multiracial child. Not only do we have to be concerned about racism toward our children because they are of color, we have to be concerned about the added element of racism toward our children *because* they are mixed. Indeed, some sociologists fear that as old racial boundaries fade and some people become threatened by America's changing complexion, pockets of hatred may grow larger.[28]

Jennifer Franks (African American), age 22, whose multiracial family includes her African American mom, Caucasian dad, African American sister and two Caucasian stepbrothers, recalls an incident on a trip to Florida. They stopped at a hotel and had "a bad experience. People were staring us down in the hallways, or they would stare us down from the balcony or at the pool. They stared as if they were about to do or say something to us. It was frightening. I think an interracial family is more surprising and gives some people a violent reaction that they don't have when they see a family that's all one race. People think, 'Oh, well, as long as all those black people stay together and breed with each other—and if there is all that black violence—whatever, I don't care.' But because our family surprises people, we have had some bad experiences."

For white parents who have grown up experiencing "the transparency of being white"[29] (i.e., never having to be *conscious* of their ethnic/cultural identity), it can be a terribly painful shock to watch our kids suffer injustice and rejection.

Diane Dillon (Caucasian), mother of a biracial son (African American/ Caucasian), relates how "as a white woman in a mixed marriage I had to learn a lot. [My husband] Leo [African American] was familiar with how white people felt and thought. He had to know. It could be a matter of survival. On the other hand white people don't make an effort to know how black people think or feel. I developed a 'radar' to pick up on things I never had to notice before. I also experienced feelings black wives and mothers have felt for generations. If Leo was very late coming home, I wondered if he was in a police station being beaten. He had been stopped before while delivering a job because he "looked like" someone who was wanted. When [our son] Lee started traveling by himself on the subway, I not only worried about bigots but about Lee getting shot being mistaken for someone else."

Although a sufficient discussion of racism in America falls outside the scope of this book, here are a few issues to consider that relate specifically to racism toward multiracial children.

Be Aware of the Meanings of Words When Discussing Race

It seems ironic that as geneticists increasingly reveal that race is an artificial construct—and as we move demographically toward becoming a more mixed-race people—we still depend on the words "race" and "multiracial" to frame discussions of these issues. If race is an artificial "emperor has no clothes" concept, and if we are all multiracially mixed to some extent—given that we all originated genetically from a handful of people in sub-Saharan Africa—why use the word? It has been said before that the concept of race is real as long as it is real in its consequences. Or, as Maria Root explains, "Race *is* an artificial construction—so why use the word 'race'? Because if we talk in a foreign language, no one will understand what we're saying—or be able to use that knowledge to help educate others."

Until that new language regarding race is invented and widely understood, terms such as "race" and "multiracial" are what we have available to frame conversations that promote change in the society in which we live.

Judiciously Expose Your Children to the Reality of Racism

Husband and wife Leo and Diane Dillon, Caldecott-winning children's book illustrators, advise, "If two people of different races decide to marry and have children they better have their eyes wide open. They should provide those children with knowledge of their history and their rightful place in the world. All children should have that, but especially multiracial children." Which means, says Mark (Caucasian) and Kelley (African American) Kenney, counselors and parents of two biracial girls, "it so important to make our children aware of the history of their cultures—especially if it's a painful history, such as the Native American experience or the black slave experience—in order to widen their knowledge base of race issues in our society."

Tracy Scholl (African American/Caribbean American/German/Caucasian), age 29, talks about how she wishes she'd been more aware of the "black experience" growing up. "I had a pretty protected existence," she confesses. "I had been sheltered from all that—I thought everyone had the same opportunities in life. That changed for me when I was 17 and I met a biracial cousin of mine who taught me all about Malcolm X and black oppression. I read Malcolm X and it was a life-changing experience. I asked my parents, 'Why didn't you *tell* me about this?' I'd been taught at school that black people *wanted* to be slaves because they didn't run away—that's what I learned."

Prepare Multiracial Children to Encounter Racist Remarks

Multiracial children may hear more disturbing racist remarks about their heritage of color than monoracial children hear because they are considered "exceptions." Jamie Doyle (Japanese/Irish/Caucasian), age 23, says, "I think a lot of people are quick to call you an 'exception' when you are biracial and they spill their racist views to you. I've heard racist comments from all sides. Some of the comments are toward Asians, but many are toward Anglos. I feel offended because they tend to overlook the fact that *I* am both Japanese and Anglo. I am both races."

Some young multiracial adults refer to what they call "white stories"[30]—racist stories told by white people about other racial groups. They expect biracial persons to laugh along with them, even though they *are* of that race and would in effect be laughing at themselves.

Do a Racial Self-Check

As we help alert our children to the racism in the world around them, we need to reexamine our own inner vestiges of racism. "Being in a multiracial family forces you to constantly examine your own prejudices," posits clinical social worker Jason Sackett (Caucasian), parent of two Caribbean American/Caucasian sons. "Everyone has prejudices. Just by being raised as a member of any race, you're raised with biases; you can't help but develop them. But part of our human thought process has to include being conscious of putting those thoughts in their proper place." This means first *acknowl-*

edging that there are times when our private thoughts (which reveal our hidden prejudices) do not line up with what we know to be the "right thing" and then recasting our way of thinking accordingly.

Perhaps we are moving ever closer to eliminating such prejudices in our society—if only one individual at a time. As one young multiracial man, Ricky Triana (Native American Pasqua Yaqui Tribe/Spanish/Mexican), age 17, puts it, "I think one of the great strengths that comes with being multiracial is that we get rid of *our* inner prejudices. You can't be half black, half white and be part of the Ku Klux Klan and hate *yourself*. It just doesn't work that way."

Amen.

CHAPTER SIX

A New Multiracial Generation in America

CURRENT CENSUS FIGURES show that, in the United States, 1 in 16 children under the age of 18 is multiracial[1] and in some U.S. counties 1 in 6 babies being born today is multiracial.[2] If the number of multiracial children continues to dramatically increase as expected, we will witness an unprecedented shift in the racial makeup of our population that will no doubt alter the way Americans live race as profoundly as the civil rights movement did half a century ago.

But as the interwoven strands in the tapestry of our nation shift color and hue, new questions emerge. First, how far-reaching is this change toward a more multiracial population? Numerous magazines have touted the changing demographics of America. *USA Today Magazine* recently commented on "how remarkably diverse" the direct descendants of Mayflower pilgrims have become today, showcasing several multiracial individuals on the cover.[3] *Time* magazine recently blurbed, "two of every 10 babies born in Sacramento are multiracial—an increase of more than 40% since 1982."[4] But the question remains, when we look behind the numbers (which only tell part of any story), how significantly is this move toward a more multiracial nation *impacting* mainstream America?

It may be useful to look at the "tipping point theory" (so named by writer Malcolm Gladwell, author of *The Tipping Point: How Little Things Can Make a Big Difference*), which isolates the three factors that converge to create a tipping point—the moment at which an emerging trend or social phenomenon becomes so far-reaching and widespread that it reaches critical mass and morphs into a *given* in our cultural lifestyle. The first of these factors, the "law of the few," holds that when trendsetter personalities in the public eye (what Gladwell terms "connectors" and "mavens") suddenly embody or represent a trend, more and more people in the general population become aware of that cultural shift, grow comfortable with it and start to emulate it in their own lives. When we have a culture in which celebrities Tom Cruise and Nicole Kidman adopt a biracial child and multiracial entertainers such as Halle Berry, James Earl Jones, Cameron Diaz, Vin Diesel, Alicia Keys, Sharika, Rashida Jones, Dean Cain, Tatyana Ali, Phoebe Cates, Tommy Chong, Ann Curry, Brandon Lee, Sean Lennon, Lou Diamond Phillips, Tiger Woods, Meg Tilly, Apolo Ohno, The Rock, James Blake, Norah Jones, Justin Guarini and Keannu Reeves reign in the public limelight, we have "the law of the few": influential people who affect the choices of others, making them more likely to (in this case) be quite comfortable marrying interracially, having multiracial children, and/or adopting mixed-race kids.

The second factor in the tipping point is the "stickiness factor": society-changing trends have wide-range impact if, when the trend occurs, it "sticks." It's not easily undone. In this case, nothing could be "stickier" than a burgeoning birthrate of multiracial children. The number of multiracial kids is not only skyrocketing along with the number of interracial marriages, but these children are very likely to marry and have their own (say, 2.5) children who will be multiracial. This generational ripple effect goes on and on, not just in terms of birthrates but also in terms of the impact our children and their children will have on the racial makeup and outlook of any monoracial family into which they might one day wed.

As Naomi Reed (African American/Russian Jewish/Caucasian), age 20, puts it, "people don't have much choice today except to view mixed people and families from a different perspective—because anyone that you hate will probably end up in your family tree."

The third element in Gladwell's tipping point theory is the "power of context," which emphasizes that human beings are more heavily influenced by their immediate environment and surroundings than we may think.[5] In the case of multiracial families, nothing could be truer. As people of different ethnic backgrounds arrive on America's coasts and borders, joining the multitudes of ethnicities already composing our communities, and as people come together via information technology, workplaces, neighborhoods, classrooms and churches, the context of our social environment—and the pool from which we partner—is forever changed. Close personal proximity leads to knowing and liking, and, as is human nature, sometimes love, sex, marriage—and children.

Another question that emerges with this growth in multiracial families is: What special insights do parents in mixed-race families and their children—those who stand at the front lines of this population shift—bring to the table regarding the discussion of race in America?

Many parents in interracial marriages say that although theirs is not always the easier choice, the rewards of being the parent of a multiracial child have altered and enriched them in unexpected ways, changing *their* identity, sensitizing them to racism across the board and deepening their connections to all aspects of the larger communities in which they live. Consider the following sentiments, by those in mixed-race families, on how a multiracial family setting, by its very nature, promotes inclusiveness and cross-cultural understanding.

Carol Franks-Randall, Ed.D. (African American), describes her marriage to her white husband this way: "If a multiracial family is going to work, then you have to be able to see things from the other's perspective. I can look at things as a black female but then I *have* to try to see it from my husband's perspective—and that is transformational."

When that "other person" is your child, understanding her perspective can be even more moving. Stacy Bell (Caucasian), director of the K and F Baxter Foundation (a nonprofit that funds foundations and research dedicated to helping multiracial kids) explains, "It's a very unique position being a white mom of biracial children. You're deeply involved with all these race issues and yet no one—to look at you—would even know it unless you're with your kids."

Bell tells of one circumstance in which "I was alone without my kids at a meeting at their school and one of the white moms said she wouldn't let her daughter walk home past the nearby middle school because, she said, 'I'm afraid of my daughter walking past those black boys.' And I started to cry. I said 'Look, my son is a black boy and that's how you'll think of him when *he's* older.' That really stopped her and she felt terrible. I have done a fair amount of advocacy on the spot because people feel safe to say things about other races in front of me, assuming I'll see it their way; things they would *never* say in front of a person of color." Still, says Bell, "I wouldn't change a thing. Being a parent in a multiracial family has opened up a whole new world for me—and a whole new way of *being* in the world."

Samantha Franks (African American), Carol Franks-Randall's daughter (whose Caucasion stepdad helped raise her), age 20, echoes these sentiments:

"Being in a mixed-race family shows you a positive side of all races that will stay with you your whole life. I'm not saying that it causes me to *always* see the good in all people, but it does allow me to see people for who they are rather than based on who I think they should be because of their skin color."

This heightened ability of mixed-race families to view humanity's color spectrum free of stereotypes is equally profound (if not more so) among multiracial individuals *themselves*. As Pearl Fuyo Gaskins (Japanese/Caucasian), author of *What Are You? Voices of Mixed Race Young People*, articulates, "Being racially mixed, you are forced to figure out your place in the world in a way that other people are not. But the journey can enrich your life. It made me more self-reflective and more knowledgeable about myself and others. It taught me to look at our society with a more critical eye and to question ideas that most Americans take for granted."[6]

Naomi Reed (African American/Russian Jewish/Caucasian), age 20, relates to the idea that being mixed race enriches one's outlook: "If I could have any wish it would be to be able to go inside people's heads and flip the little switch that controls racial categorization and racism," she says. "I would want everyone to have the ability to see things beyond the color line and to feel what true friendship and love really is. I think people would be surprised how many more genuine friends they would have if we all met each other in the dark."

But instead of waiting impatiently for the world to change the way they'd like it to, a vast number of young biracial adults are setting out to change the world themselves. Having integrated their various racial backgrounds into one confident identity (despite difficult experiences they've had with peers and strangers whose actions and remarks have often made them feel "other"), they grasp that self-esteem does not come from "what" you are but from understanding your basic worth as a human being. And they are committing themselves to "flicking that light switch on" in others.

These young adults hardly embody the supposedly self-centered and directionless Generation X and Generation Y that frequently make headlines these days. Consider their voices—and their fortitude: "I'm absolutely committed to studying multiracial individuals because there has not been a lot done on the characteristics of these groups. I want to use my background in economics to help me gather more detailed data about people like me, "says Jamie Mihiko Doyle, age 23, a graduate student in demography at the University of Pennsylvania.

Matt Kelley (Korean/Caucasian), age 23, founder and editor of *MAVIN,* the first magazine geared toward multiracial young people, explains that "I chose the name *MAVIN* because it means 'one who understands.' I wanted the magazine to be a forum where young multiracial people could come together and talk about their experiences and be understood. I felt that while child psychologists and experts might be studying multiracial kids, so little out there reflected what multiracial individuals were experiencing *themselves.* So I set out to provide that."[7]

Bethany Fry (Native American/Italian/Caucasian), age 24, is embarking on a career in college freshman diversity training—working with groups of incoming freshmen to help them be open to other students of other racial backgrounds: "I want to help incoming freshmen to understand that as they enter college and are surrounded with people from all different backgrounds they can choose to *erase* the stereotypical tapes we all have in our minds," she says. "They can say to themselves, when they do have a racist thought, 'Hey, this is stupid, this isn't how I want to think or what I want to be doing.'" Moreover, believes Bethany, "I feel that by *being* biracial I'll be able to make a bigger difference in their lives and outlook."

Jennifer Franks (African American), age 22, talks about her experience of being raised by a white stepdad, which led her to conceive of a project at Harvard "on interracial dating and how and why people so frequently gravitate to someone of the same race. I wanted to figure out how to explain that."

Yet another biracial (African American/Japanese) college student talks about her plans to "write a children's book about a family like mine because I think it's so important for young children to see families like ours as being completely normal—and there just aren't many books like that out there yet."

Not all young multiracial adults who are foot soldiers in this movement are conducting studies, developing diversity programs or writing books, however. Some among this vanguard generation are making waves simply by eschewing racial stereotypes in an *intentional* way as they go about their day-to-day lives.

Consider Nicole Brown (African American/Caucasian), age 22, who relates that for her it's important to "share what I am and teach what I am because as biracial individuals we can really help bridge gaps between races and knowledge and experiences. We can *become* these bridges."

Likewise Tracy Scholl (African American/Caribbean American/German/Caucasian), age 29, feels that "if I can change whatever negative things someone may think of my white heritage or my black culture or about my being biracial just by having them *know* me, then perhaps I can help contribute to society and to our understanding of each other, regardless of race."

All this should not be taken to imply that just because someone is born multiracial, the onus is on that individual to *be* a bridge between cultures or that our children should hold as their raison d'être the desire to eradicate racism. Neither should we view them as our society's best and last hope for racial assimilation. Not at all. Although multiracial people may well have a place, at this point in our history, in changing the way we view (and live by or venture past) racial lines, the responsibility for breaking down racial barriers is one we *all* share, no matter what kind of family we live in.

Moreover, even within this generation of mixed-race youth, individual experiences and outlook often vary significantly, depending on which "minigeneration" they are part of. For example, the difference between the experiences of mixed-race persons who grew up in the 1970s—and who are now in their thirties—is vastly different from that of a twenty-something who grew up in the 1980s—much less that of a ten-year-old today who is growing up among peers much more accustomed to the idea of multiracialness because of the rapid emergence of this population (which will have the option to check *all* their races on school and government forms, which previous generations did not have). As the racial landscape shifts, so do the experiences of those who live in it.

As Pearl Fuyo Gaskins (Japanese/Caucasian) explains, "The number of multiracial people has more than quadrupled since I was a teenager and young adult. When I was growing up in California in the 1970s I met few other racially mixed people. Mixed-race celebrities and luminaries were rare . . . some [younger people] echo the same sense of isolation and aloneness that I felt growing up racially mixed. But [others] grew up with multiracial friends, classmates, cousins, etc. They had mixed-race role models."[8]

As multiracial role models grow, some multiracial youth report feeling it's "cool" to be mixed. Consider one 16-year-old boy (Chinese/Cuban/Spanish/Austrian) who says that when he lived in Portland, Oregon, "I would say I was white." But when he moved to Los Angeles a few years later, "my jaw dropped. Suddenly it was *cool* to be mixed."[9] Another mixed-race high school student said, "I've probably had to think more about who I am than most people my age have, but I think that's given me a kind of strength. I feel like a lot of my friends admire that in me."

Real and pressing issues still exist, however, that need our careful and ongoing attention as parents. As we have seen all too clearly in this book, even the youngest of our children face the mixed messages and challenging experiences that accompany being multiracial in a vastly monoracial (and racially divided) world—a world that is still largely confused by and reactive to mixed-race people and in which deep pockets of racism (and resentment toward those who emulate the increasingly blended face of America) still run rampant. Although there has, no doubt, been progress, there is still so much to be done.

Meanwhile, as the number of multiracial children grows, so do the efforts of psychologists and researchers to examine mixed-race individuals as a group in both qualitative and quantitative terms—from the grade point averages of multiracial versus monoracial kids[10] to the mortality rate of multiracial infants,[11] and so much more. One soon-to-be-published study funded by the National Institutes of Child Health and Human Development reports that (among a small sample of multiracial seventh to twelfth graders) some youth who self-reported as being of more than one race were at increased risk for alcohol use, smoking, sex, skipping school, and experiencing physical symptoms such as headaches and aches and pains than were kids who self-reported as being of only one race.[12]

Yet there are numerous caveats to bear in mind when looking at any data on mixed-race individuals that make generalizations about them as a group. Because the number of mixed-race young adults who can be studied is not yet large, estimates based on this comparatively small cohort are, as one researcher admits, "not always very good."

Second, because each generation of mixed-race young adults has an experience that differs somewhat from that of the minigeneration before it, it is a mistake to merge the experiences of those who have already come into adulthood with those of younger children and teens who are coming of age in an increasingly multiracial America.

Third, as researcher David Harris, Ph.D. (African American), professor of sociology at the University of Michigan and father of two African American/Caucasian girls, points out, how (and whether) a person reports as being mixed race is largely dependent on the context (e.g., "Is the interviewer asking me my race based on my ancestry?" "On what I *tell* people I am?" "On how I see *myself*?" "On how others label me?" "On how my parents view me?" "On how I blend or don't blend in with the community in which I live?"), making it very difficult to know whether the data being collected is pertinent or not. How, asks Harris, "can we collect accurate data based on that?" As the researcher who studied health risk behaviors in multiracial youth reported, "We asked kids in this study to report their race and then asked them to do so again a year later—and 16 percent of them changed their race, either adding another race, taking one off or changing their racial identification altogether."

Fourth, each child's situation (based on how his parents raise him, how diverse his community and school settings are, how constant and accepting his group of friends may be, as well as his personal temperament) is unique. We must bear in mind that quantitative studies of multiracial individuals cannot easily tease out such nuances to ascertain what makes one child thrive while another falters. As we have seen in this book, multiracial youth raised to be biculturally competent (to embrace a biracial label and to appreciate and integrate both or all of their heritages) experienced greater self-confidence and a more positive self-concept than youths who were not raised in an environment that encouraged such an authentic identity. These interviewees report being less biased about other groups of people, less judgmental, more open, sensitive to and accepting of others, more likely to cite their uniqueness as a distinct strength and to find distinct advantage in being able to move confidently in and out of different worlds of people, helping build partnerships among them and enjoying a wider variety of friends.

Other researchers confirm these findings,[13] adding that multiracial individuals often demonstrate greater creativity and possess a wider range of cognitive skills that they can draw on for problem solving in difficult life situations.[14]

Biracial youth who have succeeded—with the help of their parents and the adults in their home and school communities—in achieving a strong and positive identity differ greatly in their experiences from children who have not had such support. It is therefore difficult to merge these two groups of individuals and arrive at wholly useful insights and answers that pertain to all multiracial children everywhere.

This is not to suggest that we should underplay the red flags such research raises. As we have seen throughout these pages, multiracial youth who remain insufficiently prepared for life as a multiracial individual in a pre-dominantly monoracial society *are* more likely to face difficulties. The statistics cited earlier in this book indicating the disproportionate number of multiracial youth in juvenile hall and the heightened risk of rape multiracial girls face show that such research raises real and pressing issues. But we must also bear in mind the context in which such research is conducted, *and* that it is conducted on a rapidly changing population.

Whether future studies (and there will be many, for this field is "red-hot" among psychologists and researchers) report that our children face tremendous challenges or enjoy special advantages, these discussions merely underscore the question that we, as parents, are *already* intuitively worrying over as we raise our multiracial kids: Will our children—growing up in a world that often reacts to them as if they don't fit in—be at greater risk if we do not, through mindful parenting, defuse society's often confusing and anxiety-provoking messages to them?

As has been illustrated anecdotally again and again in the pages of this book, we ourselves *are* our child's situation. The degree to which we are proactive in our approach to parenting is the most salient factor in how emotionally healthy and self-assured our children will be.

It is, after all, my concern about what I needed to know and understand as a white woman raising mixed-race children that led me to write this book; perhaps your similar concerns led you to read it. It is my deep hope that this book is the antidote to any parents' concern about whether (and *how*) they can raise emotionally resilient, biculturally competent and confident multiracial kids.

As we set out, in our role as parents, to achieve that goal, much is being said in our culture at large about whether multicultural people constitute a new "race," and whether mixed-race individuals as a group should be "racialized" (i.e., Should racial meaning be extended to this previously racially unclassified group?).[15] Certainly, as the number of multiracial children rises, there exists a unique opportunity for this generation to form its own group identity in America, articulating, through growing national and local organizations, student groups, and the like, what messages they hope to send to the culture at large.

But although our children's voices, as they come of age, can add dimension and insight to the discussion of race in our nation, and although the vast majority of multiracial people *do* share many common experiences, it is quite another thing to say that multiracial people compose a new and different "race" living in the United States. To do so seems misguided on many fronts. True, similar themes emerge from the experience of being biracial that cause people of mixed race to identify quite naturally as a group and use similar labels (multiracial, biracial, mixed-race). Yet they are markedly different from one another in their blended cultural identities. Their "group identity" has much more to do with their community of spirit than with shared ancestry or a racialized identity.

My son and daughter, for instance, are Japanese, Swedish, Danish, British and American *first*. They are "multiracial" *second*. Because their identity differs from that of other multiracial children, they can be *part* of a multiracial community, but it would be a misnomer—and a disservice to them—to say they are part of a multiracial *race*.

As one young African American/Puerto Rican woman articulates, making multiracial a "category" (whether socially or officially on the census, school applications or other government forms) "would be buying into the system—a system you've detested all your life, a system that pressures you to fit into some group. So now you have a group, and now you fit into it, but what does that do for racial problems in America? I would hate to see the creation of more racial divisions."[16] This young woman's feelings are underscored, she says, by her awareness that genetic research has come "to the realization that race does not exist—it's a *social* construct."[17]

Cutting-edge genetic research has shown, as already noted, that all "races" originated from one small group of individuals in sub-Saharan Africa and, just as strikingly, that the traditional racial categories used to "color code" people do *not* match corresponding genetic differences between these groups. *Genetically speaking,* no neat categories of race exist, proof of what we recognize all too well as we parent our children: Although it is appropriate to define people, in part, by their cultures, it is folly to pigeonhole them according to strict racial categories.

Many young multiracial individuals express hope that the dialogue their generation is stimulating will bring our society closer to breaking down divisive racial barriers, restructuring the belief system America operates on that there *are* essential differences between "races."

Nancy Brown (Caucasian), president of the Association of MultiEthnic Americans (AMEA) and mom of two African American/Caucasian daughters, agrees that the racialization of mixed-race people would be a grave mistake: "It's important that our children identify by their *ethnicities* rather than as another race. None of my colleagues and I want to make multiracial another race. Not at all. We just want our children and all multiracial people to be able to celebrate *accurately* who they are."

Perhaps Matt Kelley (Korean/Caucasian), age 23, founder and editor of *MAVIN,* the first magazine geared toward multiracial young people, expresses it best when he says, "I think too often racial community is based on exclusion instead of inclusion. I don't think it makes sense for mixed-race people to simply mimic the old model of [racial] community and create this hermetically sealed mixed-race community." For this reason Kelly focuses his magazine's efforts on helping incorporate multiracial people into mainstream society, without ignoring their separate identities and heritages. Moreover, says Kelley, rather than being labeled as yet another race, multiracial individuals—who care deeply about their cultural roots and don't want to lose their cultural identities—may help "widen the definitions of what it means to be Asian-American, Latino-American, or African-American in a positive way."[18]

Today we stand at a cultural crossroads. As families of varied racial backgrounds gather at dinner tables, weddings, bar mitzvahs, birthdays, holiday celebrations, family reunion picnics and funerals, they may well—one person at a time, one family at a time—change racial attitudes and perceptions in a way that no piece of legislation ever could or ever will.

This is not to say that we are headed rapidly toward a newfound racial nirvana. As Howard University law professor Frank Wu, author of *Yellow: Race in America Beyond Black and White,* expresses it "every generation needs to deal with [racial] issues in new and different forms. Sitting here at the dawn of the twenty-first century, we're not so smart and so enlightened we can say, 'This is it. [We have found] the solution for all time.' All we can do is strive to make things better, and the best way to do so is by sustaining an open and honest dialogue."[19]

As we expand these conversations, arguments and ponderings—as a society and as parents striving to imbue our children with an understanding and appreciation of their rich and complex identities—we may not conclude the dialogue on race, but we do have the opportunity to *rewrite* it, in our own living rooms.

I have sometimes wondered (and certainly *hoped*) that if my children's children were to one day come across this book their only response might be to ask me, "Why did you have to write this? Was being multiracial ever a *big* deal?" Although the point might be moot by then (say, circa 2050), the pleasure of living in such a world will be very relevant to *all* of us in every corner of America.

NOTES

Introduction

1. Ron Stodghill and Amanda Bower, "Where Everyone's a Minority," *Time*, 2 September 2002, 28.

2. Bureau of the Census, *The Two or More Races Population: 2000*. Prepared by the Racial Statistics Branch of the Population Division.

3. Nicholas A. Jones discussed these findings with me by telephone in an interview in November 2002.

4. This number was calculated by dividing the Census's current estimated number of multiracial children (4.5 million) into the total number of children under 18 in the United States (72.5 million). Amy Symens Smith of the Population Division of the U.S. Census discussed these figures with my by telephone in January 2003.

5. Stodghill and Bower, "Where Everyone's a Minority," 26.

6. This misguided assumption—that mixed-race children are destined to face confused, unhappy lives—originally gained popular acceptance with the publication of an article by Robert E. Park, "Human Migration and the Marginal Man," *American Journal of Sociology* 33, no. 6 (1928). Though now considered invalid and racist, such theorizing has had a lingering effect, "coloring" many people's perception of multiracial individuals to the present day.

7. When I attended a lecture by Joseph Graves, "Mixed Race Health Matters," at the national conference of the Association of MultiEthnic Americans on 13 October 2002 in Tucson, Arizona, he highlighted this point about genetics and race.

8. Nicholas D. Kristof, "Love and Race," *New York Times*, 6 December 2002, sec. A, p. 35.

9. Ibid.

Chapter One

1. For more on the ideas of Loris Malaguzzi, founder of the Reggio Emilia approach to early childhood education, which emphasizes an innovative approach toward fostering children's intellectual development through the "many languages" of words, movement, drawing, painting, sculpture, shadow play, collage and music, see Carolyn Edwards, Lella Gandini, George Forman, *The Hundred Languages of Children: The Reggio Emilia Approach to Early Childhood Education* (Norwood, N.J.: Ablex, 1994). This particular quote by Loris Malaguzzi was taken from an exhibit

based on his work displayed at the Capital Children's Museum, Washington, D.C., 2002.

2. For more on this discussion, see Joseph L. Graves Jr., *The Emperor's New Clothes: Biological Theories of Race at the Millennium* (New Brunswick, N.J.: Rutgers University Press, 2001), pt. 4, 155–200.

3. Nancy J. Nishimura, "Assessing the Issues of Multiracial Students on College Campuses," *Journal of College Counseling* 1, no. 1 (1998): 48–49.

4. Ibid.

5. Maria P. P. Root, *Love's Revolution: Interracial Marriage* (Philadelphia: Temple University Press, 2001), 148–149.

6. Lori Miller Kase, "Talking to Kids About Race," *Parents*, July 2001, 102.

7. Marguerite A. Wright, *I'm Chocolate, You're Vanilla: Raising Healthy Black and Biracial Children in a Race-Conscious World, A Guide for Parents and Teachers* (New York: Jossey-Bass, 1998), 14–15.

8. Ibid., 15.

9. Ibid.

10. From the 1958 Rogers and Hammerstein musical, *South Pacific*.

11. Dorothy G. Singer and Tracey A. Revenson, *A Piaget Primer: How a Child Thinks* (New York: Penguin, 1996), 128.

12. Maria P. P. Root, "The Biracial Baby Boom: Understanding Ecological Constructions of Racial Identity in the 21st Century," in *Racial and Ethnic Identity in School Practices: Aspects of Human Development*, ed. R. H. Sheets and E. R. Hollins (Mahwah, N.J.: Erlbaum, 1999).

13. For an in-depth discussion of preschool children's recognition and understanding of racial differences, see Louise Derman-Sparks, Carol Tanaka Higa and Bill Sparks, "Children, Race and Racism: How Race Awareness Develops," *Interracial Books for Children* 11, no. 3–4 (1980): 3–9.

14. Patricia G. Ramsey, "Young Children's Thinking About Ethnic Differences," in *Children's Ethnic Socialization: Pluralism and Development*, ed. Jean S. Phinney and Mary Jane Rotheram (Newbury Park, Calif.: Sage, 1987), 58–59.

15. Wright, *I'm Chocolate, You're Vanilla*, 26.

16. Francis Wardle, *Tomorrow's Children* (Fort Collins, Colo.: Citizen, 1999), 8–9.

17. Ibid.

18. Derman-Sparks, Higa and Sparks, "Children, Race and Racism," 6.

19. Wright, *I'm Chocolate, You're Vanilla*, 19–21.

20. Wanting children "to pass" refers to a parent's hope that others in her community will erroneously assume that her children are *all* black or *all* white or *all* Asian, rather than of mixed race, and embrace them as such.

21. This quote was posted on The New York Times on the Web: *Living Race: A Frequently Updated Selection of Responses to the Questionnaire on Race* (15 June 2000). http://www.nytimes.com. I have omitted the name of the multiracial individual quoted for privacy reasons.

22. Willie B. Garrett, "Seven Common Transracial Parenting Mistakes," *Adoptive Parents*, May-June 1999.

23. Bea Wehrly, Kelley R. Kenney and Mark E. Kenney, *Counseling Multiracial Families* (Thousand Oaks, Calif.: Sage, 1999), 68–70.

24. Susan Rosendahl, head of the preschool of the Key School, in Annapolis, Maryland, emphasized this point when I interviewed her in her office in 2001.

25. Derman-Sparks, Higa and Sparks, "Children, Race and Racism," 13.

Chapter Two

1. This study (which looked solely at mothers of boys because it was easier to differentiate the male son's DNA from the mother's DNA) is research I first reported in "Relationship News," *New Woman*, August 1996, 44.

2. David Updike, "Double Take," *Utne Reader*, November-December 2000, 46–47.

3. Beverly Daniel Tatum emphasized this point when I interviewed her by telephone on 5 October 2000.

4. Felicia R. Lee, "Bridging a Divide," *New York Times*, 30 April 2000, sec. 14, pp. 1, 13.

5. Beverly Daniel Tatum, *"Why Are All the Black Kids Sitting Together in the Cafeteria?" And Other Conversations About Race* (New York: Basic, 1997), 178.

6. Maureen T. Reddy, *Crossing the Color Line: Race, Parenting and Culture* (New Brunswick, N.J.: Rutgers University Press, 1994), chap. 3.

7. Derman-Sparks, Higa and Sparks, "Children, Race and Racism," 5.

8. Wright, *I'm Chocolate, You're Vanilla*, 95.

9. "What They Were Thinking About Race," *New York Times Magazine*, 16 July 2000, 47.

10. Derman-Sparks, Higa and Sparks, "Children, Race and Racism," 7.

11. Ibid.

12. Wright, *I'm Chocolate, You're Vanilla*, 94.

13. Developmental psychologist Jean Piaget described children between the ages of five and seven as "little scientists" because they are so busy accumulating bits and pieces of information to help them make sense of the world around them.

14. Root, "Biracial Baby Boom," 70.

15. Gail Steinberg and Beth Hall, *Inside Transracial Adoption* (Indianapolis: Perspectives, 2000), 92.

16. Ibid.

17. Reddy, *Crossing the Color Line*, 77.

18. Tatum, *Why Are All the Black Kids Sitting Together*, 181.

19. Zadie Smith coined this term in her novel, *White Teeth* (New York: Random House, 2000).

20. Root, "Biracial Baby Boom," 70.

21. Root, *Love's Revolution: Interracial Marriage*, 148.

22. Maria P. P. Root, "Experiences and Processes Affecting Racial Identity Development: Preliminary Results from the Biracial Sibling Project," *Cultural Diversity and Mental Health* 4, no. 3 (1998): 244.

23. Ibid.

24. Ibid., 244–245.

25. Ibid., 245.

26. Jaslean J. LaTaillade focused on a sample of African American/Caucasian interracial couples from the Seattle area for her dissertation research and emerged with these findings, which she shared with me by phone in February 2003.

27. Wehrly, Kenney and Kenney, *Counseling Multiracial Families*, 38–39.

28. Darryl Fears and Claudia Deane, "Biracial Couples Report Tolerance," *Washington Post*, 5 July 2001, sec. A, p. 1.

29. Ibid.

30. Wardle, *Tomorrow's Children*, 91.

31. Fears and Deane, "Biracial Couples Report Tolerance."

32. Nicholas D. Kristof, "Love and Race," *New York Times*, 6 December 2002, sec. A, p. 35.

33. Sociologist Frank D. Bean makes this observation in Fears and Deane, "Biracial Couples Report Tolerance."

34. Tatum, telephone conversation.

35. Root, "Experiences and Processes Affecting Racial Identity," 238.

Chapter Three

1. Teresa Kay Williams, "Race as Process: Reassessing the 'What Are You?' Encounters of Biracial Individuals," in *The Multiracial Experience: Racial Borders as the New Frontier,* ed. Maria P. P. Root (Thousand Oaks, Calif.: Sage, 1996), 201.

2. Derman-Sparks, Higa and Sparks, "Children, Race and Racism," 7.

3. Vivian Gussin Paley, *You Can't Say You Can't Play* (Cambridge: Harvard University Press, 1992), 3.

4. Wehrly, Kenney and Kenney, *Counseling Multiracial Families*, 70.

5. Derman-Sparks, Higa and Sparks, "Children, Race and Racism," 9.

6. Wright, *I'm Chocolate, You're Vanilla*, 102–103.

7. Derman-Sparks, Higa and Sparks, "Children, Race and Racism," 8.

8. Robert Kegan, *In Over Our Heads: The Mental Demands of Modern Life* (Cambridge: Harvard University Press, 1994), 20.

9. Dan Kindlon and Michael Thompson, *Raising Cain: Protecting the Emotional Life of Boys* (New York: Ballantine, 1999), 72–73.

10. Margaret Talbot, "Girls Just Want to Be Mean," *New York Times Magazine*, 24 February 2002, 27.

11. Root, "Biracial Baby Boom," 70–72.

12. Root, "Experiences and Processes Affecting Racial Identity," 234.

13. Williams, "Race as Process," 200.

14. Pearl Fuyo Gaskins, "Providing a Voice," interview by Anthony Yuen, *What's Hapa'ning: The Hapa Issues Forum Newsletter*, Winter 1999–2000.

15. Root, "Biracial Baby Boom," 151–152.

16. Maria Root suggested this dialogue when I spoke with her by telephone in June 2001.

17. Reddy, *Crossing the Color Line*, 61.

18. Tatum, *Why Are All the Black Kids Sitting Together*, 181.

19. Lise Fundergerg, *Black, White, Other: Biracial Americans Talk About Race and Identity* (New York: Quill, 1994), 367.

20. Some of the suggestions regarding useful responses we as parents might use when dialoguing with our children about race emerged during my telephone interview with Maria Root in June 2001.

21. Derman-Sparks, Higa and Sparks, "Children, Race and Racism," 9.

22. "What They Were Thinking About Race," 44–45.

23. When I interviewed Beverly Daniel Tatum by telephone on 5 October 2000, she discussed the importance of parents immediately undermining the authority of those who make disparaging remarks regarding an aspect of our child's appearance or identity.

24. Kase, "Talking to Kids About Race," 108.

25. These quotes originally appear in an interview with Cynthia Erdley, associate professor of psychology at the University of Maine, issued as a press release, "Finding a Friend: Childhood Friendships Are Training Ground for Adult Relationships," by the University of Maine on 3 November 2000.

26. For more on this, see Laura Sessions Stepp, "Making Something Besides Good Grades," *Washington Post*, 27 August 2000, sec. B, p. 1.

Chapter Four

1. Laura Sessions Stepp, *Our Last Best Shot: Guiding Our Children Through Early Adolescence* (New York: Riverhead, 2000), 3, 12.

2. Erik Erikson, "Identity and the Life Cycle: Selected Papers," *Psychological Issues Monograph Series* 1, no. 1 (New York: International Universities Press, 1959).

3. Wehrly, Kenney and Kenney, *Counseling Multiracial Families*, 71.

4. Wardle, *Tomorrow's Children*, 11.

5. "What They Were Thinking About Race," 44–45.

6. Wehrly, Kenney and Kenney, *Counseling Multiracial Families*, 71.

7. Nishimura, "Assessing the Issues of Multiracial Students on College Campuses," 49.

8. Wehrly, Kenney and Kenney, *Counseling Multiracial Families*, 71.

9. W. S. C. Poston's work critiques early models of racial identity development, which delineated the path to establishing one's racial identity only according to a single race heritage. Poston presents a biracial identity development model in his work, "The Biracial Identity Development Model: A Needed Addition," *Journal of Counseling and Development* 69 (1990): 152–155. For a synopsis of his model, see Wehrly, Kenney and Kenney, *Counseling Multiracial Families*, 64–65.

10. Wehrly, Kenney and Kenney, *Counseling Multiracial Families*, 71.

11. Williams, "Race as Process," 201.

12. Wehrly, Kenney and Kenney, *Counseling Multiracial Families*, 65.

13. Lisa Nichols, founder of Motivating the Teen Spirit, spoke about her personal interviews and findings regarding multiracial youth in juvenile hall at the national conference on multiracial youth of the Association of MultiEthnic Americans in Tucson, Arizona, on 15 October 2002, in a speech entitled "Treatment Issues for Multiracial Kids in the Juvenile Justice System."

14. Juleah Swanson and Kimi Kawabori, "Institutionalizing the Invisible," *MAVIN*, no. 6 (2002): 56–57.

15. Ibid.

16. Root, "Experiences and Processes Affecting Racial Identity," 243.

17. Ibid, 243.

18. Wehrly, Kenney and Kenney, *Counseling Multiracial Families*, 65.

19. Ibid.

20. Tatum, telephone conversation.

21. Tatum, *Why Are All the Black Kids Sitting Together*, 183.

22. Ibid.

23. David Carr, "On Covers of Many Magazines, a Full Racial Palette is Still Rare," *New York Times*, 18 November 2002, C1.

24. This figure comes from the 1998 National Crime Victimization Survey (NAWS), Bureau of Justice Statistics. This U.S. Department of Justice survey found that monoracial Asian American/Pacific Islander women had a 6.8 percent lifetime rate of rape or attempted rape, African American women an 18.8 percent rate, and Caucasian women a 17.7 percent rate, whereas multiethnic women reported a 34.1 percent lifetime rate of rape or attempted rape.

25. Pearl Fuyo Gaskins, *What Are You? Voices of Mixed Race Young People* (New York: Henry Holt, 1999), 229–230.

26. Maria P. P. Root, "Resolving 'Other' Status: Identity Development of Biracial Individuals," in *Diversity and Complexity in Feminist Therapy*, ed. L. S. Brown and Maria P. P. Root (New York: Haworth, 1990), 185–205.

27. Williams, "Race as Process," 203.

28. Ross Atkin, "Facing Race," *Christian Science Monitor*, 25 July 2001. Retrieved 25 January 2003. http://www.csmonitor.com.

29. Maria P. P. Root, "A Bill of Rights for Racially Mixed People," in *The Multiracial Experience: Racial Borders as the New Frontier*, ed. Maria P. P. Root (Thousand Oaks, Calif.: Sage, 1996), 11.

30. The "one drop rule" refers to the American belief—which was at times in our history law—that a multiracial person must be considered a member of their lower-status (minority) racial heritage and therefore *could not* be considered white, even in part. For example, under the one-drop rule, someone of black/white heritage would be considered fully black. This rule was applied mostly to persons of African ancestry.

31. Nishimura, "Assessing the Issues of Multiracial Students," 49.

32. Ibid.

33. Ibid.

34. Ibid., 50.

35. Ibid.

Chapter Five

1. Steinberg and Hall, *Inside Transracial Adoption*, 63.

2. Tatum, *Why Are All the Black Kids Sitting Together*, 177.

3. Yu Xie and Kimberly Goyette, "The Racial Identification of Biracial Children with One Asian Parent: Evidence from the 1990 Census," *Social Forces* 76, no. 2 (December 1997): 565.

4. Root, "Experiences and Processes Affecting Racial Identity," 245.

5. Ibid., 239.

6. Francis Wardle, "Multicultural Education," in *The Multiracial Experience: Racial Borders as the New Frontier,* ed. Maria P. P. Root (Thousand Oaks, Calif.: Sage, 1996), 385.

7. Mary Jane Rotheram and Jean S. Phinney, "Introduction: Definitions and Perspectives in the Study of Children's Ethnic Socialization," in *Children's Ethnic Socialization: Pluralism and Development*, ed. Jean S. Phinney and Mary Jane Rotheram (Newbury Park, Calif.: Sage, 1987), 25.

8. Frances Winddance Twine, "Heterosexual Alliances: The Romantic Management of Racial Identity," in *The Multiracial Experience: Racial Borders as the New Frontier,* ed. Maria P. P. Root (Thousand Oaks, Calif.: Sage, 1996), 301.

9. Tatum, *Why Are All the Black Kids Sitting Together*, 181.

10. Marybeth Lambe, M.D., "Becoming a Multi-Ethnic Family," *Chosen Child*, April/May 1999.

11. Root, "Experiences and Processes Affecting Racial Identity," 245.

12. Root, "Biracial Baby Boom," 83.

13. Francis Wardle, "Supporting Biracial Children in the School Setting," *Education and Treatment of Children* 15, no. 2 (May 1992): 163–172.

14. Ibid.

15. Wardle, "Multicultural Education," 387.

16. Ibid., 389.

17. Stodghill and Bower, "Where Everyone's a Minority," 30.

18. Wardle, "Supporting Biracial Children in the School Setting," 163–172.

19. Ibid.

20. Researcher Kimberly Cooper Plaszewski made this point during her presentation, "Social Perceptions of Multiracial Children," at the national conference of the Association of MultiEthnic Americans in Tucson, Arizona, 15 October 2002.

21. Wardle, "Multicultural Education," 388–389.

22. Edith McArthur of the National Center for Education Statistics informed me that the Department of Education requested an extension to the deadline for allowing multiracial students to "check one or more races" on school forms in order to determine how the NCES will implement this guidance, including examination of whether the Department should adopt an aggregation method for Federal reporting purposes that is consistent with other Federal agencies that collect race and ethnicity data from institutions, states, school districts, and schools. We spoke by phone in January 2003.

23. This information comes from the National Center for Education Statistics, "State Survey on Racial and Ethnic Classifications, 1998," and is available at http://nces.ed.gov/pubs98/98034.pdf.

24. Root, "Biracial Baby Boom," 84.

25. Graves, "Mixed Race Health Matters," lecture.

26. Graves, *Emperor's New Clothes,* 156.

27. Robert W. Jensen of the University of Texas at Austin made this comment during his presentation, "Single Race Bias: Redefining Privilege," at the national conference of the Association of MultiEthnic Americans in Tucson, Arizona, 14 October 2002.

28. Tatsha Robertson, "Changing Face of the Racial Divide: Mixed Marriages Alter Longtime Boundaries," *Boston Globe,* 2 January 2000, sec. B, p. 1.

29. Researcher Josef Manuel Liles of the University of California, Santa Barbara, used this term during his presentation, "Race and Multiplicity in the Lives of Mexican/White Offspring," at the national conference of the Association of MultiEthnic Americans, Tucson, Arizona, 15 October 2002.

30. Ibid.

Chapter Six

1. Smith, Population Division of the U.S. Census, telephone conversation.

2. Paula Bock, "I Consider Myself Me—Kids Come in Many Colors These Days and They'd Like a Word with Us," *Seattle Times,* 15 November, 1988, 21.

3. Cokie Roberts and Steven V. Roberts, "Beyond the Mayflower," *USA Weekend,* 22–24 November 2002, 8–10.

4. Stodghill and Bower, "Where Everyone's a Minority," 26.

5. Malcom Gladwell, *The Tipping Point: How Little Things Can Make a Big Difference* (New York: Little, Brown, 2000).

6. Gaskins, interview.

7. Ross Atkin, "Facing Race," *Christian Science Monitor*, 25 July 2001. Retrieved 25 January 2003. http://www.csmonitor.com.

8. Gaskins, interview.

9. John Meacham, "The New Face of Race," *Newsweek*, 18 September 2000, Special Report, p. 38.

10. In this study, Grace Kao explores the educational success of mixed-race students, finding that achievement scores of biracial Asian children did not differ from those of monoracial whites in mathematics, although they were lower than those of their monoracial Asian counterpoints. Kao points out that the "Asian advantage" in educational performance is linked to having immigrant parents, not to being Asian or partly Asian. Comparisons between biracial blacks and monoracial blacks are less conclusive, although Kao found that the educational performance of biracial blacks seemed more similar to monoracial black families than to white families. Moreover, how a child self-identified played an important role in determining academic performance of black biracials, but not Asian biracials. Specifically, when taking into account whether biracial blacks self-identified as "black" or "nonblack," Kao found that those who identified as "black" earned higher mathematics scores than their monoracial black counterparts, while biracial blacks who identified as "white" earned (lower) math scores comparable to monoracial blacks. For more on this, see Grace Kao, "Racial Identity and Academic Performance: An Examination of Biracial Asian and African American Youth," *Journal of Asian American Studies* 2, no. 3 (1999): 223–249.

11. Jamie Mihoko Doyle is investigating infant mortality disparities among mixed-race infants with one Caucasian and one minority parent (Asian, African American, and Mexican American) as part of her graduate work at the University of Pennsylvania.

12. Rose Maria Li, J. Richard Udry, and Janet Hendrickson-Smith, "Are Multiracial Adolescents at Increased Risk?" Presented at the Annual Conference of the American Public Health Association, November 1998.

13. Wehrly, Kenney and Kenney, *Counseling Multiracial Families*, 64.

14. Rotheram and Phinney, "Introduction: Definitions and Perspectives in the Study of Children's Ethnic Socialization," 25.

15. Williams, "Race as Process," 199.

16. Gaskins, *What Are You?* 54.

17. Ibid., 53.

18. Atkin, "Facing Race." http://www.csmonitor.com.

19. Frank Wu, "A Conversation with Frank Wu," interview by Tim Wells, *Washington Lawyer*, February 2002, 40.

RECOMMENDED READING FOR CHILDREN

Recommended Reading for
Children in Multiracial Families

Today, books featuring children of biracial and transracially adopted backgrounds are increasingly available. Here is a list of favorites—my own and those of other parents, educators and researchers in the field. Many are available at your local library.

Fiction Picture Books Featuring Positive Messages for Multiracial Children and Families

All the Colors of the Earth by Sheila Hamanaka
All the Colors of the Race by Arnold Adoff
All the Colors We Are by Katie Kissinger
Angel Just Like Me by Mary Hoffman and Cornelius Van Wright
Baby-O by Nancy White Carlstrom
Bein' With You This Way by W. Nikola-Lisa
Billy and Belle by Sarah Garland
Black Is Brown Is Tan by Arnold Adoff
Black, White, Just Right by Marguerite Davol
The Colors of Us by Karen Katz
Hairs/Pelitos by Sandra Cisneros
Hard to be Six by Arnold Adoff
How My Parents Learned to Eat by Ina R. Friedman
I'm Gonna Like Me: Letting Off a Little Self-Esteem by Jamie Lee Curtis and
    Laura Cornell
It's Okay to Be Different by Todd Park
Less Than Half, More Than Whole by Michael and Kathleen Lacapa

Little Blue and Little Yellow: A Story for Pippo and Other Children by Leo Lionni

Living in Two Worlds by Maxine Rosenberg

Nancy No-Size by Mary and Northway Hoffman

The Paper Crane by Molly Bang

People by Peter Spier

The Rabbit's Wedding by Garth Williams

A Rainbow All Around Me by Sandra L. Pinkney

Sofie's Role by Sheila Hamanaka

Starry Night by David Spohn

Straight Hair, Curly Hair by Augusta Goldin

Through My Window by Tony Bradman

Two Eyes a Nose and a Mouth by Roberta Grobel Intrater

Why Am I Different? By Norma Simon

Winter Wood by David Spohn

You Are Special by Max Lucado

You Be Me, I'll Be You by Pili Mandelbaum

Picture Books About Adoption

Being Adopted by Maxine Rosenberg

Families by Meredith Tax

Families Are Different by Nina Pellegrini

A Family for Jamie by Suzanne Bloom

Happy Adoption Day! by John McCutcheon

Horace by Holly Keller

How it Feels to be Adopted by Jill Krementz

Katie-Bo: An Adoption Story by Iris L. Fisher

A Mother for Choco by Keiko Kasza

The Mulberrry Bird by Ann Braff Brodzinsky

Real for Sure Sister by Ann Angel

Tell Me Again About the Night I Was Born by Jamie Lee Curtis

Through Moon and Stars and Night Skies by Ann Turner

We Adopted You Benjamin Koo by Bobbie Jane Kates

The White Swan Express: A Story About Adoption by Jean Davies Okimoto

Nonfiction Picture Books
Featuring Children of Many Cultures

The Color of Man by Robert Carl Cohen

Hands Around the World: 365 Creative Ways to Encourage Cultural Awareness and Global Respect by Susan Milord

Kid's Multicultural Art Book: Art and Craft Experiences from Around the World by Alexandra M. Terzian

The Kids' Multicultural Cookbook: Food and Fun Around the World by Deanna F. Cook and Michael P. Kline

The Multicultural Game Book by Louise Orlando

The People Atlas by Philip Steele

A Photographic Journey Around the World by Maya Ajmera and Anna Rhesa Versola

Your Skin and Mine by Paul Showers

Magazines

Click. www.clickforparents.com

Ladybug. www.ladybugmag.com

RECOMMENDED READING FOR TEENAGERS

Recommended Reading for
Teenagers and Young Adults in Multiracial Families

Some of these novels address mixed-race issues in the United States during an earlier and more problematic era for multiracial individuals.

Fiction

All But the Right Folks by Joan Kane Nichols
The Brave by Robert Lipsyte
The Broken Bridge by Philip Pullman
Half a Heart by Rosellen Brown
I Only Made Up the Roses by Barbara Ann Porte
Mary Dove by Jane Gilmore Rushing
Molly by Any Other Name by Jean Davies Okimoto
Rain Is Not My Indian Name by Cynthia Leitich Smith
Ramona by Helen Hunt Jackson
Tancy by Belinda Hurmence
Whale Talk by Chris Crutcher
With My Face to the Rising Sun by Robert Screen

Nonfiction for Teenagers, Young Adults, and Parents

As We Are Now: Mixblood Essays on Race and Identity by William S. Penn
Crossing the Color Line: Race, Parenting and Culture by Maureen T. Reddy
Beyond the Whiteness of Whiteness: Memoir of a White Mother of Black Sons by
    Jane Lazarre

Black, White and Jewish: Autobiography of a Shifting Self by Rebecca Walker

Black, White, Other by Lise Funderburg

Caucasia by Danzy Senna

The Color of Water: A Black Man's Tribute to His White Mother by James McBride

Different Worlds: Interracial and Cross-Cultural Dating by Janet Bode

Everyday Acts Against Racism: Raising Children in a Multiracial World edited by Maureen T. Reddy

40 Ways to Raise a Nonracist Child by Barbara Mathias and Mary Ann French

Growing Up Adopted by Maxine Rosenberg

Half and Half: Writers on Growing Up Biracial and Bicultural by Claudine Chiawei O'Hearn

"I Am Who I Am" Speaking Out About Multiracial Identity by Kathlyn Gay

Of Many Colors: Portraits of Multiracial Families, photographs by Gigi Kaeser and interviews by Peggy Gillespie

What Are You? Voices of Mixed-Race Young People by Pearl Fuyo Gaskins

Magazines

MAVIN. www.mavinfoundation.org or call 1-888-77MAVIN

ACKNOWLEDGMENTS

This book was a team effort.

In the early days of this book idea—when it still existed only as a conversation—Elizabeth Kaplan, my literary agent and friend, called me on a weekly basis to ask, "Are you writing this yet?" Without her gentle nudges this book would not exist. I thank her for this and for the way in which the line between our friendship and work relationship has always been so gratifyingly blurred.

This book would also not exist without Stephanie Von Hirschberg, who, in the never-ending story of our friendship, went through every stage of the emotional process of book writing with me. It is hard to say what was more helpful—the support she unfailingly offered or her sage advice on troublesome pages from proposal to final manuscript. I am also indebted to Mark Levine for the many ways in which he contributed to this project with a breathtaking generosity of time and spirit, the magnitude of which led me to refer to his good deeds as "The Mark L. Levine Foundation for Needy Writers." Thank you.

To my editor, Marnie Cochran, a thousand thanks for beings a writer's dream—not only full of editorial insight but a writer's champion to boot. Who could ask for anything more? I am also grateful to senior project editor Erin Sprague for her dedication and the graceful editorial suggestions that enhanced this book.

For their unfailing support of friendship, I'm indebted to Kimberly Minear, Kary Stadlin, Susan Harrington, Tracy Oliver, Barbee Whittaker, Sabra Hill, and Sandy Goodman. These pinch hitters helped with my children when last minute edits needed to be made, or simply understood when I didn't return a phone call for days (or both), and were still there when it was all said and done. I am also grateful for the support of my family—Jay and Janice Jackson, Don and Betsy Jackson, and Chip and Emily Jackson—and of course my mother, Marcia Strok, who was always ready to help.

To experts in this field, most notably Maria Root, Nancy Brown, Matt Kelley, Nicholas Jones, Amy Symens Smith, Willie B. Garrett, David Harris, and Kelley and Mark Kenney, I thank you for your time, your wisdom, and for laying the groundwork that allowed this book to become a reality. Thank you, too, to Mary Jane Milner and the teachers at The Key School for generously sharing your knowledge.

To the many children, teenagers, young adults, and parents in multiracial families who gave of their time, energy, thoughts, and insights, thank you. This book is your book.

And then there is the other half of my home team, my husband, Zenji Nakazawa, to whom I am more grateful than words can convey, not only for the emotional support he tendered, but for believing in the mission of this book and for putting his actions behind his words in every way. Thank you.

This book is dedicated to my children, Christian and Claire.

INDEX

Adolescent years, 121–128
  and dating, 133–135
  and education, 178–183
  and problem solving, 138–139
  recommended reading, 215–216
  and self-identity, 128–133,
    138–148
Adoption, xiv, 21, 53, 212
Adoption Council of Canada, 22
African Americans, xiv
  children, 16. *See also* Multiracial
    children
  and family identity, 19
AMEA. *See* Association of
  MultiEthnic Americans
Amirthanayagam family, 62, 67–68
Ancestry, 61–66, 106–108
Ashanti to Zulu (Dillon and Dillon),
  29
Ashton, Judith, 21
Association of MultiEthnic
  Americans (AMEA), 25, 28, 55,
  66, 106, 144, 169, 175, 198
At-risk multiracial children, 195

Bean, Frank D., 74
Bell, Stacy, 148, 191
Bender family, 76, 85, 124, 131, 134,
  149
Bicultural competence, 169

Bilingualism, 174
Biracial children, xiii. *See also*
  Multiracial children
Birth rates, xii
Black Americans, xiv
Black Student Alliance, 153
Books and magazines about race,
  29–31, 32, 211–216
Boys, 89–90, 135–138
Brown family, 29, 30–31, 73, 81, 82,
  114, 124–125, 127–128,
  135–136, 160, 165, 176
Brown, Nancy, 25, 28, 31, 55,
  175–176, 198–199
Brown, Nicole, 150, 193
Bureau of Justice, 106(n24)

Caucasians, xiv
Census statistics, xi–xii, 181, 189,
  201(n4)
Center for the Study of Biracial
  Children, 16
Center for the Vulnerable Child, 12
College years, 150–155
Color-blindness, 6–11
Community and multicultural
  children, 157–163
Confidence, 115–118. *See also* Self-
  identity
Coping skills, 21–28, 111–115

Counseling Multiracial Families
   (Kenney), 49, 95, 134, 168, 171
Craig family, 68
Criminal acts, 130–131, 136,
   206(nn13, 24)
*Crossing the Color Line: Race, Parenting
   and Culture* (Reddy), 50–51
The Crown of Columbus (Erdrich and
   Dorris), 146
Cultural differences, 84–86
Cultural identity, 168–176. *See also*
   Self-identity

Dating, 133–135
Demographics, xi–xii
Dialogues about race, 28–29
   grade school years, 54–55
   middle childhood years, 92–97,
      99–105
   preschool years, 28–29, 34–38
Dillon family, 29–30, 31–32, 105,
   117, 184–185
Diversity. *See* Community and
   multicultural children
DNA, 44, 203(n1)
Dolls, 32–33
Dorris, Michael, 146
Double categorization, 14
Douglas, Frederick, 179
Douglass, Ramona E., 66–67, 106,
   117, 144
Doyle family, 125–126, 144–145,
   152, 154, 158, 173, 186, 192
Doyle, Jamie Mihoko, 192, 209(n11)
Dumas, Alexander, 179

Education, 176–183, 209(n10)
Egocentrism, 13–14
Elementary school. *See* Grade school
   years

*The Emperor's New Clothes: Biological
   Theories of Race at the Millennium*
   (Graves), 183
Erdley, Cynthia, 115, 205(n25)
Erdrich, Louise, 146
Euro-Americans, xiv

Fairness, 88–89
Families
   backgrounds of, 61–66, 178–179
   cultures of, 170–173
   with dysfunctional parents, 70
   extended, 174–175
   multiracial, 191–195
   organizations for, 175–176
   See also individual family names
Fiction picture books, 211–213
Filling out forms, 139–141, 181–182,
   208(n22)
Finch family, 54
Franks-Randall family, 57–58, 60, 65,
   97, 151, 165, 167, 184, 191–192,
   193
Friendships. *See* Peer interactions
Fry, Bethany, 147, 155, 171, 193
Fu family, 7, 45, 56, 66, 171

Garrett, Willie B., 10, 22, 23–24, 27,
   31, 170, 172–173
Gaskins, Pearl Fuyo, 92, 137, 192,
   194
Genealogy. *See* Families: backgrounds
   of
Generation X, 192
Generation Y, 192
Genetics, 179, 183, 198
Girls, 90, 135–138
Gladwell, Malcolm, 189–190
Gottman, John, 72–73
Grade school years, 49–53

and developmental tasks, 52–53
dialogues about race, 54–55
and education, 178
and family backgrounds, 61–66
recommended reading, 211–213
and self-identity, 52–53, 66–71
Graves, Joseph L., 183
Guibault family, 56, 80
Guibault, Leceta Chisholm, 22

Hall, Beth, 58
Harris, David, 69, 146, 195–196
Hazing, 130–131
Heterogeneous socializing, 181. *See
also* Peer interactions
High school years. *See* Adolescent
years
Horowitz family, 26, 30, 174
Howard family, 27, 114

Identification with one race, 19–21,
123–128, 202(n20), 207(n30).
See also Self-identity
Identity labels, 97–98, 141–145, 198
Interracial family organizations,
175–176
Interracial marriages, 71–74

Jensen, Peter, 183–184
Jones, Nicholas A., xi

K & K Baxter Family Foundation,
148, 191
Kansas Juvenile Justice Authority, 130
Kao, Grace, 209(n10)
Kelley, Matt, 81, 127, 140–141,
143–144, 147–148, 164, 193,
199

Kenney family, 50–51, 96–97,
106–107, 110, 113, 118, 134,
171–172, 175, 185
Kenney, Kelley, 10–11, 14, 35, 49, 95,
145
Kenney, Mark, 49, 95, 134, 168
Kindlon, Dan, 89
Kroll family, 93, 131–132

Language and racism, 185
Lass-Gordoa, Katie, 179
LaTaillade, Jaslean, 71, 204(n26)
"Law of the few," 189–190
Lazare family, 25, 51, 74, 86,
105–106, 175
Locale and multicultural children,
163–168

McArthur, Edith, 208(n22)
McGowen-Kaul family, 26, 57,
169–170, 174
Magazines about race, 213, 216
Majority population, xv
Malaguzzi, Loris, 5, 201(n1)
Malcolm X, 186
Marriages, 71–74
MASC. *See* Multiracial Americans of
Southern California
Matrix of races, 146–147
MAVIN magazine, 81, 127, 140–141,
193, 199
Media and race, 31, 32
Meyers family, 78–80, 85–86, 94,
125, 164
Middle childhood years, 77–82
and coping skills, 111–115
development in, 83–89, 116–118
and education, 178–183
emotional life, 91–99
and family backgrounds, 106–108

peer interactions, 115–116
and self-identity, 114–118
and stereotypes, 108–111
See also Grade school years
Middle school years. See Adolescent
    years
Miller family, 26–27
Minority population, xv
Mixed race children, xiii. See also
    Multiracial children
Mortality rates, 209(n11)
Moss family, 87
Motivating the Teen Spirit, 206(n13)
Multicultural children and racism.
    See Racism
Multiculturalism, 168–176
and bilingualism, 174
and community, 157–163
and education, 176–183, 209(n10)
Multiethnic children, xiii. See also
    Multiracial children
Multiracial adolescents. See
    Adolescent years
Multiracial Americans of Southern
    California (MASC), 127, 175
Multiracial boys, 89–90
Multiracial children
as adults, 148–150
at-risk, 195
best-case scenario, 167–168
books and toys for, 29–34,
    211–216
college years. See College years
comments about, 21–28, 58–61
and coping skills, 21–28, 111–115
and cultural identity, 168–176
dialogues about, 28–29, 34–38
with dysfunctional parents, 70
and education. See Education

and family backgrounds. See
    Ancestry; Families
grade school. See Grade school
    years
and identity. See Self-identity
identity labels, 97–98, 141–145,
    198
middle childhood years. See
    Middle childhood years
mortality rates, 209(n11)
and neighborhood, 163–168
and physical features, 38–42, 44–49
preschool. See Preschool years
reactions to, 21–28, 55–58
realities of, xii
recommended reading for,
    211–216
research about, 195–196
statistics, xi–xii, 181, 189, 201(n4)
teasing of, 89–91
Multiracial college students, 9
Multiracial entertainers, 190
The Multiracial Experience: Racial
    Borders as the New Frontier
    (Root), 8, 9–10, 62, 130, 159
Multiracial families, 191–195,
    211–216. See also Families
Multiracial girls, 90

Nakazawa family, 1–6, 24–25, 28, 39,
    43–44, 62–65, 68, 95–96,
    107–108, 160–162, 173
National Center for Education
    Statistics (NCES), 182, 208(n22)
National Crime Victimization Survey
    (NAWS), 136, 206(n24)
National Institutes of Child Health
    and Human Development, 195
NAWS. See National Crime
    Victimization Survey

NCES. *See* National Center for Education Statistics
Neighborhood and multiracial children, 163–168
New York State Citizens Coalition for Children, 21
Nichols, Lisa, 206(n13)
Nicknames, 173
Nishimura family, 126
Nishimura, Nancy J., 154–155

Odd Girl Out: The Hidden Culture of Aggression in Girls (Simmons), 90
"One drop rule," 148, 207(n30)

Pact, An Adoption Alliance, 58
Paley, Vivian Gussin, 83
Parents, xv. *See also* Families
Parker family, 104–105, 110, 134–135, 151–152, 166
Peer interactions, 83–84, 86–87
  adolescent years, 123–128
  middle childhood years, 115–116
  scripts for, 99–105
Personal names, 173
Physical features, 38–42, 44–49
Piaget, Jean, 13, 203(n13)
Picture books, 211–213
Population Division of the U.S. Census, xi–xii
Poston, W. S. C., 128–129, 206(n9)
"Power of context," 190
Pregnancy, 43–45
Preschool years, 1–6
  books and toys, 29–34, 211–213
  dialogues about race, 28–29, 34–38
  and education, 178, 201(n1), 203(n13)
  and race, 12–18

recommended reading, 211–213
and self-identity, 18–21

Race
  and preschoolers. *See* Preschool years
  books about, 29–31, 32, 211–216
  dialogues about. *See* Dialogues about race
  differences in, 84–86
  and filling out forms, 139–141, 181–182, 208(n22)
  identification with one, 19–21, 59, 123–128, 202(20n), 207(n30)
  issues of. *See* Racism
  matrix of, 146–147
  and media representations, 31, 32
Racially Mixed People in America (Root), 53
Racism, 84–86, 88–89, 105–106, 183–187
Rainbow Support Network, 10
Raising Cain: Protecting the Emotional Life of Boys (Kindlon and Thompson), 89
Randall family. *See* Franks-Randall family
Recommended reading, 211–216
Reddy, Maureen, 50–51
Reed family, 30, 61, 151,155, 190, 192
Reggio Emilia approach, 201(n1)
Relationship Research Institute in Seattle, 72
Rittenhouse family, 4, 56
Root, Maria, 8, 9–10, 19, 23, 39–40, 53, 62, 69, 75, 93–94, 96, 130–131, 146, 159, 177, 182

Sackett family, 3–4, 31, 132, 157,
   186–187
Scholl, Tracy, 153–154, 186, 193
Schools, 176–177. *See also* Education
Scripts. *See* Dialogues about race
Self esteem. *See* Self-identity
Self-identity, 5–6, 194–195
   and adolescent years, 128–133,
      138–148
   and grade school years, 52–53,
      66–71
   and middle childhood years,
      114–118
   and preschool years, 18–21
   See also Cultural identity
SHADES, 154
Siblings, 74–78
Simmons, Rachel, 90
Social interactions. *See* Peer
   interactions
Statistics, xi–xii, 181, 189, 201(n4)
Steinberg, Gail, 58
Stereotypes, 108–111, 192
"Stickiness factor," 190
Student groups, 154
Summer camps, 173

Tallchief, Marie, 179
Talking about race. *See* Dialogues
   about race
Tatum, Beverly Daniel, 32, 38, 48,
   74, 99, 124, 133, 136, 158, 159,
   170, 205(n23)
Teasing, 89–91
Television. *See* Media and race
Thompson, Michael, 89
Time magazine, 189

*The Tipping Point: How Little Things
   Can Make a Big Difference*
   (Gladwell), 189–190
Toys, 32–33
Transracial adoption, xiv, 21, 53, 212.
   See also Multiracial children
Triana, Ricky, 187

Unfairness. *See* Racism
U.S. Department of Education, 181
U.S. Department of Justice, 206(n24)
Updike family, 47–48
USA Today Magazine, 189

Videos. *See* Media and race

Wardle, Francis, 16
Watson family, 32–33, 45, 117
*What Are You? Voices of Mixed Race
   Young People* (Gaskins), 92, 137,
   192
"White stories," 186
*"Why Are All the Black Kids Sitting
   Together in the Cafeteria?" And
   Other Conversations About Race,*
   (Tatum), 32, 48, 99, 158
Why Mosquitoes Buzz in People's Ears
   (Dillon and Dillon), 29
Williams, Teresa Kay, 142
Wright, Marguerite, 12, 15–16
Wu, Frank, 199

*Yellow: Race in America Beyond Black
   and White* (Wu), 199
You Can't Say You Can't Play (Paley),
   83
Young adults. *See* Adolescent years

ml   7/03